PRIVATE PRACTICE ESSENTIALS

Howard Baumgarten, LPC

Foreword by Chris E. Stout

PRAISE FOR PRIVATE PRACTICE ESSENTIALS

"Howard's work in this book serves as a virtual Swiss Army knife of tools and techniques that are clearly explained and critical to one's success… This book is a great single resource for the private practitioner."

— Chris E. Stout, PsyD
Originator of the book series
Getting Started in and *Getting Better at Private Practice*

"Within an ever-changing healthcare environment, *Private Practice Essentials: Business Tools For Mental Health Professionals* offers those in private practice just what they need today: a steady, smart business path that they can easily follow with good results. The book presents a complete business plan and answers the many questions that overwhelm new therapists. Howard Baumgarten writes a clear guide filled with examples, information, options and exercises to help readers set up a safe and profitable practice."

— Lynn Grodzki, LCSW, MCC
Master Certified Coach
Author of *Building Your Ideal Private Practice, 2nd Edition*

"*Private Practice Essentials* is an excellent resource for any clinician venturing into or already in the world of private practice. As a former student of Howard's graduate school course, his mentoring helped me start and grow my practice into a successful business with a full caseload for the past 7 years. If you want a thriving practice and are having difficulty seeing yourself as a business person, the time-tested and proven methods in this guidebook are a must read."

— Joel Bruns, LMHC, NCC
The Green Room Counseling LLC

"If you ever thought that being an effective therapist while adding on the role of business owner and entrepreneur was too difficult a path, think again. *Private Practice Essentials* provides a clear, precise, and comprehensive road map of everything you'll need on the journey to success--both in business and as a caring and compassionate clinician. Author and psychotherapist Howard Baumgarten has crafted a gem—filled with step-by-step real-life business tools, an understanding of the complexities of running a therapy practice, and filled with insightful and helpful stories that are sure to resonate. Many of us starting private practices started one the hard way, learning from our mistakes. Why not avoid all the guesswork and undo financial and emotional stress? *Private Practice Essentials* is like having your own personal mentor and business coach for building a sustainable practice right now. Highly recommended!"

— Donald Altman, LPC
Bestselling author, *The Mindfulness Toolbox*,
101 Mindful Ways to Build Resilience, and *One-Minute Mindfulness*

DEDICATION

For Joanne,
A Pioneer of Change,
A Champion in Life!

ABOUT THE AUTHOR

Lori J. Photography

HOWARD BAUMGARTEN, a Licensed Professional Counselor, has been in private practice since 2000 and has over 25 years of clinical experience, working with children, adolescents, adults, couples and families. His clinical specialties include adolescent development & dynamics, communication trust & intimacy in relationships, and helping men heal emotionally.

He is the founder of Smart Practice Central, a business-building platform that values intelligent, ethical, and clinically minded practice development, and he provides clinical practice business consultation to private practices and healthcare agencies.

Howard has lectured around the country on the integration of mental health and business, including topics such as practice development, working within managed care systems, and the impact of health care legislation on mental health care. In addition, he is an expert trainer to businesses and organizations on wellness, stress management, resilience, work/life balance, teamwork, customer service, and burnout prevention.

Howard developed and implemented one of the first practice building business curricula in a graduate level accredited counseling program in the country while teaching at the University of Colorado.

When not counseling, lecturing, teaching, writing, presenting or consulting, Howard enjoys skiing, traveling, running, hiking, and spending time with his wife and two boys!

TABLE OF CONTENTS

ACKNOWLEDGEMENTS

This book would not be a reality without the growing need in our professional helping industry for business knowledge and experience. Never anticipating that I would end up carving out a small but important niche in the area of business education and consultation in private practice, the opportunity really found me in both a general sense and then specifically with respect to authoring this book. I am ever grateful to the clinical practice community at large for demonstrating a high degree of clinical competence, coupled with an awareness of knowing when something not known like business building and management skills leads to a demand for practitioner-led business advice from me and others like me. Specifically, I appreciate you the reader for selecting my volume to help you in your journey toward building your clinical practice.

My work on this project comes with extreme gratitude for the many people who supported this project and me throughout the process of putting it together. Numerous individuals directly involved in the book deserve notable mention. First, I am extremely grateful to my former student, intern, and colleague Veronica Tunis for her assistance in chapter writing, preparing many of the appendices, conducting interviews, preparing and monitoring the clinician survey, aggregating and analyzing data, and formatting parts of the book. In addition to her hard work, I greatly appreciate the routine meetings that helped keep me progressing with writing and the project itself moving forward.

Lori Johnson and Becky DeGrossa were willing, honest, and open about sharing their expertise in social media and website building, which added great value to the marketing chapter. And, thanks to Becky and others for helping spread the word about our search for practitioner stories. I am extremely grateful to the practitioners from all over North America who responded to my request for stories of practice building, sharing challenges, triumphs, and personal advice with readers. Though we couldn't share all the stories received, we were able to print pieces of many stories of practice building.

To the publishing team at PESI (PPM), specifically acquisitions editor Karsyn Morse and publishing production specialist Hillary Jenness, your patience with my process and flexibility with deadlines, as well as your thoughtful ideas and collaboration on a routine basis were well accepted, greatly appreciated, and instrumental to successful completion. I am also grateful to have a wise and thoughtful editor in Donald Altman LPC, a highly accomplished author and writing professor. I could not have asked for a better team.

There are countless others not directly involved with the completion of the book, some of whom bear mentioning because if it weren't for these individuals, the book may not be a reality. Marsha Wiggins, the professor who pushed me as a young graduate student, the program chair who believed in my private practice curriculum idea inviting me on board as non-tenured faculty instructor, the colleague who supported and continues to support my work in the field, thank you for your time, energy and support. Gratitude also must be shared for the generosity of the University of Colorado at Denver Association of Lecturers and Instructors who thought this project worthy and gave a helping hand along with public recognition to the entire UCD community. Thank you. Tom Giles, Patrick Schwartz and Tom Kalous are three mentors whom I am grateful to have met early on in my private practice career, each of whom in their own individual way gave me countless opportunities and advice that allowed me to develop and practice my knack for growing business in mental health, and in their case on a much larger scale than I had foreseen.

Finally, there are many people outside the field of mental health who are to be thanked for their encouragement and support throughout this process. The entire clan of Zeiler intellectuals (my wife's family) without whom I wouldn't have the courage to risk my academic insights, I thank you for your suggestions, ideas and support. To my own family of origin, thank you for your open arms, your listening ears, and the support you have given me from day 1 at the age of 12 when I first wanted to be a helping professional, through tough times and great times, and into the future. Thank you. To my dearest and closest friends, you know who you are, each of you know exactly how to take me away from intensity and into lightheartedness, and you did your job perfectly throughout this process. Thank you. To my wife Diana, and my children Eli and Aden, during a time of much responsibility and with the challenges of balancing the work and our personal lives each one of you knew just how to take me away from insanity and into wholeheartedness. I thank you for your patience and your support throughout this process.

FOREWORD

Starting a private practice is the dream of many a graduate or medical student. It has never been an easy or even clear path, and I'd say it has gotten even more difficult today. Sadly, such challenges cause too many students who transition into professional, clinical work to give up on their dreams of opening their own practice.

Others go on to try to open a practice, but quickly fail as they do not realize all of the important considerations and proverbial moving parts that need to go into the development and growth of a successful and sustainable practice. The desire to help others may overshadow the need to have a well-defined, realistic, and actionable business plan. Without such a model in place, the budding private practitioner cannot help those in need.

In both of these scenarios there may be a lack of understanding that creating a private practice is creating a business. The clinician must also be an entrepreneur. Applying the discipline and energy that was marshaled for getting into and through graduate or medical school will likewise be required for a successful, thriving private practice that helps those in need and provides a sense of accomplishment and security for the practitioner.

Howard's work in *Private Practice Essentials* serves as a virtual Swiss Army knife of tools and techniques that are clearly explained and critical to one's success. Much of what nascent private practitioners need is demystification of what the world of private practice is like. While much of my career has focused on professional presentations, various peer reviewed articles in APA journals, and a shelf's worth of books on getting started and getting better in private practice, using evidence-based practice, and various assessment and treatment tools, this book is a great single resource for the beginning private practitioner, or those readers who are just curious to learn how private practice works, what's involved and thus whether it is indeed something to be ventured into.

Even though the focus may be more so toward readers who hold counseling degrees and credentials, most of the content is quite generalizable to any behavioral healthcare provider—psychologists, social workers, psychiatrists, marriage and family therapists, substance abuse counselors, etc. Howard has clearly organized the myriad of components necessary to launch a private practice within any specialty. His provision of sample forms is an accelerant to establishing the structure critical to good operational functioning as well as risk mitigation and management. But this book is not all just a nuts-and-bolts manual, Howard also covers the more introspective aspects of the reader's story, as well as his own journey.

I wish you, the reader, all of the best in commencing your journey into private practice. It will be challenging but also very much worth the effort—both for you professionally as well as for those you will be able to help in your clinical work. I think you will feel sufficiently prepared, as well as enthusiastic, in commencing the next stage of your career after learning what Howard has to teach.

Chris E. Stout, PsyD
Originator of the *Getting Started In* and *Getting Better at Private Practice* series

INTRODUCTION

I always knew I wanted to be in private practice. Yet, I had no idea what a successful practice in the 21st century really looked like. Neither did most people I learned, as our country experienced a shift away from practitioner-centered care to patient-directed care, driven by consumer powerlessness, a financially failing healthcare infrastructure, and overseen by some enabling of outdated 20th century government policy. Into the first decade of the 21st century, healthcare costs soared to 16% of the nation's GDP, the most costly of any countries' GDP. Switzerland can claim second place among the civilized countries of our world at 11% in its country's GDP. It's like the U.S. is Secretariat at the Belmont, winning one award it would never want, and by many "lengths."

With rising healthcare costs, frustrated consumers struggling to understand the system and take their own measure of control of their care, it's no wonder practitioners moving into or already in private practice under-value themselves, and therefore often place themselves in positions of low income, not pursuing their dreams, their passions. Why just become another cog in the wheel that is healthcare delivery?

That's why this book is stuffed with highly effective, practical information, and real-life tools you need for building a great practice! Hopefully it will inspire and teach you how to unlock the passions you feel inside about doing meaningful work in your community—and doing it at a highly successful level.

If you are already succeeding and feeling value, loving what you do as a helping professional, then this book will become a tool to help reinforce confidences about being in practice while challenging you to work smarter and build even more. I will, in fact provide a few extra tools, as well as creative ideas for you to work on practice building at your current level. By no means can anyone, including myself, be perfect in practice, as we often need resources and advisors to help us learn what we are doing well, and what we can do differently.

You may be reading this book because you are about to make the transition into starting your own practice or you are struggling with getting things moving in the right direction. This book is full of personal vignettes of success and failures (yes I said failures, and more on that later) that lead through a path of fulfillment in your helping business.

Throughout this book, I offer both practical and needed tools to help with the set-up, management, and growth of your practice. I also offer excerpts of personal experience on my road into and through practice, as well as stories of other practitioners I trained throughout the country. Many of my former graduate students who studied the business concepts you are about to learn, are now successful private practitioners. You will learn from their experiences of transitioning from graduate school into practice.

Before you dive in, I want to familiarize you with my three-stage developmental theory of the emerging private practice owner in the helping field. In other words, what three stages of practitioner development make for the "seeds of success" in private practice?

Stage one is that of EMPLOYEE. In this initial stage of professional growth, you work under the direct supervision of one or more individuals, and though you choose to be employed somewhere, you have little or no choice about who supervises you. Additionally, you are charged with defined responsibility that is the overall mission of whatever agency, group, or other setting where you work. Though levels of independence vary from one setting or place of employment to another, as an employee the structure and definition of work is more defined, closely monitored, and especially in healthcare enlists heavy amounts of teamwork to get the job done. Oh, and did I mention that compensation is defined by being a W-2 wage or salary earner. You make the same amount of money, often with benefits, and though you get raises at times, there are limits to what you can earn.

That said, there are many benefits to being an employee, and some drawbacks. Regardless, I hope you agree that being an employee in your fieldwork, for at least a few years, can build value, character, needed clinical skills, and most of all experience. Some of my students who opted to try their hands at a private practice right out of graduate school with no clinical experience failed and learned a hard lesson. While I support their ambition, I only support this decision when there's prior experience working as an employee in the field. And, even then it's wise to build a practice part time while working full or part time in an agency or hospital setting. Being an employee is an important form of private practice preparation.

The moment you open the doors of your practice (perhaps your doors are already open) you become an EMPLOYER. As an employer, you call the shots! You have freedoms in business that you previously did not as only employee. You are now employee and owner. You bear the responsibility of both titles. And, with two important titles comes more challenge and risk. With more responsibility, you work harder, and there's more potential for reward! This reward is meaningful as is of course the work itself, because you are creating the work largely from within. As employer there is also more potential for failure and you must become comfortable with this notion.

Once you master the experience of practicing both employee and employer, you are ready to become an ENTREPRENEUR. You may even be ready shortly after entering ownership, or it may take many years. For most people, though, the true nature of entrepreneurship takes hold around five to eight years after becoming an owner. You may possess big ideas upon entering ownership of your practice. However, most successful owners focus on putting systems in place that make running the business itself profitable and valuable. Entrepreneurship grows with ownership experience and creative planning of programs, service delivery systems, branding, marketing, and other areas that occur once the practitioner understands fundamental success and failure. The entrepreneurial phase can and usually does last throughout a large portion of the ownership phase. Unfortunately, few practice owners take the chance to act on their entrepreneurial ideas. It is my hope that wherever you are in your professional development—employee, employer, or entrepreneur—you are empowered by the ideas throughout this book to take risks, work hard, and make your practice dreams come true!

Part I

GET READY TO BUILD

The first phase of any practice building process involves a lot of thinking, preparation, and planning. Whether you are just starting out, or revamping important areas of your business, you need to get ready to build by writing ideas down. These ideas become a blue print for execution, a step-wise process that might lead to certain success while teaching you something of value in the midst of failure. Part I of this book will help you prepare by guiding you into your passion through the retelling of your story that led you into this business. A solid and structured business plan and process will assist you in moving your personal story into well laid out professional plans. Finally, you will learn exactly how to implement important business mechanisms and supports for starting and staying on solid ground. Even if you are already in practice, reading this section is essential in case you missed steps along the way in the early stages of your practice. Seasoned practice owners certainly wouldn't want a crack in the foundation of a growing practice.

CHAPTER ONE |
WHAT'S YOUR STORY?

Take a moment to stop and think: How did I arrive at this place? Am I really a professional in private practice or about to be one? Believe it or not, you are! And, you are a good one too. Could it be, with all the bills to pay, marketing to do, clinical information to retain, not to mention the business of your personal doings, you simply haven't stopped to ponder the story of your many accomplishments up to this point.

Reflecting on your story can be quite revealing and energizing. You came to this field for a reason, quite possibly several. And, now you are reading a "how to" book on private practice building so that you can bring that story to life and impact others in your way! And, if you are already bringing it to life, then perhaps your aim is to take your practice to the next level. Or, maybe you have been in practice for a while and success eludes you. **This book is about how you can bring your story alive while reaching your greatest potential, earning a profit, doing beneficial work in your corner of the world!**

Why not start this very moment? Right now, reach inside those reasons you came into the field, think about how you found yourself in practice or on its doorstep, and most important write these thoughts down. Do it now! It's okay. (I can wait.) When you come back from jotting those inner thoughts down, note how motivated and refreshed about your "mission" you feel. You may even want to take things a step further, and actually revisit these ideas with a loved one or trusted friend. Your story is by far the most important and relevant part of building your successful practice. Without it, you lack authenticity, meaning, and purpose—virtues that are crucial to your success.

While authenticity, meaning, and purpose are necessary virtues on your journey, it is aspiration, inspiration, and perspiration that form the basic building blocks. Becoming familiar with how each works individually and together is essential before moving into the nuts and bolts of practice building.

ASPIRATION

Regardless of your current practice stage, there is always something you aspire to do.

What are aspirations really? An aspiration in our field is a meaningful act, outcome, or state of being, which affects positively one or more beings in your particular area(s) of interest. For example, you might aspire to assist elderly persons with aging issues, or help depressed people alleviate symptoms of depression. You may wish to assist children in overcoming grief and loss.

EXERCISE 1.1 | Aspirations

Whatever your aspiration(s), write them down in the space below:

_____

_____

_____

INSPIRATION

The best part of inspiration is that you inspire to do for others based on your own discovery and in return you are the benefactor of inspiration from those whom you help change! One helpful way to write about inspiration is to think of those who have inspired you during your work in the field. Then, look for the reciprocal relationship. How do you inspire that person who inspired you?

Remember your story? What or who in your own story inspires you most? If just starting out in practice, think of who inspired you growing up. Pick three areas or more. For example, maybe you are inspired by the child's life you changed while working at an after school program in college. And, because of how you have helped children, you have become inspired to work with children.

As you search your story for these inspirations, take note of how many people and issues inspired you already.

EXERCISE 1.2 | Inspiring People and Experiences

Choose three that are important to you today and write them down in the space provided.

_____

_____

_____

PERSPIRATION

You have just returned from that long run, finished the long hike, performed on the piano, or whatever activity makes you perspire. Perspiration is the carrying out of your inspiration so that you can reach your state of aspiration. This is the action part of the equation. What is your level of perspiration? You can have wonderful aspirations and be inspired, but without perspiration nothing gets done. How hard do you work to tap into your inspirations, and reach the stated levels of aspiration you just wrote down? Are you a consistent worker? Can you string together days of doing what you love; performing well even on those days that you might not love it so much?

You might be thinking, "How can I plan what I am going to do when I have personal as well professional responsibilities, and even unexpected duties that come up?" While these thoughts may be true, place an accurate guess as to how consistent you are and what you are willing to do on a day-to-day basis to make things happen positively in your work. Even reading this book is part of the work you're doing, so give yourself credit for that! In the space below, make a note of when you do your best work. How often do you do it? How many minutes or hours per week are you willing to invest in building your best practice from this point forward?

EXERCISE 1.3 | Committing to Build

In the space below, write down commitments of your time in answer to the questions above.

_____

_____

_____

COMBINING THE THREE

Now that you've explored your aspirations, inspirations, and perspirations, the real secret is to see how they fit together. Most people start with aspiration in their minds. And, it's easy to get stuck there. How often have you started doing something with your goals only to never complete them? Or worse, you fantasize and make plans in your mind only to fail to even get started let alone follow though. Human beings often aspire first and never get to work or feel inspired!

That's why this equation can help:

1 PART PERSPIRATION + 1 PART INSPIRATION = 1 WHOLE ASPIRATION

You need two important parts to yield successful aspirations.

Why perspire before inspiring? The answer is simple. While you know what inspires you, the discovery of inspiration happens through your experience. Examine your past, and you'll find that the discovery of your passion and joy occurred as a result of experience. Experience is perspiration.

As you combine these three concepts over time, something magical occurs. Confidence and trust are built. You develop trust in your work, while others build trust in you because of good outcomes. Then, your confidence grows with diverse and random reinforcements. These reinforcements come in the form of money, client appreciation, colleague appreciation, community appreciation, and so on.

PASSION, TRUST, AND STORY

Trust in self unlocks passion that leads toward success. In the area of smart business development, self-trust builds from experience. As you experience reading and working with the material in this book, your trust in building your practice will grow. I'd like to earn your trust by sharing my story about how people, experiences, and the power of passion helped my journey toward building an ethical, meaningful successful private practice and a desire for business elements in practice:

> What led to private practice and ultimately a strong interest and investment in business matters in the helping professions? My mother, with no college education spent her working life in the business world. Her disdain for oppression, second class-gender identification, and the general status quo, modeled for me a willingness to risk, at times in unpopular and unconventional fashion! Following numerous administrative positions, starting with secretary for a land developer, she developed her own successful small business, using connections she had made through all previous work experience.

> My father, and paternal grandfather had a hand in my passion and inspiration for business. Morris, my grandfather and a true inspiration, owned restaurants in the Chicago area from the late 1930's into the 1970's. Three restaurants spanning four decades, working sixty to seventy hours a week, Gramps' passion for his craft never waned. Then there's my father's business background. His business modeling came by quietly moving up the ranks from sales to management positions in various companies, often taking on leadership roles within organizations he served. Both my father

and grandfather served their communities in their respective roles well. Without a college degree, they didn't earn millions or care about notoriety. Each made many mistakes, learned from them, and defined success by living their passion. Humility and honesty were their unspoken mottos!

Another inspiration is my paternal grandmother's brother, a lawyer and leader in state government. My great uncle, Edward Pringle, served as a Justice on the Supreme Court of Colorado from the late 1960's to the early 1980's, I admired his way of being in an important leadership role in the community. His work and role in government is an inspiration and made a huge impact on my life!

Others are credited with making impressions on my career development. My older brother's success in business also helped move me toward my passions. Experiences outside the family obviously helped shape my interests. Growing up with a part liberal, part conservative Jewish background, including the experience of becoming a Bar Mitzvah, serving leadership roles in a youth organization, and of course my experiences as a camper, counselor and administrator at an overnight summer camp all shaped my interests and helped create passion for counseling, business, and professional leadership.

In college I studied psychology, religion, writing, history, business, and many other fascinating subjects, all of which quenched my thirst for knowledge. There were countless camp counselors, handfuls of camp directors, teachers, and professors, as well as other leaders who mentored and taught me important lessons and values, which eventually led to discovery of passions I never imagined! The impression these experiences and people had on me during my formative years led to interests in business, leadership, justice, and helping others.

During graduate school, I stopped working, borrowed more money, and invested time in leadership roles, while attending classes and studying hard. I accepted an appointed position as Graduate Student Liaison to the Colorado Counseling Association, which lent itself to exposure to the greater counseling community beyond the academic environment. This risk also allowed for other leadership positions on the board, including numerous public speaking opportunities. The value of these early experiences while in graduate school far outweighed the financial costs of giving up paid work for a few years.

After obtaining my license while working at a residential treatment center for adolescents, I opened my practice in 2000, signing on with a group that turned out to be mismanaged. Noting the administrative challenges of that situation, I left after only eight months and some back pay owed to me by the group's owners. I fortunately exited just before the group collapsed, while sadly it was too late for many others who were never paid what they were owed.

I found another group practice in 2001, and this time did plenty of research into the business philosophy and management practices of the company. This experience became quite opposite of my previous entry into the world of private practice. The two partners running this practice started the endeavor three years earlier, upon the request of their former managed care employer. At that time, the group contracted with a few large and growing managed care companies, and housed about six providers. Therein lay a problem, and an opportunity. A well-diversified available managed care contract base along with the lack of enough geographic representation of providers became a problem for a larger community in need! Approaching the owners with nothing to lose but my pride, I suggested they expand these two arenas to remain solvent, and that if their business model was to work, they would have to diversify by adding more managed care contracts, and a greater spread of providers in outlying areas of the community.

A short time later, in addition to running a full time clinical practice, I found myself in the position of building the infrastructure of this group practice at the request of the owners. This seven-year in-house consulting job included accomplishments building the group to over forty providers, with a psychiatry service division, and adding ten new insurance contracts, several of them with successful rate renegotiations every few years. I left the group in 2010 to pursue private consulting, public speaking, training, and writing, while continuing to grow my clinical work. I am grateful to both owners for taking a chance on my passion and youthful wisdom, and for their support and mentoring.

Another experience turned passion is my relationship with a graduate school professor who challenged me academically like no other. As our postgraduate school relationship blossomed, having been invited to come back to give talks to the honors society and in classes of existing students, I inquired about whether the graduate program could ever house an entire course on private practice building. She replied by asking whether I would be interested in designing and teaching a curriculum for such a course. With her support, and my drive, I developed the first course in the country on private practice building housed within an accredited graduate level counseling program, which I taught for about fifteen years.

Today, I work to leave a legacy that I am proud of through my work as a clinical practitioner, business consultant, trainer, public speaker, advocate for health and wellness and now author of a book about honest and ethical business development in private practice.

My story of passion for business, counseling, teaching, speaking, and training is unique, just like yours. So, it's time to write *your* story! Take a few pages out of your own book and write or re-write your story. Go back in time to discover and re-discover your passion(s) that led you toward a career in this important work. Write about your particular interests in the field and how each interest developed. Be specific. The more detailed and the more connections drawn from your developmental process, the better. You are great at getting your clients to do this type of work. Now it's your turn.

EXERCISE 1.4 | Write Your Story

Below are a few tips to remember when writing your story of how you came to work in this field you love. When writing your story, just write, free form. You can go back later and polish it if you'd like. The important thing is to get your thoughts and feelings onto paper and start connecting! Here are your tips:

1. **Who are my major influencers during childhood? Adolescence? Adulthood? Currently?**
2. **What lessons/values did I learn from these people?**
3. **What are my major experiences in life?**
4. **What did I learn from these experiences?**
5. **What am I passionate about in my field? What areas? Specifically?**
6. **How do these passions connect to earlier lessons/influences or stories?**

Upon completion of this exercise, take a moment to step back. Reflect. How am I feeling about what I just wrote? Does my soul resonate with each word on the page, each piece of my passion puzzle? Pay attention to what is congruent. Consider sharing your story with another person and obtain feedback. What does it feel like to share your story?

FORWARD MOTION : PATIENCE, RISK AND ACTION!

Put your pen down now and trust in yourself, as I trust you, and it's time to move forward together in this journey of practice building. But first, let's do a little reframe around three very important concepts you'll be using the rest of the way: *patience, risk and action!*

Success isn't made in a day and doesn't occur overnight. You are almost certainly going to make more mistakes than experience successful outcomes, especially in the beginning! If you were selling widgets, let's say, and you spent just one hour on the phone contacting ten people to tell them about your amazing widgets, how many would you sell? One, maybe two if you are lucky? That's a failure rate of eighty percent! Suppose the next day you spent ten hours calling prospects about your widgets. You call nearly one hundred people. How many widgets are you likely to sell? I venture to guess ten to twenty, again an eighty percent failure rate. "That's a lot of failure!" you think. True. It's also a great success! Your hard work in the extra nine hours you spend above the one-hour of work you did the previous day landed nearly 10 times the number of sales compared to your earnings from only one hour of work the previous day. You went from one sale to eight sales in a day, *and* you still failed to complete a sale much of the time.

Remember, you must have *patience* for failure. You often have to *risk* new behaviors and put them into *action*. Risking and taking action to create forward motion and momentum over time is a recipe for success. With this in mind, you are about to embark on creating an effective, meaningful, and purposeful private practice plan, one that is unique to you, which is born out of the *story of your passion.*

CHAPTER TWO |
THE PRIVATE PRACTICE PLAN

While risk is an important component of success, planning your risk is essential. "I am not a risk taker," you think. Or, "Every time I risk, I fail miserably. I don't know where to begin." These are very common internal thoughts of the highly capable, extremely competent clinician. You are not alone in thinking such thoughts. As I travel around the country training clinicians on matters of business planning and implementation of their craft, time and again I am told of risk aversive business behaviors that are counterproductive. It's my job to teach each clinician how to unlock and change views through the creation, adoption, and revision of an individualized Private Practice Business Plan.

Some practice consultants will tell you that you don't need to create a business plan to be successful in practice. While this may be true, without a solid plan you will run the risk of business organization problems, poor decision making, and lack of follow through. To be honest, I never had my own plan in the beginning of my practice. No one taught me to think that way, and there certainly wasn't a lot in print nor anything in the form of live business trainings for practitioners at the turn of the century when I began my practice. I had to wing it, and if it weren't for the graces of the insurance companies, and my experience with the successful group practice I helped build, I am certain I would not have made it without a business plan.

With the explosion of the Internet and larger numbers of clinicians moving into part or full-time practices, it's becoming ever more challenging to move in the right direction. There are many more options today around practice specialties, and the make-up of a private practice than there were twenty years ago. While this is great news for both practitioners and clients, our "new mental health field" requires a carefully thought out, value aligned, and solid plan for a successful practice.

Think of this plan as your blueprint for calculated risk. This notion should take away some of the fears of risk, as through the development of your plan confidence will ensue, along with a greater willingness to take risks, in a thoughtful manner.

A plan is so important that in the graduate level training course I designed, creating a written comprehensive private practice business plan was a major assignment worth 60% of the final grade. Broken into an outline, followed by a rough draft, and the final plan, the students completed the plan in 3 stages over about 10 weeks (roughly the final two thirds of the course). Then, each student created a 30-minute presentation that they provided to the rest of their classmates to get experience sharing their ideas. If you'd like to take a look at an actual completed business plan of one of my students, you can visit www.smartpracticecentral.com and in the "resources" tab you will see "sample business plan."

To reduce your fears and build your confidence, here's a simple 10-step process to help you with your risk process:

Step 1: Create a practice plan template

Step 2: Work thoughtfully on each section of the template

Step 3: Review your plan

Step 4: Practice with consistency what's outlined in your plan

Step 5: Evaluate outcomes as successful or needing more work

Step 6: Repeat processes that lead to successful outcomes

Step 7: Re-write parts of the plan that didn't work well

Step 8: Practice the new re-writes

Step 9: Repeat steps 4–8

Step 10: Take time to enjoy your growth and sustainability

This 10-step process is your patience, risk and action business model. Your private practice business plan is a blueprint of your future, the process of the now, and the archive of outcomes. As you work throughout your practice years, these areas will shift and change, always maintaining a presence within your plan! As a mentor of mine once said, "Plan your work, and work your plan!"

Your Private Practice Plan Template

After many years of putting together and teaching the process of creating business plans, what I learned is to keep it simple and well defined. If you are having any trouble understanding the sections, or wish to adjust them to better fit your business needs, feel free to do just that. This general template is merely a way of helping you guide your business planning process. In this section, I describe each section of the Private Practice Plan Template. You can also find a full template without description in Appendix A.

Executive Summary: The executive summary is a brief explanation of the contents of your entire plan. It's not a list or table of contents. Rather, it's a one-page written summary of the main points of your practice plan. Think of it as your abstract to the research paper you have just written, after you have conducted your research. Since your plan is not yet written, it's best to skip this part and save it for the very end. When you are done writing your comprehensive plan, you can sit down, say "last but not least" to yourself, and write this section.

Mission Statement: In the previous chapter I shared my story and journey into practice and through life, which led to my passions and current involvements. Hopefully, after reading my story, you are busy remembering and writing about your development as a professional helper. Your mission statement is a brief description of the passion itself. The story that led to your passion is being told in the here and now experience of what you do today and aim to change tomorrow. It's a thoughtful, well-written statement or two of the small but important contributions you are making to the world!

Here are examples of mission statements:

- *General clinical practice mission statement*—"Helping people **build** and practice new skills, in order to **change** that which is painful, damaging, or otherwise intrusive to living, to mindfully **grow** and become truly authentic."

- *Relationship therapy mission statement*—"Establishing a greater relational foundation, while repairing conflict and avoidance through building **communication, intimacy, and trust.**"

- *Smart Practice Central business mission statement*—"To raise the standard of how we do business as practitioners, creating systems of success that are transparent to clients, colleagues, and community, while encompassing the values of **smart business decisions, strong ethical behavior, and clinically mindful treatment.**"

The examples above are all related to my current passions and endeavors! Yes, you can actually have more than one mission statement. Remember, this is *your* business plan.

I like counseling in general and have an overall philosophy relating to what makes people change. By nature I have discovered that I am a behaviorist. Practical about change, I have found over the years that change comes from building upon one's strengths, and behaviorally managing difficult symptoms, while setting and reaching new goals. Hence, I developed a very simple, easy to understand philosophy of treatment, which I can market to the average help seeker. Terms like "build, change, and grow" are simple and catching.

Because I love working with couples and have developed my own easily-understood theoretical model about what makes couples successful in counseling, I created a mission statement for my couples work. It provides enough interest in my philosophy to get interested partners asking the right questions about therapy under my direction.

You know your mission statement is good when you get that gut feeling it fits you and what you do. You know it's great when that feeling turns into a sense that your prospective client is already starting treatment as you are   with them about your mission.

EXERCISE 2.1 | Mission Statement

Take a few moments and write a mission statement. Put your ideas on paper. Write several, one or two versions for each and every passion or major area of interest in your field!

Here are few important points to think about when creating a solid mission statement:

- What's your passion or interest?
- List short-term and long-term goals
- Make it creative
- Use simple language

_____

_____

_____

_____

_____

_____

_____

Tagline: Not all businesses use a tagline. While it's certainly not a requirement, a solid tagline can truly enhance the message of your mission using a short phrase or series of words. Your tagline is a way of "branding" your practice! The tagline may have words that are used in the name of your practice, or it can contain key words directly from your mission statement. And, if you think about it, it's a great way to help market your services.

My Taglines:

- *Private practice tagline*—"Build, Change, Grow" (This is also the name of my website!)

- *Couples therapy program tagline*—"Connective Communication, Diverse Intimacy, Growing Trust" (This tagline uses words from my theory that communication, intimacy and trust are essential to healthy relationships, and thus the basic arenas in which couples therapy takes shape.)

- *Smart Practice Central business tagline*—"Smart Business, Strong Ethics, Clinical Integrity"

Do you notice anything that these three separate taglines have in common? They each have aspects of "three" in them. For me, breaking ideas into three exclusive and connected parts is helpful in creating my taglines. This may be a helpful way for you to create your tagline. You don't have to follow this exact idea. If you have a way of coming up with a tagline that works well for you, by all means create it in your unique way.

EXERCISE 2.2 | Tagline

Go back and read your mission statement. Now it's your turn to take a crack at creating your tagline.

A few pointers about taglines:

- Keep it brief enough to fit under the name of your business or a logo
- Make sure it captures the spirit and meaning of your mission statement
- Be creative with wording
- Say a lot in just a few words

_____

_____

_____

Logo: The creative tagline you just developed needs a brand or "logo" above it that also speaks to your mission. The logo is a picture, graphic, or original artwork that gives consumers a sense of your services, and is about you the practitioner as well as your mission. It's extremely important to either craft your own original image, or make certain that if you are using an existing image, it's either fully free for commercial use, or that you have written permission from its creator.

Branding! Combining Tagline & Logo: Once you have your logo design it's time to blend it together with your tagline for a professional and eye catching brand that is about you, your mission, and those you serve.

One of my high-achiever graduate students created her business around individuals and families recovering from various addictions. She appropriately named her business "Rooted in Recovery." Thus, as you might imagine, you see a beautiful piece of original artwork in the form of roots winding around the trunk of a large tree inside a circle. She commissioned the work to be done solely for her business branding. Under her logo, the business name exists, and beneath the business name are two taglines, one that shows three simple words: *"Acceptance, Growth, Freedom,"* followed below by *"Discover your path to personal transformation."*

FIGURE 2.0 | Branding Example

Rooted in Recovery Counseling, LLC

Acceptance   Growth   Freedom

Discover your path to personal transformation

This example ties the logo, tagline, and practice name together on the back of a business card.

Figure 2.0 shows her branding design as it appears on the back of her business card. (The card background is green, a calm earth-like tone that has many extrapolations: Green is clean, promotes calm, symbolizes growth and blooming, leaves of a tree providing shade and shelter.)

EXERCISE 2.3 | Creating Your Logo

Whether or not you have creativity in your genes, on a piece of paper write a description of what you see in your mind as your logo.

1. What do you want others who seek your services to see?
2. Imagine for a moment that you are seeking your own services. What would you like to see? What is your visual cue that draws you in?
3. Think about design, color, and content. Write something for each of these three areas.

Design: _____

Color: _____

Content: _____

4. Take out another piece of paper and try drawing a mock up of your logo after using the space provided following #5 to draw your quick doodle.
5. You can also look online through Google Images Search to get ideas of pictures and clip art. (Be certain that you do not copy existing material that is not otherwise denoted as free for reproduction. You can find what's free for reproduction by going to the "advanced search" tab in Google Images—"Settings" on the lower right. Once in the "advanced search" page, scroll down to "usage rights" and choose the "free to use or share . . ." option that fits best) Use the space below to draw a quick doodle idea of your logo:

The Four C's of Private Practice Business Planning

If you have ever purchased a diamond, you might recall the important Four "C's" one must know: Carat, Color, Cut, & Clarity.

In business planning, one should become more self-aware by assessing the following areas: *Strengths, Weaknesses, Opportunities, Threats (SWOT)*. You may have heard or seen these terms before if you have ever seen or completed a business plan. To create easier terms that resonate more with therapists, I prefer to think of these as *The Four C's of Private Practice Business Planning*.

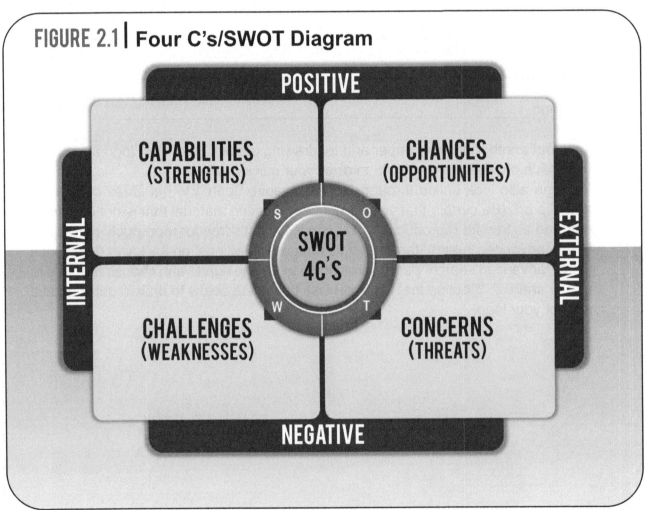

FIGURE 2.1 | Four C's/SWOT Diagram

THE FOUR C'S INTERNAL/EXTERNAL AND POSITIVE/NEGATIVE AXES

In the figure above, you can see that *capabilities* and *challenges* are internal in nature, while *chances* and *concerns* revolve around external influence. Additionally, *capabilities* and *chances* are positive influences, while *challenges* and *concerns* carry negative influences.

Take a look at Figure 2.2 below. This is a true sampling of some of my Four C's. Notice how some are repetitive in different categories.

FIGURE 2.2 | Author's Four C's

	PERSONAL	PROFESSIONAL
Capabilities	• Caring, passionate, thoughtful • Ambitious • Extrovert • Ethical, Responsible	• Business minded & intelligent • Passionate about helping others • Strong interest in science of psychology • Ethical, Responsible
Challenges	• I worry too much • I over-commit at times • Occasional verbal diarrhea • Mild organization issues	• I over-commit at times • Listening/Talking balance in session • Organization • Overly flexible with schedule • Public speaking proficiency
Chances	• Earning a living doing what I love! • Personal growth/benefit that stems from professional training	• Working with children, teenagers, men and couples • Providing professional consultation/training programs to clinicians • Product development
Concerns	• Balance of personal/professional • Physical/Mental consequences of over-commitment	• Not enough time/money to reach the masses with my message/passion!

Over time, the lists in each category change. For example, I always thought I was organized. As responsibilities in my work increase, not to mention my advancing age, I realize that organization issues are rapidly becoming a personal challenge. Thus, it recently made my list. The idea is to get a snap shot of you in each box, with a "status report" approximately once a year (just like an annual medical check up), during which updates are made, pulling items off a particular box that no longer fit, and adding new items that are relevant to you now.

Here are final thoughts on your "Four C's" of your plan:

1. Pull out your smart phone

2. Take a picture of your chart

3. Store the picture somewhere safe

4. Take it out and look at it, read it from time to time to remind you to be aware of these areas in your personal and professional spheres

5. Schedule your formal "annual review" when you will update and change what's needed in each area!

EXERCISE 2.4 | My Four C's

Complete your "Four C's" in two different areas: *personal* and *professional.* Note that you may end up seeing overlap in terms of putting the same thought down in personal and professional areas, and even across more than one of the Four C's, just as I did in mine.

	PERSONAL	PROFESSIONAL
CAPABILITIES		
CHALLENGES		
CHANCES		
CONCERNS		

By now you have discovered your mission from within your passions, developed one or two creative taglines, and even created a mock-up of your logo design to blend into your brand. You worked on your personal and professional analysis of *capability, challenge, chance, and concern!*

The next section of your plan is perhaps easiest to write. It's easy because it's everything about your training and what you intend to do in the future with your training and experience. Whether you are just beginning your practice or trying to reach the next level, your services plan plays a pivotal role in the success and joy of your overall business.

Services Plan: Do you remember your Journalism course in junior high or middle school? Recall the "rule of 5 W's and H" when writing an article. Your use of this rule as applied to your services makes it much easier to think, create, and write this section. In case you forgot . . . here's the breakdown: *who, what, where, when, why, and how!*

Who—are you working with? List your ideal client who you prefer to see. For example, I work with children/adolescents, couples, individual males, females, students, employees, and employer groups, as well as groups in general.

What—are the types of issues you treat? List all issues, both issues that exist diagnostically, as well as general areas or problems you treat. For example, diagnosis-wise, I treat depression, anxiety, PTSD, ADD/ADHD, and other diagnoses. I also work with narcissism in males, relational trust, emotional healing from trauma, confidence and self-esteem issues in children/adolescents. This part of your plan is crucial in helping you be aware of the diverse services you provide.

When—are you offering your services? When would you like to make yourself available to your clients? What are your general office hours? When would you like return calls, or have out of session consultations? When will you perform essential administrative functions? The "when" is about structuring your day. It's important to create structure for yourself, and do the best to stick to that structure, keeping your time boundaries with your clients.

Where—do you do your work? Don't simply put down your office(s). There are many places you may be doing your work or hoping to do your work. Any time you go into schools and provide a program, or to court to testify, or hold an educational seminar outside of your office, or visit your patient in a hospital, you are doing work in places other than your "primary" location. So, mention your primary and secondary areas where you perform your duties, as well as those places you'd like to get into for sharing your gifts. The latter may include teaching a course at a university, seeing patients an afternoon a week in a doctor's office, presenting at conferences, or even traveling, regionally or nationally, providing seminars/workshops.

Why—are you providing your services? This is a simple answer: "See mission statement!" Your reasons go back to your passions. And, now that you have written much about your passion in your mission statement, you have many ways that you can share the "why" of your services plan.

How—exactly are you performing or providing your services? Discuss the interventions you use as a practicing clinician. You may, for example, share that you use the following techniques: Cognitive Behavioral Therapy (CBT), Emotionally Focused Therapy (EFT), Behavioral Therapy, Solution-Focused Techniques, etc. List your favorite techniques first.

Does your services plan have diversity, depth, and definition? A good way to include all three of these elements is shown in figure 2.3. Like a dartboard, the center represents your "bulls-eye" or ideal client, or specialization area(s). The next circle might represent the areas of focus where you like to work and have expertise, but which aren't necessarily considered a specialty. The outer circle represents clients or issues within the scope of your training that you are willing to see.

FIGURE 2.3 | Circles of Services

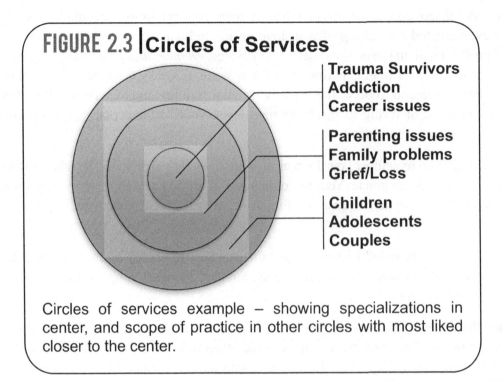

Trauma Survivors
Addiction
Career issues

Parenting issues
Family problems
Grief/Loss

Children
Adolescents
Couples

Circles of services example – showing specializations in center, and scope of practice in other circles with most liked closer to the center.

EXERCISE 2.5 | Circles of Services

Complete the figure with your specialties in the bulls-eye or inner circle and those areas you like but aren't highly specialized in the next circle, followed by other areas you treat that are within the general scope of your abilities in the outermost circle. Now you have your ideal client(s) defined as well as those with whom you work in general. Put this graphic in your business plan once completed.

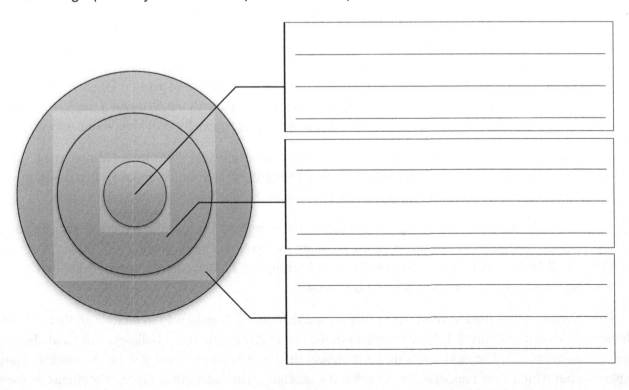

Networking/Marketing: Client referrals are perhaps the most important aspect of your business. Without a consistent flow of clients who are a good fit for your particular practice areas and style, you won't be running a successful business.

Since this section of the plan is so important, there is an entire chapter dedicated to this subject. When you arrive at chapter 4, *Systematic Structure & Facilitation,* you will study my uniquely defined networking and marketing concepts which are specifically designed to help you not simply get clients, but actually get the clients you would like in your practice. Stay tuned for targeted exercises and information, including how to create your very own "referral wheel," a concept for finding good clients that I developed and successfully implemented in my own clinical practice!

Practice Administration: What are the essential tasks that must be performed, often on a routine basis, in your business? While you may perform many of these non-clinical, administrative functions in the beginning of your practice, at some point you will need to hire people to help you carry out these tasks, especially when you are busy seeing clients! Who are the people you need to support the administrative processes of your business?

EXERCISE 2.6 | Practice Administration Breakdown

Create the beginnings of your administration plan. Below is a chart of common administrative tasks involved in routinely running your practice. These tasks are shown on the left side of the chart. On the right side of the chart, fill in the name(s) of the person(s) responsible for those tasks. Several names might be yours when you are just beginning, however you may need to start looking for another professional, as you get busy with seeing clients.

ADMINISTRATIVE TASK	ASSIGNED INDIVIDUAL
Appointment Scheduling	
Website Development/Upkeep	
Office Supply Orders	
3rd Party Billing	
Bookkeeping	
Tax Preparation	
Organizing of Client Files	
Managed Care Contracting	
General Marketing	

Financial Growth and Management: As you practice, it's vital to create and sustain financial value in your work, in order to build greater value and provide higher quality services to your community as you grow professionally. It's important that you keep your personal quality of life at a reasonable standard. I talk about reasonable standard of living because most practitioners undervalue their practice or worth as a clinician. While managed care contract rates are often far lower than your usual and customary rate, there are methods to help you retain your true value financially and grow your business while still working with managed care insurance panels. We will discuss these methods throughout the rest of the book.

For now, you need the basic structure of growing and managing your finances. This structure includes setting up proper banking accounts, in a manner that is seamless, efficient and thorough. It also includes having a routine financial program and process for tracking receivables and payables. It also involves knowing and following tax codes and procedures to the letter. And, finally, creating and working a personal saving and investing plan is extremely important!

You will learn much more about protecting, managing and growing money in Chapter's Three and Nine. It is important that you read these chapters before actually completing these steps. For now, here are a few basic steps to get you started on putting financial management information into your business plan:

6 Steps to Financial Protection, Management, and Growth

Step 1: Talk with an attorney about becoming a corporate entity
Step 2: Set up bank account(s)
Step 3: Create a process for tracking receivables & payables
Step 4: Talk with your tax preparer about tax planning, for both business and personal
Step 5: Talk to an insurance professional about types of insurance that will protect assets
Step 6: Create financial savings and investment plan (Financial planner as needed).

Professional Growth & Development: Your professional growth is extremely important when it comes to getting better at what you do best. In Chapter Ten, you will develop a comprehensive professional development and growth plan that entails designing what specific trainings and/or professional certifications you will complete as you develop your practice. For now, start thinking about the areas where you'd like more specialty training.

Personal Growth: It is easy to become overwhelmed by wearing the two hats of business owner and clinician. Managing your work/life balance is essential when it comes to building and maintaining a strong clinical practice. Creating and following a personal growth burnout avoidance plan is extremely important. Many clinicians I know take care of their clients and the people in their personal lives, with very little focus on caring for the self. Your personal growth is essential to the success of your business. Start thinking about the ways you take care of yourself. Chapter Ten will outline four key burnout avoidance techniques for self-care, while helping you further your personal growth ideas.

Diversity Inclusion: Most clinicians never think about how to plan for inclusion of the numerous types of diverse individuals who walk into their offices! In fact, if anything, often you are trained to "specialize" in working with certain populations. Though I told you to create concentric circles, with specialties in the center of your dartboard, a diversity inclusion plan is something quite different from treatment specialization.

For example, a client suffering from a degenerative eye disease, her sight slowly disappearing, one day noted that the elevator in our office building had no Braille. I immediately called the building manager to request Braille be put in the elevator and in common areas, and sure enough (it's the law by the way), within two days there was Braille for all buttons in the elevator. Some clinicians put artifacts from other cultures in their offices; others put "LGBTQ" friendly material in their offices and statements on their websites.

Your diversity inclusion plan is really about your sensitivity to other people of varied culture, sexual orientation/preferences, gender, socio-economic status, religion, ability, age, and the list goes on. As time passes our culture grows, changes, and becomes ever more diverse. At some point in your life, you were taught diversity sensitivity. Now it's time to apply that sensitivity to your practice.

EXERCISE 2.7 | Diversity Inclusion Plan

Create a diversity inclusion plan for your office. Explain how you are currently sensitive to others different from you and others. Build new ideas into your plan about how you can become more aware and inclusive of differences in your office setting, and throughout your marketing plan.

_____

_____

_____

_____

References & Resources: As you might guess, references and resources are the last section of your comprehensive business plan. The references part shows the tools you used to create the plan. And, there's a second section to your "references." This list includes all reading material you compiled throughout your career and that you would recommend to clients, and perhaps colleagues. Your resource guide includes all resources that you accumulate throughout your practice journey. These resources might include community agencies, hospitals, hotlines, specialized programs, colleagues, unique websites, and other ideas. Make sure you update these lists about once a year.

EXERCISE 2.8 | Books and Resources

Start a list of all the books you read related to your profession, as well as all the community resources you know within your community.

Books I read and recommend: _____

_____

_____

_____

Resources in my community: _____

_____

_____

_____

Congratulations! You are now an expert in knowing how to plan for a successful business and practice. This business plan template has been refined over years of consulting and teaching. You may use sections that are relevant to you, or even create a template that is entirely different than the one outlined in this chapter. What matters most is that you create a solid plan wherever you are in the development and building process of your clinical practice. I recommend you show your plan to others you trust as you are in the development and refining process. Feedback from other trusted professionals in the field, as well as family and friends may be invaluable. Just remember you are the ultimate designer and engineer of your plan. As you work through the rest of this book, take time to go back to your plan and add to or modify it as you see fit. Remember, plans often change, and outcomes will look different in reality than within the plan itself.

CHAPTER THREE |
PRACTICE PROTECTION, ADMINISTRATION & MANAGEMENT

Inefficient administrative systems, poor protection, and subpar management have caused countless talented private practice owners to fail. The goal of this chapter is to help you make certain you have a properly designed business infrastructure in terms of liability protections, effective administrative systems, and top-notch management strategies. You are creating a small business that needs low overhead, without compromising quality and efficiency. And, you must set these systems in place in an organized, honorable, ethical, and legal fashion. Let's investigate each one, placing an emphasis on practical answers and solutions.

Business Protections: Do you carry malpractice insurance for your private practice? If you are just starting out, have you looked for liability plans that fit your needs? Do you know the limits to your plan, or the limits you need? Most insurance carriers and agencies require minimally $1 million per occurrence and $3 million aggregate of annual liability coverage. Cost for your coverage depends on how much you practice (e.g. part-time, full-time), geographical location, policy type including limits and add-ons, claim history, and other miscellaneous factors. While liability coverage is a must, you cannot afford to stop there when it comes to protection.

What happens, for example, if a client trips over a cord in your office, breaks a leg, and tries make you liable for their medical treatment? Or perhaps you are out with your friends on a beautiful weekend rock climbing and fall and hit your head, discovering that while you survived the fall, you have a serious brain injury that will keep you from responsibly performing your duties for at least 12 months? You are rendered disabled and have no income from your practice. Consider a dispute with a contracted insurance company, or a business partner with whom you share ownership of a program or even an entire practice, and one of these entities or individuals believes you have broken contract, and sues you.

A malpractice policy alone is not enough to cover expenses that occur from any of these examples. In fact, you could experience a great deal of financial loss, including the possibility of losing personal holdings such as your house, savings, or other assets by not setting up proper protections for these and other possible "attacks" on your business, personal holdings and/or basic livelihood.

Let's go back to our three examples now. Can you guess what protections you need for each of them? Give it a try:

EXAMPLE 1

Your client trips over a cord in your office and comes after you for medical expenses!

The Business Key Policy or Premises/Theft Insurance policy should be put in place to protect you when a client is injured at your office. Additionally, this coverage protects items that are stolen from your office. When setting up your policy, you will be asked by your insurance agent to estimate the value of items you own in your office and in some cases you may be required to list some or all of the items you would like to have covered. Most commercial property management companies actually require this type of policy be in place and this is stipulated in your commercial lease.

The insurance company that holds your malpractice or liability policy may be a good resource for purchasing your theft/premises (business key) protection. In some cases, you can add this type of coverage on to your Malpractice/Professional Liability Policy. It is important to compare coverage options with any insurance policy. Some policies have lower premiums. Lower premiums may translate to less coverage. So be sure not only to look at a premium price point, also check into the content of coverage. Your insurance agent can help, but remember the agent earns money based on type of coverage and how much is sold to you. So, it's important that you talk with colleagues about their coverage(s) and consider discussing such matters with a professional consultant in your chosen field.

Answer: Premises/Theft Insurance or Business Key Policy

EXAMPLE 2

You experience head injury from a fall and can't work for 12 months!

Disability insurance is one of the most important types of coverage. More professionals get injured versus dying while in the thick of their career, and yet for some reason more practice owners carry life insurance, but no disability insurance. I often hear owners say, "Why do I even need disability coverage? If I break a leg I can still use my mind to help people!" In the example earlier, a head injury was the hypothetical accident.

Answer: Disability Insurance

A real instance actually occurred in my practice. In early 2011, I was out on a cool February Friday evening with my wife and mother enjoying dinner and what would be a movie afterward. While we were waiting for the movie to begin I felt a little queasy and mentioned so to my wife. The movie began and the odd camera angles and continuous motion of the images made me dizzy, and I began feeling like I needed some fresh air. Ten minutes into the picture, I arose from my seat walking briskly up the ramp to the exit doors, and the last thing I recall was hitting the double doors, slamming into a porcelain wall in the lobby (knocking my head on the wall) and finally waking up on the cold tile floor of the vintage movie theatre. Yes, I gave my wife and mother a big scare, inconvenienced the other movie-goers, the staff, and most significantly received a concussion. It could have been much worse, as I am thankful that I recovered fully and returned to my job as a professional counselor. Though I returned without missing any days, one of my first thoughts upon awakening from my blackout was, "Thank goodness I have medical insurance, and good disability coverage!"

EXAMPLE 3

You encounter a legal dispute with a contracted entity (not your client) in which said entity sues you.

This example illustrates one of the simplest, low cost mechanisms for protecting liability and assets, and yet many professional helpers fail to investigate and commit to becoming a legal entity such as the most common small business entity, the Limited Liability Company (LLC). The idea behind obtaining this kind of protection is in separating your business from you personally. Implementing this protective mechanism means your business and what it owns becomes the first and only layer of assets that can be extricated should a judgment occur against your business, thus protecting you and the assets you personally own, such as your house and personal savings. Attorneys use a unique phrase to illustrate what this legal protection actually does. They say your entity is an important layer of protection that keeps others from "piercing the veil" into your personal assets. The veil is the legal business entity. Let's come back to the specifics and issues revolving around obtaining and maintaining your legal entity a bit later in this chapter.

Answer: Legal entity (e.g. LLC, S-corporation, or other legal business entity)

In our discussion of these numerous protections, it's important you know that each of these protection layers alone helps in certain areas, and under unique circumstances, but not enough standing alone. Together, however, they represent a powerful and solid structure making your business and personal life's assets a virtual Fort Knox. Impenetrable. While it's impossible to set up all these protections in a short amount of time, I recommend working on the important ones first, and adding further as you are able. However, here are a few protections that you MUST put in place prior to ever earning your first penny or seeing your first client.

MALPRACTICE OR PROFESSIONAL LIABILITY INSURANCE

If you learned anything about liability protection in graduate school, the one piece that should be driven into your mind is the need for malpractice or professional liability insurance. This type of protection is a must before entering into any professional helping relationship. It is your main protection against liability in the practice of your craft. As mentioned in the beginning of this chapter, you need to make sure you have the right limits to your policy, and know that most third party payers require minimum coverages. In addition to how often you practice and geographical location, your annual premium will also be determined by your discipline. Psychiatrists, for example, typically pay more for their malpractice policy than say a clinical social worker because their liability is assessed to be greater by the insurer based on claims history for that discipline, as well as the liabilities of prescribing medication and performing other duties not performed by a social worker. Again, it's important to compare policies and understand what you are purchasing. For information about where to begin looking for your professional liability policy, see Appendix I.

BUSINESS KEY POLICY OR PREMISES/THEFT INSURANCE

Though I already discussed the nature of a "business key policy" or premises insurance, please remember the following tips about purchasing such a policy:

Tips on getting the right business insurance

1. *Make sure your coverage includes theft & slip/fall injury*
2. *Investigate whether your malpractice carrier offers this coverage type*
3. *Get three good quotes as a comparison*
4. *Remember lower premiums may translate to less coverage*

LEGAL BUSINESS ENTITY

Let's return now to one of our examples and our discussion on creating a legal entity. Creating a legal entity such as an LLC or sub-chapter S-Corporation is not like purchasing an insurance policy. A legal entity is your way of further protecting assets and personal liability when founded claims go beyond the limits of malpractice coverage, or when your malpractice coverage won't protect you. The example given earlier shows how you might be sued and not be covered by your malpractice policy due to the non-clinical nature of the infraction.

When creating a legal entity, most professional helpers are concerned with the types of entities available and what will be best for them. Perhaps you are stuck in the same situation, not knowing what is right for you. Stout and Grand (2005) outline numerous types of legal entities. It's important to research the best option and certainly helpful to consult an attorney regarding types of legal entities available in your state, and which entity is recommended for your particular situation.

Once you choose an entity right for you, an attorney should draft proper documents defining and supporting how the entity operates. For example, if your company is going to be a corporation, then your attorney will draft Articles of Incorporation, which define the necessary rules of how the business operates. In the case of a Limited Liability Company (LLC), the document needed is called the Operating Agreement, which also outlines how the company operates. If you have a business partner(s) and choose to create a Limited Liability Partnership (LLP), you would then need a Partnership Agreement for the purpose of defining how the business operates through the partnership entity. Without such an agreement, your state's general rules governing how businesses operate becomes your default agreement. In most cases states' rules are too general to adequately define how your particular business operates, rendering your legal entity more penetrable if you do not have an exclusive agreement described.

While your initial entity filing process with the state takes less time than watching your favorite sitcom episode and costs anywhere from $50 (if you work in Iowa) to $615 (if you work in Illinois), your professional agreement will cost an additional amount when drafted by an attorney. Attorney's fees depend on how detailed the agreement and the time it takes to complete the work. Some attorneys charge a flat fee, while others use their hourly rate. Occasionally corporate attorneys give discounts to those who provide numerous clients at the same time. An example is one attorney who charged half his going rate to come out to a central location and draft operating agreements for 5 different therapists who had an office in the same building, but wanted separate legal entities. You should budget as little as an additional $500 and as much as $2,000 for your specific Operating Agreement, Partnership Agreement, or Articles of Incorporation.

You may wonder whether you can get away with only filing your entity with the state without the proper agreement. A legal entity without Articles of Incorporation or an Operating Agreement is like a bottle of water without the water. You are not actually protected in court when a judge or opposing counsel asks how your business is defined under the protection of your entity. Once you say, "it's not, your honor," the judge could find you personally liable when there's a judgment against you.

In addition to the supporting documents, once your legal entity is filed with your state (your attorney will do this on your behalf if you choose), you need to either assign your attorney, yourself, or another trusted individual to process any routine reviews by your state. In my state of Colorado, business owners must file annual review documents, which most states allow you to do online. Colorado has an email reminder system for annual reminders that tell you when a filing deadline is approaching and even offers the website link for simple filing. As with most filings, there is usually a fee. Stay on top of your deadlines or the fee for annual review is often greater. Remember, filing fees differ according to state. The filing fee for an annual review for an LLC in Colorado is $10 online. In Florida, the annual review filing fee for the same legal entity is just over $138. Please make certain to check on these fees and filing frequency in your state. For further information about initial filing and annual renewal fees see Appendix I, Legal Entity Resources and Fees By State.

One important aspect about your legal entity you should remember is that in order to properly operate your company as the entity you choose, you need to put the legal name of your business on every clinical form, all marketing materials, including each and every webpage on your website, and even on the name plate of your office suite or office door. The more you identify and operate as the entity you choose, the less likely you are going to be held accountable personally for any wrongdoing.

Tax Implications of Legal Entity

There are certain tax-related implications that depend on the type of legal entity you choose. For example, the Limited Liability Company (LLC) is a simple flow through entity that allows you as the taxpayer to simply file a Schedule C for your business dealings, instead of a completely separate business return. If you are a subchapter S-Corporation, you must file a separate business tax return along with other tax-related documents throughout the fiscal year. It is important that you consult with your accountant or tax adviser about how your choice of legal entity will impact your tax filing process and cost.

Where The Money Goes

Proper financial behavior is always required in order to comply with legitimizing your business. While you will learn more about financial management and taxes in Chapter Nine, you need to know that for purposes of properly running the financial end of your legal entity, you must obtain a business checking account, into which you will deposit all money coming from your clients in order to account for your business as a financial entity separate from yourself. You will also only flow money from your business account into other accounts and never the other way around, unless you are lending your business money that you are accounting for in your bookkeeping. The next two figures properly illustrate how to financially operate the flow of money in your business.

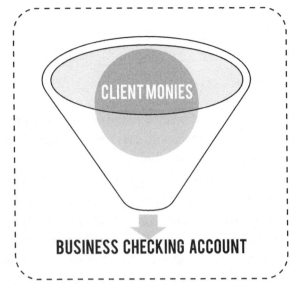

Figure 3.1: Illustration of how all client payments are deposited into your business checking account

Figure 3.2: Illustration of how money in the business should flow from your business into your personal account(s)

While these two figures illustrate a fundamental business behavior financially, you must never underestimate the importance of operating the financial process of your business in this basic manner. The financial behaviors illustrated in Figures 3.1 and 3.2 are essential as they help define your business as a legitimate business. Money comes into your business entity bank account, and then "passes through" into your personal holdings, using the business account as a holding account for just enough dollars to manage your monthly business expenses plus $1,000.00 or so.

You will learn more about financial behaviors, including banking and investing strategies in Chapter Nine. For now, protect your hard-earned dollars by becoming a legal entity, with specified documents on how your company operates, and behave as a legitimate business as well!

Remember, you are a good clinician and I hope you never face an issue in which you are found guilty of wrongdoing. However, in the outside chance you receive a legal complaint, and in the even less likely chance of a judgment against you, owning and operating under a legal entity provides the necessary protection to make it extremely difficult for any person or company to "pierce the veil" and get into your personal holdings.

Below is a simplified checklist for obtaining and maintaining your legal entity:

EXERCISE 3.1 | Legal Entity Checklist

- ○ *Work with an experienced attorney who can assist you with choice of legal entity and then draft and file any necessary documents or legal agreements.*
- ○ *Research and choose the proper legal entity for your business needs.*
- ○ *Consult with tax adviser or accountant about tax implications.*
- ○ *File your entity with your state's business offices, usually Secretary of State.*
- ○ *Draft and file operating agreement or articles depending on which entity you choose.*
- ○ *Note your legal entity's annual review date and file reviews accordingly.*
- ○ *Put your legal entity name on all marketing materials, clinical forms, and physical location to properly show you are operating as your business.*
- ○ *Set up a business bank account and flow all income into that account and only draw monies from business into personal, and not the other way around.*
- ○ *Always practice according to state and federal laws and ethical standards of your profession.*

DISABILITY INSURANCE

Remember a few pages ago I shared how in 2011 I fell and hit my head at a movie theater, receiving my one and only concussion? Though I didn't have to miss work, it really rattled my brain (no pun intended) about human fragility! Often, you think you can handle anything and "it will never happen to me" until it does and you're sitting at home pondering how you wished you'd secured a disability policy for this exact day. You fail to think about what you might need, until . . . **YOU REALLY NEED IT!** This philosophy won't work when you are opening or already operating your practice. Change your philosophy and get a disability policy (and other policies mentioned in this chapter).

Now that I have your attention, disability premiums gave me a bit of sticker shock. The monthly premiums for such policies are higher than your malpractice, business key, and even life insurance premiums. I currently pay only $30 more per month on all three of these premiums compared to my monthly premium for my disability policy. If you are planning on forgoing the disability policy because of monthly premiums, please go back and re-read the previous paragraph once again. Your chances of lowering your disability premium increase when you are extremely healthy and deemed less of a risk to the insurer.

LIFE INSURANCE

As is the case with your disability insurance, you are foolish not to have a life insurance policy in the event of your untimely death. You wouldn't want to leave loved ones with your debts and an inability to continue living the same lifestyle you helped create, would you? You have a responsibility, as a small business owner, and honorable human being to be sure not to leave loved ones in the lurch with your financial burdens, should you have any at the time of an untimely death.

Many think of life insurance as something they don't need or can obtain later. I recommend that you secure this insurance sooner than later. Even if you aren't quite ready to open your practice, purchasing life insurance at a younger, healthier age, will result in lower premiums. Just like disability policies, and even more so with life insurance, your overall health has much to do with risk factors for dying when the insurance is active, and that impacts the determination of your annual insurance premiums. Health issues such as smoking, obesity, chronic illness, and previous surgeries can lead to higher premiums as your physical condition and age determine your risk factors for death and therefore your premium (the cost to insure you).

While there are many life insurance policies to choose from, I can best explain selecting life insurance policies by breaking them into two main categories: (1) Term Life Insurance (2) Whole Life Insurance. Let's discuss each.

Term Life Policy

A term life insurance policy is a policy that has a beginning and an end date otherwise known as a defined "term." You are essentially covered when the policy term is active. You select the term, or length of time the policy exists, based on the products (policies) available. The premiums for such policies are based on the individual's health at the time the policy is initiated or when it is renewed into a lengthier term. If you are a smoker, or overweight, or trying to get a chronic condition under control such as high blood pressure or high cholesterol, I recommend visiting with your physician and asking what you can do to get healthier (and stay healthy!) in order to get and keep a low life insurance premium. The two most obvious health choices I recommend are to be a non-smoker, and keep your weight under control.

Here's the good news. Term insurance is overall relatively inexpensive. In addition to health being a driving factor on the premium, so is the length of the term and the amount of payout should you die when the insurance is active. Determine coverage amounts you need to pay off debt and keep your loved in the same lifestyle you helped build. For example, if you are 40 years old, and want to take out a 20-year term, at 1 million dollars of coverage, and you are relatively healthy, depending also on where you live, you may end up paying around $80 per month.

Some believe that term life insurance is really all you need given that when you are 60 years of age, for example, and reach the end of your term, most of your major bills, especially your home are paid off and you have hopefully saved enough to semi-retire or enter a full retirement. (Don't worry; retirement savings is covered in Chapter Nine).

Whole Life Insurance

While you can renew into a new term if you choose after your term expires and stick with the term insurance plan, whole life is a life insurance policy that never expires and actually serves as an investment vehicle. It is not your traditional retirement plan, like a 401K. Rather it's an insurance that pays out just like a term policy, only your premiums earn you money and you can borrow against what you've saved without penalties. Different policies have different rules, so it's imperative that you talk with your insurance agent or financial advisor about options that are best for you. Because whole life insurance is also an investment vehicle, many financial institutions offer this type of insurance. You may end up discussing insurance options with your financial firm or advisor as well as your insurance agent. It's also important to know that because this type of insurance does not ever terminate, and it's an investment as well, the premiums are much larger.

Regardless of which life insurance policy you choose, it's important to choose one, and stick to it. Here are a few easy steps regarding life insurance:

Steps for obtaining life insurance:

1. *Talk to insurance agent and financial advisor about what's right for you*
2. *Stop smoking, control weight, stay healthy*
3. *Get this insurance going early in life (at least term life)*

UMBRELLA INSURANCE

"What is Umbrella Insurance, and why would I ever need it?" you wonder. An umbrella policy is one that covers any claims that fall outside monetary caps and limitations of other policies you own. For example, when a theft claim turns out to be over your theft policy's coverage limits, rather than needing to reach into your pocket to pay the difference, which in some instances can be a lot of money, a well-designed umbrella policy, custom written to fit your projected needs, can cover some or all of the remainder of the cost of the claim.

Here's the best part. Umbrella policies are extremely inexpensive. I pay around $11 per month for this coverage. Be advised that premiums once again depend on the coverage you need, geographic location, and other factors. Umbrella policies have limitations as well. Make sure when you check into this coverage with your insurance agent you ask about limits to your coverage.

REVIEW OF POLICIES

Let's review so far what you've learned about getting your practice organized. Here is your checklist for setting up and safeguarding your financial foundation. As you complete each task, place an "X" in the space provided, knowing that you are putting in place a solid financial foundation:

- ○ Malpractice Insurance (Also called Professional Liability Insurance)
- ○ Legal Entity (LLC & S-Corp are most popular, remember you must have a business account)
- ○ Disability Insurance
- ○ Life Insurance
- ○ Umbrella Policy

Make a note in the administrative section of your business plan now of which areas you need to take action and what exactly that action entails.

These are my top 5 most important safeguards that I believe should be put in place before ever seeing your first client in private practice. If you don't put this grand safety net in place in the beginning, you are more likely to put it off further into other developmental stages, and in those future stages you hope to be much busier with marketing, networking, training, seeing your clients, and other related activities, that you will likely keep putting it off and as many clinicians do, you will completely forget to obtain one or more of these 5 essential safeguards! Don't be the person who puts this off or forgets entirely. It may pain you on the front end to pay costly premiums for something you hope to never need or use. But, believe me, you wouldn't want a lack of coverage or protection should you be one of the few unlucky ones. All it takes is one theft, one lawsuit, one physical injury in your office, or one unfortunate fall hitting your head in a movie theater!

EXPERT PROFESSIONAL SUPPORT

In the Administrative section of your business plan in Chapter Two, you saw a template of administrative tasks you need filled and a space to write the actual names of people who could fill certain administrative support roles in your business. Take a closer look at what is typically needed and let's get a little more detailed about what these experts offer. Think about whom you already engage, while evaluating how those professional relationships are working for your business. Do an assessment of the people you already pay to help you run your business. Ask yourself, is this individual helping my practice in a way that I need? Are there areas in our business relationship that need clarification? If you don't have a "go to" person in one of the areas below, go back to the chart in your business plan and make note of those experts you need to hire to help with your business. As with any professional support service, some of areas will matter less than others, and even a few you might not need yet, or ever. For example some clinicians prefer to do their own billing. Some don't need an assistant. You get the picture.

Most clinicians in private practice choose to engage the following list of professional experts at one time or another in their clinical practice.

Corporate & Estate Attorney

By now, you obviously understand the need for an attorney. While I won't bore you once again with the corporate entity side of legal work, you need an estate attorney for to help you create a will. Some business attorneys also offer services such as preparing wills and trusts. Or, you may need to hire a different attorney to draft documents related to your estate. Creating a will is one of the least desirable actions, yet it's extremely important.

Whoever you hire, make certain your attorney outlines what will occur should you die suddenly while running your practice. Without a legal plan, or any plan for that matter, your grieving loved ones will be left with the burden of shutting down your practice, including contacting every one of your active clients, I recommend you engage a trusted and qualified colleague to contact your patients for referral, and a trusted and experienced administrative individual to help your loved ones with the closing of the administrative parts of your practice. Your attorney will outline how this process works.

You may try and save a bit of cost by using a "do it yourself" software program. If you use this method to get something in place, you may want to meet with an estate attorney at a later time to review the document and make changes as needed, when you are in a position to afford to engage someone professionally.

Medical Billing Professional

Which private practice owners need a medical biller and which do not? First let me explain the duties of a billing professional. A trained and trusted medical billing specialist files claims on your behalf directly to insurers and other third party payers, and keeps you organized with your system of tracking client co-payment, co-insurance, deductibles paid and owed to you. Some even help you with the paperwork and "red tape" of getting on managed healthcare (insurance) panels as an in-network provider. Some help by calling insurers to learn about client benefits, dealing with unpaid or problem claims, and clarifying complicated third party payer issues. Additionally, a medical billing professional bills your clients directly for outstanding or ongoing balances, and collects monies on your behalf. Finally, your medical biller generates and sends you reports on how your overall practice is doing with regard collection of your fees from all entities, clients and third party payers alike.

Based on this description above, do you require the services of a professional billing specialist? Some owners prefer to forgo engaging a biller at a few hundred dollars a month (depending on how much billing you need), and do the billing on their own. Some use a billing software program in lieu of a medical biller. For more information on where to find these programs, see Appendix I, Mental Health Practice Management Software.

For those who see only direct fee for service clients, most of these owners never engage a medical billing professional. The few clinicians who use such a person, do so to generate patient statements, send invoices and collect on private pay fees, so that as the clinician they don't have to wear the "financial hat," thus removing a large portion of a financial role with your client.

What does a medical biller charge? Rates depend on how your specialist bills you. Some medical billing professionals charge by the hour, while numerous bill a percentage of the monies brought in from your clients and/or insurance claims. The latter is usually a fair and customary manner most suited to the practice owner. The reason I like fees based on percentage is you want someone who actually has incentive to go after the money you rightfully earned. The billing specialist who bills garnering a paycheck based on a percentage of the money collected is more motivated to bring in your money than one who gets paid by the hour. Percentage charged by the billing specialist will largely depend on where you work geographically, your medical specialties, cost of living, and years of experience of the biller. The industry average is around 7–10%. Some larger firms require contracts and some have initial start up fees. Be advised that there are billers who charge a percentage, and also use an hourly rate for extras like calling insurers for benefits and/or authorizations.

Regardless of who you engage as your medical biller or what software program you use in lieu of a medical biller, it's important that you get three or so good quotes. Interview at lease three medical billers. Working with an excellent billing specialist you trust and who works hard to obtain your money is highly desirable. Contracting with someone you can't trust and doesn't properly do the work may be disastrous for your business.

Virtual Assistant

Let me ask you something? If you are a current practice owner and used to fielding calls, scheduling appointments, sending appointment reminders, and dealing with many other front and back end administrative tasks, I'd bet you experience what I call "administrative burnout!" The administrative tasks are the stressors you bring home at night and not so much the emotional issues of your clients. If this pertains to you then it's probably time to investigate either purchasing a software program that helps with these administrative tasks, or hiring a virtual assistant. For more information on what programs are available, see Appendix I, Virtual Assistant Resources.

What can a virtual assistant do for you? A good assistant is flexible and offers a variety of front and back office services to assist you with practice efficiencies that manage your time more effectively! When searching an assistant, not only is flexibility a must, so too is the assistant's willingness to tailor their services to the unique needs of your practice. This person must be willing to be trained by you, and you must alternatively be willing to properly train the assistant. Patience and trust building on both ends are key components! For example, if one of the tasks you'd like your assistant to help with is triaging calls, then you must properly train the assistant in appropriate screening technique and boundaries to fit your practice and the profession.

Suppose you are in the set up phase of your practice. In your case, it may make more sense to investigate using a software program initially and then adding the virtual assistant when your practice administrative needs increase. Some practices actually use both software and an actual person. The virtual assistant may even use the practice management software program to help you stay organized.

Not ALL practices benefit form one or the other or both. Some practices elicit the help of family members and use other volunteer or occasional paid assistants as needed for non-routine projects to help stay organized. It's perhaps most important to remember that you cannot make your private practice work without the help of others. While you may not engage a virtual assistant or even run software to assist you right away, rest assured someone sometime from somewhere in some particular area will assist you with running its operations.

Webmaster/SEO Specialist

Did you ever think that your success as a face-to-face practitioner would need so much work online? We visit online marketing later in Chapter Six, but for now, remember that most clinicians used to quite literally "hang a shingle," obtain third party insurance contracts, and clients would show up. This "Field of Dreams" no longer works. Your newest playing field for getting and keeping clients involves interfacing on the World Wide Web. If you want to succeed in the business of helping others, you must construct and maintain your own website and you need to build your website's presence in the search engines. You can learn to do this on your own, or hire a Webmaster and/or Search Engine Optimization (SEO) Specialist.

Consultant

Not everyone needs a private consultant to help with practice building. In fact I might add that no one actually "needs" to hire a consultant to become successful or more successful in the business of private practice. In actuality, the individuals I help, say on the front end they thought they needed my help, only to realize that what they really want is support, expertise, and a little push. The desire to become successful in your business is a very personal experience, and equally as personal is the choice to engage a professional consultant. Because of the unique nature of the close work that a good consultant brings to your business building process, it's highly critical that you take time to interview a few people who do professional practice consulting work, and that you find the right fit. This includes understanding and agreeing with the consultant's approach, values, and process of working with you.

You may decide at some point to hire a consultant for a brief time, perhaps even for just one meeting, or you might engage your consultant for a longer period of time. While expense is higher for longer engagements, most fair consultants offer longer-term packages at lower per hour rates. Be sure to inquire about how the financial arrangement works prior to full engagement.

Bookkeeper

Are you bad at keeping up with your finances? Do you often forget to enter checks and amounts into your check register? Do you find it tedious and challenging to categorize your transactions and prepare for tax season? Are you struggling with managing your accounts? If you answered yes to any of these questions, consider hiring a bookkeeper to help you stay organized and up to date on a consistent basis. This professional support individual can either be hired as an independent contractor or an employee. Regardless of the contractual set up, trust is extremely important when one works with your finances. This area of your practice is extremely personal and information must be highly guarded. Make certain you have the right person helping you. Check references, interview more than one professional and, once hired, monitor their work progress. Chapter Nine covers more on financial management.

Accountant

While a bookkeeper assists with keeping you up to date on financial management by preparing you for tax season, you may need professional help filing your taxes. Starting out it's easy to think you can complete and file your own taxes, especially when you use a great software program. While you may continue using the program or simply file tax returns on your own, my advice is once you become busy enough to increase your client load and you are making more money or your tax status is more complex, it's highly advisable to have a tax preparation individual upon whom you can rely!

There is a wide range of accounting professionals who can prepare taxes on your behalf. Each individual or firm charges differently, depending on your needs. It took three tries for me to find the right fit of a good tax preparation professional. First, I hired a firm that didn't really understand the needs of the small business professional. The firm was extremely thorough; however, their fees were way outside the range of working with individual small business professionals. They essentially charged for every minute on the phone, every document prepared and by the end of that year, I paid over $3,500 for fairly simple returns and projections. This initial try was a firm of CPA's (Certified Public Accountants). Then I hired a tax attorney whose services were mostly tax preparation. While he was reasonable financially, he was often responding slowly and finally just disappeared one year. Strange, but it happens. Finally, I found a gentleman who specializes in financial planning and tax preparation and he's been a perfect fit ever since. He understands the needs of the small business professional. I know exactly what I am paying for his professional services, as he is always upfront with me. I value transparency. He always returns my calls, emails, and other communications (and doesn't add extra charges for them). And, he is extremely efficient and thorough! Oh, and he's on the up and up! He doesn't cheat or recommend cheating! All of these qualities are highly important to me.

Financial Advisor/Manager

Do you currently have a financial advisor or manager? You may not think you need one just yet. If you are doing some of your own investing and enjoy managing your finances including obtaining advice through your own research, you may never even need to hire a financial advisor. However, to have a second set of eyes on your finances from a professional perspective is extremely helpful.

Let's say you are in a financial bind because you want to grow your business and need short-term capital in order to do so. You have several options, including taking out a small business loan, borrowing from a family member, or perhaps boot strapping the expansion by minimizing your financial loss and working harder to bring in more revenue. I advise discussing this kind of decision with a professional who knows something about small business loans. Making informed decisions is hard to do when you are juggling your clinical work and other administrative responsibilities, not to mention trying to enjoy your personal life. Making the time to talk with a financial advisor is a good idea.

A financial advisor's main purpose is to help with larger and more long-term growth decision-making, while helping you maintain financial stability in the short-term. Such decisions may include how to save for retirement, creating a life insurance plan, and structuring your financial savings and investing in a way that helps meet your long-term goals, without breaking your bank in the short-term.

Investment Banker

Investment bankers focus on a very specialized area of your financial picture. This professional is interested in helping you invest your money properly. A good investment banker helps with investment options that fit your age and risk variables, as well as taking into account your comfort level with risk. Investment bankers are found within local banks, and often when you have several banking accounts within the same bank, their investment advisors/bankers will reach out to you to invest your savings within their bank. Your bank has a huge incentive in your investing within their bank because YOUR money remains within their banking system.

Insurance Agent

You may already be working with an insurance agent. Even if this is the case, you may want to hang around and keep reading since there are a few important points about working with an insurance agent to consider. Insurance companies and agents are a dime a dozen. Companies offer different policies, and try to out bid, out write, out premium, out benefit their competitors. Make sure your agent is interested in YOUR insurance needs. You must have clear communication with your agent, letting him/her know exactly what you need, while allowing the agent to recommend coverage and policies that make sense for your needs. A good agent asks the right questions in their assessment of your personal and professional needs, while also matching you with the right products. Your agent should reach out to you on an annual or routine basis to review your changing and growing needs. Earlier, I talked about the types of policies you should look into when it comes to covering your business and personal life. Make sure to review the policies you need.

Commercial Real Estate Broker

Finally, in your pursuit of office space, whether renting or purchasing space, consider engaging a Commercial Real Estate Broker. Brokers help reduce a considerable amount of legwork required when finding the right location, office space, grade of office building, lease terms, and tenant finish. The broker typically gets paid through a commission that ultimately comes from within the lease you signed, or the purchase price of property when you buy space.

When purchasing a space, such as a small building, it's important that you cover rent out the amount of space you purchase for more each month than you have to pay on whatever loan you secure, so that not only is your purchase a long-term investment, it also keeps you in the black in the short-term as you are paying down the loan. If you are purchasing a small office inside a larger building, commonly known as an "office condo," remember while the purchase price is typically smaller than a free standing building and you won't necessarily need to worry about renting other office suites out, OOA (Office Owner's Association) fees apply on top of your monthly loan payment. Regardless of the type of purchase, it's always important to ask for income and expense statements of the prospective property for the previous 5 years, and inquire about vacancy rate history, property taxes, and any other information that is helpful when making this kind of investment. Most clinicians don't purchase their space because there is not enough money for a down payment, they are risk aversive, or simply not interested.

If you are renting office space, it is extremely important that you negotiate your lease options and terms well before signing the lease. For example, you need to decide the length of your lease. Certain circumstances may factor into that decision. How new you are to the area, how confident you are that you want to stay in that space, etc. Also, the "tenant finish" must be considered when signing a lease. Tenant finish refers to what work shall take place to make the space "move in" ready, according to your specifications. When it comes to tenant finish, talk to the leasing company about sound attenuation. Sound attenuation is one of the most important considerations next to office configuration.

It's your job as business owner to negotiate in your lease what you want in terms of sound attenuation. Because commercial spaces often aren't set up for this level of sound reduction, Chapter Four contains a comprehensive list of sound attenuation ideas. A contractor hired by the management company usually completes tenant preparation or finish. The extra labor and materials that go into your tenant finish is paid over time through your lease term. Longer lease terms likely reduce your overall monthly payment, and can be especially helpful when you are doing a high-cost tenant finish.

You should not be surprised that it takes a considerable degree of professional support and assistance to fully run your practice. Now that you have more definition in terms of professional support, go back to that chart in Chapter Two (figure 2.6) or use the business plan template in Appendix A, and add your administrative support needs and potential candidates for those who will support your practice professionally. Additionally, you may want to note planned follow-up conversations with those professionals who already work for you.

EXERCISE 3.2 | Qualities to Look for in the Professionals You Hire

Corporate & Estate Attorney:_____
_____
_____

Medical Billing Professional:_____
_____
_____

Virtual Assistant:_____
_____
_____

Webmaster/SEO Specialist: _____
_____
_____

Bookkeeper:_____
_____
_____

Accountant: _____
_____
_____

Financial Advisor/Manager:_____
_____
_____

Investment Banker:_____
_____
_____

Insurance Agent:_____
_____
_____

Commercial Real Estate Broker: _____
_____

INTEGRATION OF PROTECTING, ADMINISTERING, AND MANAGING YOUR PRACTICE

Once you complete the basics of creating your practice foundation through obtaining office space, setting up your legal entity, starting your business bank account, branding your practice, getting the right kind of insurance policies, and contracting with necessary individual professionals, you must administer the processes and manage the people supporting your practice. This integration consists of routine planned meetings with your professional supports, and regularly evaluating your processes for quality and efficiency. Implementing smart administrative systems is vital to practice success! Once you reach a point of healthy integration and your foundation feels strong, you are ready to take on further development, diversification, and delivery of your services!

Part II
DEVELOP, DIVERSIFY, & DELIVER!

In this section of the book, you are entering what I commonly refer to as "Phase II" of practice development. Regardless of whether you are just starting out, or are a seasoned veteran, the second phase of practice development building is characterized by creating systems of structure and practice facilitation, strong diversified revenue streams, a solid multi-layered networking and marketing strategy, and finally your own unique, dynamic, and original one-of-a-kind programming and products that carve your niche and establish expertise over time! The following chapters cover these important practice-building modules!

CHAPTER FOUR |
SYSTEMATIC ORGANIZATION, STRUCTURE & FACILITATION

Now that your foundation is complete, or you fixed the repairs needed in your foundation as a seasoned practitioner, it's time to develop your practice further. In this chapter, you learn certain practice procedures that help you work more efficiently, while providing your services with ethical responsibility and clinical integrity. Additionally, I train you on aspects of practice organization that many clinicians fail to consider both upon start up and throughout the process of practice development.

ETHICAL AND CLINICAL TIME SAVERS

Responsibly saving time when you are both in session with your clients and while not in session puts you ahead of the business curve. Let's tackle the latter first. In order to create a solid clinical routine, develop administrative processes systemized in such a manner that you can quickly access, process, and file your clinical paperwork. A thorough and routine clinical charting system makes for saving time and an effective practice.

Clinical Paperwork

There are now many ways you can take and keep notes for your official patient record. The key is to create a note taking system that maximizes efficiency and organization. For you, this process may involve a traditional paper method, or it could be an electronic medical record keeping system. More agencies and hospitals are moving to an electronic medical record keeping system or EMR. In fact, the Patient Protection and Affordable Care Act (2010) specifically outlines a gradual increase in moving from the costly use and inefficiencies of paper records to EMR systems.

While many larger medical facilities began moving to EMR as early as 2012, private practice owners are moving less quickly, largely due to a lack of availability of cost-effective software programs, and what appears to be unwillingness on the part of the practice owner to change course. Seasoned practitioners become set in their ways, especially administratively. There is good news for all private practice owners when it comes to EMR software for therapists. Finally, numerous developers are creating cost-effective EMR software programs specifically for the private practice owner and small practice groups. See Appendix I for further information on EMR programs for medical and mental health professionals in private practice. While it's only a matter of time before all helping professionals use electronic medical records, whatever you decide to do, make sure your paperwork is uniform, compliant with state and federal laws, the guidelines of your specific profession, and has your legal entity name on each page.

On your website, upload your initial intake packet and make it easily available. This method of providing the intake packet means your client doesn't need to come in early to complete paperwork, making the administrative hassle of getting the client to complete the paperwork minimal. All you have to do is tell your new client to go to your website, download, print, and complete the initial paperwork. Of course you will remind your client to bring their completed intake packet, along with their insurance card, if you take their insurance, to the initial appointment. Other methods include the client uploading the completed packet to through a secure server so that you have the information well before the client's initial evaluation session.

While many new clients like the option of completing the intake packet in the comfort of their home or office, some prefer filling out the paperwork at my office just before their initial appointment. For example some individuals seeking therapy have other people living in their house who they prefer not know about their treatment and thus don't want to fill out paperwork at home. Therefore, when triaging the client before setting up their first appointment I offer new clients the option of completing the packet at my office in the fifteen or so minutes prior to their first visit, or doing it at home.

Regardless of whether you use EMR or paper records, your intake packet consists of certain important forms. Below is a summary and brief explanation of what's generally inside most intake packets. Remember these packets will vary depending on your state (the laws on informed consent differ from state to state), your specialty, and preferences. The list below describes the forms legally required along with other intake forms that are the standard of practice.

FIGURE 4.1 | Critical Intake Forms

IN TAKE FORM NAME	IN TAKE FORM CONTENT
Mandatory Disclosure	Informed Consent, Patient Rights/Responsibilities, Professional Background, Theoretical Orientation & Techniques, Urgent/Emergent Matters, Confidentiality Limitations, Fees & Policies
HIPAA	Protection of Patient Privacy
Patient Admission Questionnaire	Symptom Checklist, Presenting Problem Description, Brief Health History Including Current Medications, Treatment History, Drug/Alcohol History, Strengths/Challenges, and other assessment information you deem necessary
Release of Information Form	Consent to allow information to be released to a third party
Patient Information Form	Patient Name, Date of Birth, Contact Information, Insurance Information
Missed Appointment Policy Form	Spells out specific consequences and fees regarding missed, late or canceled appointments
Social Media/ Electronic Communication Policy	Explains why you don't accept connections with clients on social media or respond to emails with clinical information
Consent For Treatment of Minor	Used only when seeing minor client. Provides written consent by parents and/or guardians to treat the minor patient

Summary of intake packet forms to give to patient and brief definitions of each form. See Appendix B for actual sample forms.

A well-designed comprehensive Clinical Evaluation Form rounds out the intake paperwork. The clinician completes this form during and shortly after the initial session. It's important to include history, presenting issues, a *DSM-5* diagnostic narrative, and a well-defined treatment plan with goals, objectives, planned interventions, and goal-measurement process. See the sample Clinical Evaluation form in Appendix B.

In addition to the intake packet, several other forms are necessary for routinely running your practice. Other forms you may need include but are not limited to:

- Clinical Summary
- Letter to Court
- Overpay Return Form
- Safety Contract
- Child Abuse Reporting Form

When you have templates/forms built into a "forms" folder on your computer, it takes far less time to complete the work. This forms storage method creates a smoother operation of your practice, so you worry less about cumbersome paperwork, and focus more intently on client contact. While these forms are available in Appendix B at the end of the book, think about other forms specific to your practice areas and start developing your own forms folder.

EXERCISE 4.1 | Formulating Forms

Build a section into your business plan by writing down the forms listed that you need in your practice, and add any forms you'd like to develop that will make your practice run more efficiently, and keep you organized clinically. Then, create a timeline with deadlines for completing the development of your forms. Use the sample forms in Appendix B to get started.

Office Organization

The physical layout, aesthetics, organization, and privacy of your office space are critical to saving time, practicing responsibly, and creating excellent first and lasting impressions with your clients. The place you spend much of your waking life is your office! So, it's extremely important that you plan with careful attention to the details.

First, think about the most important "rule" of our profession. The all-important covenant of CONFIDENTIALITY is at the top of the list. Think about client privacy and confidentiality, when you are planning and/or building out the office interior, and throughout your daily practice. Regarding the set-up of your office, it's crucial that you plan for sound attenuation. Here are my hard and fast tips around sound attenuation in office space:

Sound attenuation tips

- Make sure all windows are double paned, and preferably triple paned.

- Whenever possible, choose your office in a space that does NOT face large or busy streets, or is not close to ground level. Sound from traffic travels easily through even the best exterior office windows. A space that is on a higher floor when adjacent to a busy street might be okay.

- If building out the space, use the thickest drywall possible and space out walls with more joists and certainly use a lot of insulation everywhere possible to reduce sound travel.

- Minimize air vents to only what's needed. The more air ventilating, the more opportunity for sound to travel. But, don't make it so that your ventilation is uncomfortable to you and your clients.

- Put insulation between the ceiling and the floor above. (This is extremely important.) Definitely do so above all interior walls.

- Have a carpet pad installed under your carpet. Most office spaces don't include carpet padding. It's an upgrade that is well worth it.

- Use weather-stripping and bottom doorstops, including a drop-down rubber barrier that drops to the floor upon closing of door.

- Carefully place in-ceiling speakers in your waiting area and have soft music playing through the speakers. This helps keep other sounds away and assures privacy in session as well as a pleasant experience for those waiting for a session. The last thing you want is a client waiting for an appointment and hearing a couple yelling at one another during the session, even if it's unknown what is being said.

- Make sure all of your interior doors are made of a solid core. Hollow doors are not going to prevent sound from traveling from room to room.

OFFICE FURNISHINGS, EQUIPMENT AND SUPPLIES

While it may be challenging for some to think of what's needed to fill office space, there are really three main categories: furnishings, equipment, and supplies. It's possible you won't ever worry about these challenges if you sublet from another clinician. If you don't want the responsibility of creating your own office space, subletting may be a better option. Some clinicians prefer to sublet for other reasons, such as using several offices around town as a way to build a client base more rapidly and keep the referrals flowing. If you are planning your own office or already have an office you manage, here are some ideas in each of the three categories.

Furniture

Office furniture comes in all shapes, sizes, and colors and of course varies according to price. You know your particular tastes and want your office to reflect an environment you'd like your client to experience, and represents you, your interests and values. Consider your client population and what each client might be experiencing when sitting in your office. When a client is in my office I imagine I am in the client's home, and wonder how to help them bring me into their world, even though they are sitting in my office. Everything matters when it comes to the experience of your client.

Think about diversity and inclusion in terms of variance of socio economics, gender, religion, race, culture, etc . . . A good example of inclusion is making sure you take into account clients' physical size and weight. Outfitting your office with furnishings that don't properly support variances in weight and size won't be inviting to clients who are unable to fit into the dimensions of your client chairs. Your office ought to be relevant both to you and to your clientele.

One of the most important pieces of furniture you will ever purchase is the chair you sit in during therapy sessions and, if it's not the same chair, the one you use at your desk. Both chairs should be ergonomic, with proper back support. Trust me, even when you're young and can handle any chair, your posture, physical health, and positioning is extremely important as you spend hours, days, months, and years sitting in your office working.

Creating a calm, inviting and safe sitting space for your clients is essential. Think about the populations you treat when it comes to the space for your clients. For example, if you see children and do play therapy, you are going to want items that are "child friendly" such as a beanbag chair or a comfortable place to sit on the floor. Many clinicians who work with kids use a separate room for play therapy specifically designed to appeal to the tastes of children, while keeping a more formal office for adults. Some clinicians use furnishings that are interchangeable, or items used for both children and adults. The key to finding the right furniture is to know your population, and think about and carefully layout how to use your office space.

Finally, you don't need to spend tens of thousands of dollars on furniture. Big box department stores, hardware stores, boutique shops, and some online retailers all have something for the smart business-minded therapist. It's easy to find bargains, just know what you are getting, and don't go so inexpensive that the furniture falls apart after a year. For more detail on the actual items I recommend, see Figure 4.2.

Equipment

There are numerous considerations when purchasing office equipment. Should I buy new or used? What do I really need in the way of equipment? What if my equipment breaks down? How do I properly maintain office equipment?

First, let's address the issue of what you need. Most practices need a good copier. Because you will be printing from a computer, likely faxing, scanning and emailing documents, it's an excellent idea to get an "all in one" machine that also offers a wireless connection. Most of these machines are rather inexpensive and may be purchased online or through your local retailer. The higher expense comes with purchasing ink cartridges for the all in one machine. Make certain you find out more about print cartridge costs, read reviews and talk with others to learn about their printer experiences. A good efficient machine is important and saves time when copying, printing, scanning or faxing.

In addition to the "all in one" printer, most clinicians need a computer. I recommend an easily transportable lightweight laptop. In the case of numerous office locations you need the flexibility of having your information readily accessible and thus need a portable system. Using only one device that you lock and transport with you at all times complies with HIPAA (Health Insurance Portability and Accountability Act, 1996) regulation. There are numerous ways to use a computer or computer network. As cloud-based computing and storage becomes more popular, practice owners will store files within "the cloud." Many cloud programs, especially those that are free, are not HIPAA compliant. Make certain that your cloud-based storage system is HIPAA compliant. Typically you can find that information on the cloud vendor's website or by simply contacting the vendor directly.

Other popular equipment clinicians use regularly include fireproof locking file cabinet(s), a smart phone, internet wifi modem/service, and a credit card machine. Regarding the latter, be certain that your card reader is at or above current industry standard, and that you are compliant with all credit card information storage guidelines, as well as compliant with HIPAA. Figure 4.2 below shows a summary of equipment items discussed.

Supplies

Creating an efficient and economical system for purchasing supplies is important. In the beginning of my practice building, I took my office supply list over the local office supply store, which took me over 15 minutes each way, and then spent at least 20 minutes blazing through the store aisles filling my cart and then making my purchase. On trips where I bought large quantities of paper and/or other large supplies, it took longer to get the items from my car to actual office storage. By the time I was done with the entire trip, moving supplies to and from the car, at least an hour passed, and often my back didn't feel so great.

There's this amazing new way to shop for supplies now. It's called the Internet! Shopping for office supplies online is a convenient way to save time and money. Internet purchasing and FREE delivery takes the legwork out of carrying heavy boxes up your stairs. I recognize that, from time to time, you want to go to the actual store. That's fine. Just think of the savings, over time of the trips you don't need. They add up and you will make better use of your time either seeing actual clients (money in your pocket while helping others) or getting other more important administrative tasks completed, or even spending more time at home.

The figure below shows a general list of supplies that I recommend. If you use paper medical charting, your greatest expense will be the medical file folders with the metal tabs. They are costly and you'll need them routinely. One of the benefits of using a HIPAA-compliant online charting service is not having to buy the physical charts. However, online medical record keeping alone may be just as costly with monthly access fees. It's important to do your financial homework, and adopt a system that is both cost-effective and user friendly to your practice!

FIGURE 4.2 | What Goes in Your Office

FURNITURE	EQUIPMENT	SUPPLIES
Desk Chair	Copier/FAX/Printer/Scanner	Medical File Folders
Desk	Locking File Cabinet(s)	Black Pens
Book Shelf	Computer	Sticky Notes
Pictures	Credit Card Machine	Steno Pads
Couch/Settee/Comfy Chair	Smart Phone	Stapler/Staples
Soft Lighting Lamps	Land Line Telephones	Paperclips
Side Table(s)/Coffee Table	Internet Wifi Modem	Paper
		Extra Toner Cartridges

What generally to buy for your office. You may not need all of these items. This list is not complete and comprises only the basics.

SESSION FACILITATION AND MANAGEMENT

Saving time while not seeing clients is important. Set up systems of organization that save time, help with practice efficiency, and create more opportunity to see clients. Implement numerous strategies within your clinical session that help you stay organized, efficient, and successful.

In-Session Note-Taking

Throughout the building of my business, I tried numerous time-saving, practice efficiency strategies. Some worked and many did not. For example, I tried typing notes into a tablet while working with my client, and it took away from the connection and interface with my client. However, when I took notes on a clipboard while being present with my client, it actually made more sense, and didn't take away from the session. I even found note-taking to be clinically relevant as a technique or intervention. Sometimes, as a therapist, you need to look away from the client and looking at your notes is a strategy to give your client the space needed to take a moment and emote. Sometimes it's good have to the chart right there so I can look up information from a previous session. It demonstrates transparency and session continuity. Very occasionally, when stumped for a creative and accurate intervention, I examine the chart, or document for a moment in the interest of buying a little time to think about my next intervention.

Discover your own value in taking notes during session. When doing so, it's always important to ask your client for permission at the onset of treatment. If a client says "no" whether verbally or through their body language, then it's likely not a great idea to take notes during session. Another reason you should not take notes during session is when it's counter indicated treatment wise. For example I don't take notes in front of clients with paranoid symptoms or severe personality issues such as Borderline Personality Disorder. Obviously you will cease taking notes in a session where it's just not appropriate. Sometimes it just feels "right" to put the chart down and pay 100% listening attention to your patient.

When I survey clinicians who chart notes at the end of the day, many therapists share that it takes them an average of at least an hour per client day to complete their notes. It takes me up to about an extra 15 minutes daily to finish the one or two notes that I couldn't complete during my client sessions. On average I am saving about 45 minutes per day in real time. In any service profession time is extremely valuable. More time for seeing clients, networking, doing other business-related activity is crucial to the success of your business. On a given week I gain 3 to 5 full available 45-minute session times by note-taking in session, still highly respecting the client experience and process in therapy. Even when I cannot use the extra time for client sessions, I put that time to great use by working on other areas of my business, such as marketing/networking, administration, or even spending time with family or friends. Could you use an extra few hours a week to see more clients, get more referrals, spend your personal time more effectively?

45-minute Hour & Session Stacking

Where taking notes in session leads to time saving and practice efficiency, there's another strategy I ask you to try. Whether you work with insurance panels or not, medical insurance companies set a high standard of care in the healthcare world. Insurance companies, along with government programs, determine the rate of pay for a given service. That given service in the private practice outpatient world is for a designated amount of time. The most common time billed in the outpatient world is the 45–50 minute hour. Many clinicians, whether they accept insurance or not, will do a 50-minute hour because they believe that is the normal time limit of outpatient therapy. When you work efficiently and manage the session properly you can get just as much work done by facilitating a 45-minute hour, which pays the same rate as the 50-minute hour by the insurer. (For purposes of example, I am using the most common hourly rate billed. Certainly consider longer sessions for clients who need them, with the same general idea of using the minimum time allowed for the maximum payment contracted.)

Allotting 45-minutes for the session instead of 50 and getting paid the same saves you a little time each session. In this case, when you see an average of 27 clients per week and all are on the 45-minute hour, you actually gain 3 additional 45-minute slots to use how you want. Let's say you filled those slots and gained 3 more from the savings of note-taking discussed earlier. You can now increase your average weekly client load by 6 sessions, taking you to about 33 clients. Assuming you don't mind seeing 33 clients a week and your average rate of pay is $65 per session, the additional 6 clients weekly for 48 weeks (you have to have some time off during the year too), would amount to additional annual revenues of $18,720.00. That's a pretty nice boost just based on the strategies of taking notes in session and using a 45-minute hour, then enrolling 6 more clients who visit your practice weekly. For more information on increasing client enrollment, see Chapter Five.

Don't stop at saving 6 weekly client session times. Practicing efficiency and smart time management leads to more success. Many clinicians start their therapy session at the top of an hour, allotting 10 minutes (15 if you are doing the 45 minute recommendation) to use the restroom, make a quick phone call, or decompress from a tough session.

In the beginning of my practice journey, I tried the traditional top of the hour start with a small break between sessions and found that my break caused more distress and disruption to my day and patient flow. Often I went over the allotted time, knowing that I had the window of time until the next client. I gave valuable non-paid time away to my clients when it seemed they needed the extra few minutes. Even when I ended on schedule, there wasn't enough time to return phone calls, use the bathroom, or do anything else. I wondered how other therapists spent their 10–15 minutes between sessions and decided to do an informal survey of clinicians I know. Sure enough, therapist after therapist answered in like form, "I never seem to have enough time between sessions, and often go over the allotted time, knowing there's a time window before the next client."

I tried something different. I call it "Session Stacking." When I stack my sessions together back-to-back in blocks of how ever many I can handle in a row, I take longer breaks in between. I started by grouping client sessions into threes, taking a 30-minute break between each block. By doing so, I actually save 15 minutes of down time, since each session technically yields a 15-minute break. If you did this exact practice, you would save 30 minutes a day, or one full hour per week (assuming you work a four-day week). That's another full session gained per week. Add another weekly session and the number of added clients is now at 7 per week (you are now efficiently seeing 34 clients weekly) and the extra 7 weekly sessions at a modest rate of $65 per session in a 48-week year, yields you an extra $21,840 of total revenue annually, assuming you use your time savings to build in more clients. Alternatively, look at this gain from the lens of obtaining more time for hobbies or with family and friends. This brings value to your practice from a work/life balance perspective.

The following figures illustrate how session stacking compares to the traditional method of seeing clients.

FIGURE 4.3 | Sample Schedule Using Traditional Client Hour

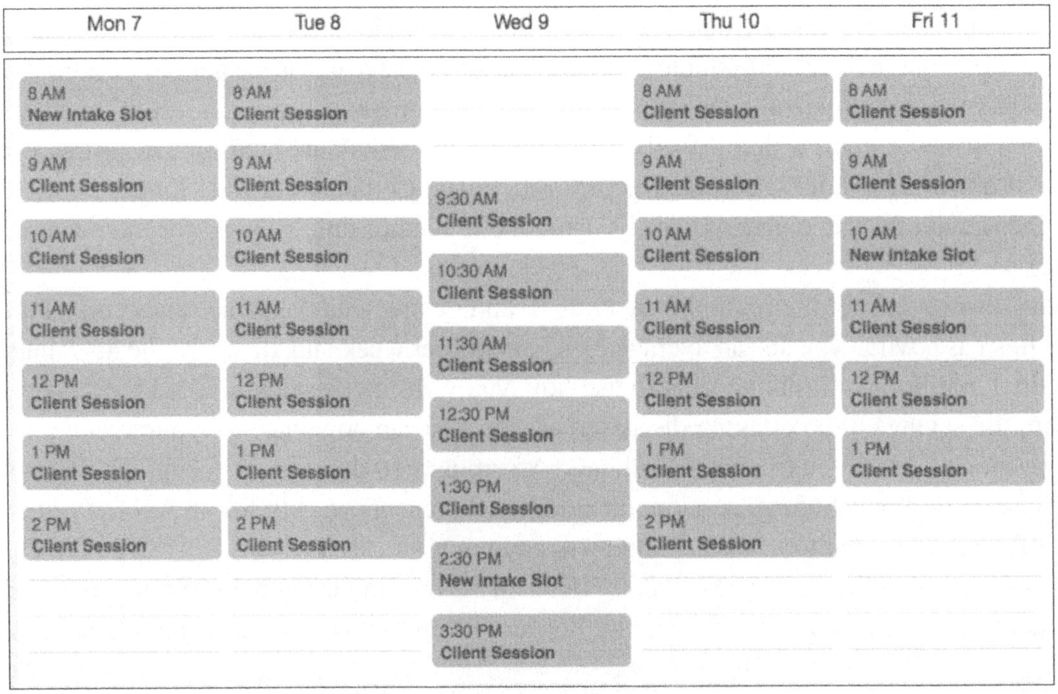

Sample schedule using the traditional method of seeing clients every hour, with a 10 or 15-minute break in between each client. Note that the provider's total hours of seeing clients are 34 per week. This chart represents 30 open follow-up spots and 3 new intake spots weekly. One might assume that 26 clients are seen on average weekly. At $60 per session, your revenue would be $1,560 per week. Not bad. Now look at the next chart.

FIGURE 4.4 | Sample Schedule Using Session Stacking

Mon 7	Tue 8	Wed 9	Thu 10	Fri 11
8 AM New Intake Slot	8 AM Client Session		8 AM Client Session	8 AM Client Session
8:45 AM Client Session	8:45 AM Client Session		8:45 AM Client Session	8:45 AM Client Session
9:30 AM Client Session	9:30 AM Client Session	9:45 AM Client Session	9:30 AM Client Session	9:30 AM New Intake Slot
10:45 AM Client Session	10:45 AM Client Session	Client Session 11:15 AM Client Session	10:45 AM Client Session	10:45 AM Client Session
Client Session	Client Session		Client Session	Client Session
12:15 PM Client Session	12:15 PM Client Session	12:30 PM Client Session	12:15 PM Client Session	12:15 PM Client Session
1:30 PM Client Session	1:30 PM Client Session	1:15 PM Client Session 2 PM New Intake Slot	1:30 PM Client Session	
2:15 PM Client Session	2:15 PM Client Session		2:15 PM Client Session	
		3:15 PM Client Session		
		4 PM Client Session		

Sample schedule using the session stacking strategy, in which there are no more than three back-to-back sessions, with 30-minute breaks built in. Note this schedule shows 35 each follow-up times, and 3 new intakes weekly. It also accounts for a late day and an afternoon off every Friday. 38 total sessions available. Assuming 30 are filled each week and at $60 per session, your weekly revenue is approximately $1,800. Your actual clinical time is one hour less in the office than in Figure 4.3. There are 33 hours of in-office time in this sample..

Session stacking isn't for everyone. Some providers need time alone between sessions in order to be ready to move into the next session. When ready to try my new model of seeing patients I, too, felt concerned I wouldn't take care of myself when I needed downtime due to an intensely difficult session prior to the next client. What I learned really surprised me. More often than not, I didn't need any time alone to be ready for the next client, and I felt energized moving right into the next session. In only rare circumstances I needed to be alone between clients, and then quickly told the client waiting that it would be just a few minutes and that I would be right with them. To my surprise, I didn't need 10 minutes to "unwind" from the session. I didn't even need 5 minutes. I really needed about 2 minutes to breathe and gain perspective going into the next session. I now find I cherish the 30 minutes I give myself after three 45-minute sessions in a row. That's meaningful time alone. In essence, I habituated myself into a non-traditional, time-saving, clinically-effective, pattern of providing services. When I need to use the bathroom and can't wait 2 hours, I simply and politely let the next client waiting know that I will be with them shortly, and start the session a few minutes late, giving the client their FULL session time.

Think about your common experience sitting in the waiting room of a doctor's office. Wait times for most medical doctor appointments average 19 minutes and many offices make you wait longer. Though I am usually on time, I am never more than 10 minutes behind schedule. When I am a bit behind, the client always receives the full session time at the other end of the session. However, when the client is late on their end, the time ends at the scheduled time. Put this policy in your intake paperwork to make your clients aware ahead of time. Additionally, when I know I am a few minutes behind schedule, I ask the current client if I can poke my head out and let the client waiting know I am a few minutes behind and that I will give that next client their full session time. Never has there been a situation in which my client was bothered by my needing to step out to let the waiting client know about running late. In fact, it serves as an excellent reminder to the client in session that the time is nearing the end and it's a good "wrap up" cue for the client currently in my office.

Transparent Clinical Consultation & Collaboration

A final "in-session" strategy that is an amazing time-saver in your clinical practice, of course used only when it's in the best interest of the client, is to perform collaboration and consultation with other professionals with your client present in session. I do not recommend doing in-session collaboration with other professionals in crises situations in which the consultation is not pertinent to the current crisis or when the client's diagnosis and/or clinical presentation is such that it would do harm to the client if the client were present during a consultation. Do not use this method when the client simply prefers that their session not be taken up with professional consult time. In most cases, when I ask a client or parent if they'd like me to contact their psychiatrist or primary care physician right now in the session, the client responds with relief and a resounding yes because usually that client already reached out to their professional and reports that their professional hasn't responded.

Situations that occur which require consultation outside of the clinical hour should be dealt with on a case-by-case basis. That said, I recently adopted a policy that I share with all new clients regarding clinical consultation outside of the therapy hour. I charge a rate per quarter-hour for outside consultation/collaboration that the client is told about when they begin their therapy course.

There are reasons for charging a consultation rate. First, I believe a therapist ought to be paid for work provided outside the clinical hour. Attorneys charge for every minute of work on client material, including research, preparation, and time with client and in court. They charge an hourly fee that is on average 50 to 75% higher than a therapist's usual and customary rate, while roughly the same amount of training is required for both professions (Psychologists must complete even more education than attorneys). Second, in 2013, some insurance companies added a billing code that allows certain medical providers (sometimes therapists as well) to bill for outside consultation, or consultation with another professional outside the clinical session. As soon as these new codes allowing clinicians reimbursement for outside professional consultation rolled out, insurance companies set a new standard allowing for clinicians to reasonably charge for services outside the clinical hour. It's disappointing to learn of how many therapists in private practice still give away their time doing consultation, writing letters, etc . . . never asking for a penny from their client or billing the client's insurance as appropriate.

If you are wondering about other types of outside services that should carry a charge, make a list of the types of services you perform outside your clinical hour and determine a reasonable fee for those services. Your reasonable fee should take into account (1) your experience, years of service, certifications, and training (2) geographic location, including how many other providers are available to do what you do and (3) the type of service.

Regarding the latter, I charge more per hour for appearing in court than any other service because it's a fairly stressful and exhaustive process. The higher charge is justified by the extra work it takes to prepare as well as travel. Here's an exercise: Pick the services on the list that you perform and make a general services "price list." Though there are sample prices below, they may not be representative of your actual charges. I encourage you to use the guidelines mentioned when considering your actual charges.

FIGURE 4.5 | Sample Non-Direct Services and Charges

TYPE OF SERVICE	CHARGE	SLIDING SCALE Y/N
Clinical Letter	$100 hr	Y
Clinical Treatment Summary	$250 Flat Rate	Y
Clinical Consultation	$25 per .25 hr.	N
Out of office meeting (e.g., IEP, School, Agency)	$200 minimum, +$100 per hour more beyond 2 hours	Y
Copying and Sending Notes/ Clinical File	$50 minimum flat charge, + .05 per page	N
Program Preparation (if you do seminars)	$100 hr	N
Missed Appointment/Late Cancellation	Usual and customary charges	Y
Travel time to an outside meeting	$50 per hour	N
Court/Legal Proceeding	$500 minimum +$100 per hour more beyond 2 hours	Y
Other:		
Other:		

The table above is a fictitious representation of examples of outside of the therapy hour services and sample charges either flat rate or per time increment, along with whether a sliding scale is offered or not. This list of service types is not exhaustive and should be geared toward the outside services of your specific clinical focus/practice.

Session Facilitation & Management

Finally, here are insights on managing and facilitating each clinical session. Are you pondering exactly what I mean, given that your training says the client simply brings up material and directs their session? I agree with client directed therapy, that it's necessary to empower your client to share clinical material. Still, you are actually the engineer, facilitator and manager of each session. You must do your best to know how and when to intervene, as we were taught in graduate school and other professional clinical trainings. From a business standpoint, it's imperative to properly manage the session, facilitating organizing and integrating business matters such as re-scheduling the next appointment, receiving the client payment, etc.

Here's a good rule of thumb when thinking about session structure. Use the first few minutes, 5–10 minutes, to help the client settle into the session. This may include small talk around the weather, the traffic getting over to your office, how their week is going. Stay away from politically charged topics. Next, briefly review your previous session with the client and ask what current agenda items they would prefer to discuss during their time in today's session. Make sure you build in time to review their homework if you recently gave the client some out-of-session work. Finally, be sure to begin wrapping up the session about 6 to 8 minutes before the end of session time, and leave about 3 minutes to collect money, if you haven't already done so, and re-book for another follow-up appointment. I usually begin wrapping up at 10 minutes prior to ensure the session actually completes on time. A good way to segue to the administrative part is recommending another homework assignment revolving around the topic discussed that session. In rare cases, when the client is highly emotional and not quite ready to transition, slow down and let the client have a few extra minutes. It's not the end of the world to be behind by a few minutes, especially for this kind of reason.

So, in a 45-minute individual session, the general time management breakdown is:

1. 10 minutes—Settling in
2. 25 minutes—Session Work and Process
3. 10 minutes—Transition, Fee Collection, Re-booking

You may be surprised that 25 minutes of actual session work doesn't seem like much. If you work efficiently and transition at the right times, and you are extremely thoughtful, focused and diligent during that middle part of the session (25 minutes or so), your client will work hard as well. In my experience many clients can't do much more work than about 30 minutes intensely. With individuals who need more time in general I offer 60 minutes for individuals and 90-minutes for couples and families (non-insurance reimbursed for the 90-minute session), still with a break down on the front and back ends of the session that involves transitioning.

Respectful Approach & Clinical Sensitivity

As I often recommend, it's important to track your progress in the areas of change you decide to try. At the end of each month take a look at your numbers and compare them to previous months when you weren't seeing clients the same way. In Appendix E you can find a sample tracking form that tracks the number of sessions and clients per month, and it can even be divided into managed care companies and other 3rd party payers. You may not want to try all of the strategies I recommend. I suggest you try one or two of the changes mentioned for a while, and add in others as you see fit. You may think about new ways to save time, while improving value in your practice. Don't be afraid to test the waters. In these examples you just read, if you successfully performed just a few of these ideas, you'd free up enough time to create more work/life balance, perform more marketing and networking, see more clients, and make more money.

Finally, please remember to always have your client's best interest in mind, including being extremely clinically sensitive about what might be going on for your client, and always be respectful in your integrated approach to solving client problems with efficiency and meaning.

CHAPTER FIVE |
GET THE WORK YOU WANT
& GET PAID WHAT YOU ARE WORTH

Did you ever worry that you couldn't find enough avenues for your work? This chapter describes in detail the multiple sources—from government programs to Employee Assistance Programs and others—which you can tap to build a robust and thriving practice. In fact, you'll learn how these different sources function and operate in order for you to collaborate with them. While getting work is paramount, getting paid for it is a close second. There's no doubt that getting paid for your services is one of the most important aspects of running your business. You cannot run a successful practice and do what you love if you are not paid, paid on time, and paid at a rate that is commensurate with your experience, the overall field, and the geographic location where you work. So, how do you set up a system of reimbursement that works for your practice? While every practice has its own methods for setting up payment and working with revenues, my best advice for creating practice success is to create a model that utilizes diversity in entities that pay you, along with monetary variances for different services. Let's begin with setting your fees.

SETTING FEES

Whether a seasoned practitioner or just beginning your practice, you need to set a reasonable fee for each service you provide. That fee, commonly called the "usual and customary fee," or (UCF) is the fee you ALWAYS charge your client or third party payer, regardless of whether you participate with insurance panels, other 3rd party payers and/or use sliding scales.

Private practitioners are paid in real time increments. Think of your charges in two broad categories: direct client service, and other services. Direct client service occurs when your client is in your office or treatment location and seen for an actual in-office session. For this category, your UCF is based on the length and type of therapy session. The table below shows the most common session lengths and a sample of usual and customary charges.

TABLE 5.1 | Common Session Types, Lengths, and Fees

SESSION TYPE & LENGTH	USUAL & CUSTOMARY FEE (UCF)
60-Minute Initial Evaluation	$110
60-Minute Follow-Up	$100
45–50 Minute Follow-Up	$80

Sample of common session type and length used and billed to managed care companies, with sample UCF for each session type. Note that the fees shown may not be reflective of your actual UCF fees nor are they a recommended fee for services for each session type, nor are these fees an accurate reimbursement fee from a managed care organization.

The other category, non-direct client services, are fees you charge for services outside of direct in-office therapy. These fees may include non-scheduled out-of-office client consultation, professional consultation, formal document preparation, outside of office meetings involving client, and missed appointment or late cancellation fees. Additionally, when you create and facilitate clinical trainings for professional development or other purposes and charge for that service, you need either an hourly rate or "per project" rate. Create fees for these services that are both affordable to your target population, and commensurate with your geographical location, the field specialty, your experience and expertise. Do a little research into each of these areas by asking questions of others, and studying reputable resources, whether these sources are online or not. The table below shows a more comprehensive list of "non-direct" client services and proposed sample fees from practice start-up to 10 years at 5-year intervals.

TABLE 5.2 | Non-Direct Client Service and Fees

NON-DIRECT SERVICE TYPE	FEES AT START-UP	FEES AT 5 YEARS INPRACTICE	FEES AT 10 YEARS INPRACTICE
Professional Consult	$20 per 15 Min	$30 per 15 Min	$40 per 15 Min
Brief Clinical Letter	$75	$85	$100
Comprehensive Summary	$125	$150	$175
Outside Meeting	$100, plus travel	$125, plus travel	$150, plus travel
Court Appearance	$300	$450	$600
Missed/Late Cancel Appointment	$80	$120	$150
Chart Copies	$20	$30	$40
One Day Professional Training Program	N/A—Not training until year 5	$800, plus travel	$1,000, plus travel

List of "Non-direct" clien-related services and usual/customary fees (UCF) for therapists at varying levels of experience. This table shows fees at 3 separate career intervals. These sample fees do not take into account geographic location, and other factors such as special certifications. This table is merely for illustrative purposes.

While the table above illustrates some of the non-direct client service charges, it is not exhaustive, as there may be other costs for services provided that are non-direct to your client.

WORKING WITH MANAGED CARE ORGANIZATIONS

Now that you completed the process of setting your usual and customary fees, and determined whether and how you are sliding the fees, it's time to turn your attention to the world of *Managed Care Organizations (MCOs)*. Common synonymous terminology for MCO's include 'insurance company,' 'healthcare organization,' or 'provider panel/insurance panel.' Consumer insurance policies are named "plans." The type of plan depends on what the member/patient chooses from the plans purchased by the patient's employer.

In general two main plan types exist in the insurance world. There are PPO plans; short for Preferred Provider Organization plans. And, there are more traditional HMO plans, an acronym referring to Health

EXERCISE 5.1 | Client Services Fee Planning

Now it's your turn. First, make a list of the direct services you offer. Break those services into service type, like "initial intake, follow-up session, etc.," and time increments, and list reasonable Usual & Customary Fees (UCF). Next, make a list of non-direct services you provide or will provide, along with your UCF for each service, either by time or by service. Finally, create a projected timeline, and reminder system of when and how much you estimate rate changes and service modifications. Hint: you do not need to change all rates at the same time. Often I evaluate which rate is most appropriate to change. On rare occasions, I lower a rate because it's not accurate or reflective of the service. Remember once you set a rate for direct care, it is the rate you ALWAYS charge for that service for a reasonable time until you evaluate and officially change that rate across the board.

NON-DIRECT SERVICE TYPE	FEES AT START-UP	FEES AT 5 YEARS IN PRACTICE	FEES AT 10 YEARS IN PRACTICE

Maintenance Organization plans. Patients in HMO plans used to need a referral from their Primary Care Physician in order to see a specialist such as a mental health provider. Over time, HMO plan premiums increased while out of pocket member/patient cost in these plans remained steady. Frustrated, consumers in the early to mid-1990's needed a different option, and the private insurance industry rolled out the PPO plan, which lowered premiums and allowed members/patients to choose which doctor they could see, returning more control of healthcare management to the patient/member.

Why share this historical detail about insurance terms and products? If you already work with insurance panels, you know the answer. It's highly important to know what "products" you are dealing with (HMO/PPO, or otherwise), as well as the insurance-related terminology. Knowing this information helps you make intelligent, educated decisions as a professional in the mental health field, assisting your client through their issues, as sometimes the very issue consists of finding your way through the maze of insurance. While it is the patient's responsibility to know their insurance policy, you the practitioner must possess a working knowledge about insurance in order to get paid, generate the proper referrals for your practice, work with provider contracts and credentialing processes, patient benefits and claims, and referral and support processes.

You might be thinking, "I don't even work with insurance. What do I care?" Or, "I am NEVER going to work with insurance panels. So, what does it really matter whether I know this information?" If you never sign on with even one panel, this information is still important. Patients often inquire, "Will you take my insurance?" They do not understand what it means when you are not a contracted provider for their insurer. When you don't know an answer to such a question, or anything about the insurance policy your patient carries, the patient and the practitioner may miss out on the information needed to provide the patient with an accurate and proper referral. Even clinicians who are out of network, and not contracted with insurance panels must know about how insurance applies to the business side of patient care, something you will learn more about in just a few moments. Perhaps more importantly, as the economy turns and shifts your business may benefit from and need the visibility and referrals that come from being paneled in an insurance network. You may simply experience a change of heart after reading the rest of this chapter. If so, you will have knowledge of how to get on insurance panels, what you should expect in terms of extra paperwork, reimbursement, and contracts, and what to do to maintain a great professional relationship with the panel(s) that contract with your business.

MANAGED CARE PARTICIPATING PROVIDER CONTRACTING PROCESS

If you already contract with managed care panels, then you obviously know how to become paneled as a network provider, and may wish to read this section for your review or skip to the next section on rate re-negotiation. If you are not on a panel and think you'd like to join one at some point or aren't sure, read this important section so that you know how the process works. Even if you don't think you'll ever join managed panels, please read this section anyway with an open mind, as you may think differently after reading and giving it some thought!

There are a several steps to getting credentialed with a managed care company as an individual practitioner. Let's keep in mind a few important concepts. First, when applying to be paneled with a managed care company, you are NOT becoming an employee of that organization. You are still the owner of your business and get paid an independent contractor fee, for which you receive a tax form 1099 from each insurance company that paid you during the year. Your role is one of "Independent Contractor" and that means you bear the full burden of both the employer and employee portions of the income tax. It also means that your contract with the insurance company is an extremely important business document as it defines the terms of the relationship between you the provider and the insurance company. I highly encourage you to spend time reading your contracts before signing them. Even think about hiring an attorney to help you look over your contracts prior to signing on the dotted line. The moment of leverage in your relationship with any managed care company is typically after you are given a contract to join the panel, and before you actually sign the contract.

The distinction of your network status as a provider is important. Know the differences in terms of "in-network" and "out-of-network" provider. Let's deal with the latter term first. A provider who is out-of-network is simply not currently contracted in the provider network of a particular insurance company. This means that the company doesn't list you on their website. You have no contracts with this insurer. As such, there are no agreed upon provider-contracted rates. Still, when it comes to reimbursement rates for services provided, certain insurance companies won't pay your full usual and customary rate. These companies pay out-of-network providers a rate up to the "allowed amount." The "allowed amount" is their determination of the maximum amount allowed based on numerous determination factors. The amount is typically higher than a "contracted rate" as an in-network provider (more about in-network status and rates in a moment). But, the allowed amount is typically lower than a provider's usual and customary fee, especially if you charge a higher rate because of your experience, certifications, location, and other factors that help determine your usual rate charged.

In-network status, also known as being a "contracted provider" for a given insurance company, means that you actually apply for membership within the insurance company provider panel, must be accepted, and sign a contract that includes their rate of reimbursement. Rates of reimbursement vary by insurer, geographic location, and type of licensure and service delivered. There may also be other factors that determine your rate. When considering applying for "in-network" contracted provider status, it's important to make an informed decision. The following list includes a set of questions that, once answered, will assist you in making the right decision:

1. Are you currently accepting new providers in your network?
2. What minimum qualifications such as years post-license, training, supervision are required for consideration of being accepted into your provider network?
3. What specialties, geographic locations, or other criteria might help in getting accepted into your network?
4. What are your reimbursement rates for the most common services under my discipline?
5. How many member lives do you cover in the zip code of my office location? In my city? In my county?
6. Once accepted into your network, how long does it take to become fully credentialed for me to able to start seeing your members for treatment?

TABLE 5.3 | Common Services

CURRENT PROCEDURAL TERMINOLOGY (CPT)	SERVICE TYPE
90791	Initial Assessment
90834	45–52 Minute Follow-Up Session
90837	53–60 Minute Follow-Up Session
90847	Couple/Family Therapy Session
90853	Group Therapy Session

Common services provided by private practice mental health clinicians, that include CPT billing code number on left and description of service on right.

RATE OF REIMBURSEMENT

Remember, when joining a managed care organization as an in-network clinician, you are agreeing to their "contracted rate" of reimbursement. Rates vary based on insurer. You should know exactly what your rates are as previously noted, and know this information before you sign your contract. You wonder, "What are fair contracted rates of reimbursement?" While this depends on where you practice geographically, your specific discipline, and which insurance company, your general contracted rate for most services will land somewhere between $50 on the low end, and $125 on the high end, for a therapy hour visit. This wide range of reimbursement possibility further reinforces the importance of knowing exactly what you are getting. Please use the exercise on the next page to fill in actual or proposed rates based on insurer so that as you contact each provider relations representative, you can evaluate and determine the impact of each rate on your practice. This chart helps you with projections of overall income based on specific insurers and assists you in determining whether to participate with specified insurers, and when it's time to renegotiate your rates.

EXERCISE 5.2 | Contracted Rate Analysis for In-Network Status by Insurer

INSURANCE COMPANY	90791–RATE	90834–RATE	90837–RATE	90847–RATE	90853–RATE

Proposed or current contracted rate analysis for in-network status by insurance company.

NON-CONTRACTED, OUT-OF-NETWORK STATUS

As a non-contracted provider, you are out of the network of the insurer. This means that you collect all of your fees directly from your client. You don't deal at all with the insurer. Instead, once fees are paid, you provide an invoice to the client like the sample invoice below. It is then up to your client to send the invoice to their insurer so that they can get reimbursement or credit toward their deductible according to out-of-network benefits. It's very important that the invoice or "super bill" as it's sometimes called, include the phrase: "Patient accepts assignment of reimbursement" or something similar, so that the insurer doesn't send the check directly to you in your name. Remember, your client already paid you.

On the following page is a sample invoice for a client who intends to seek payment out of network. Your client submits your prepared invoice directly to their insurer.

GETTING CONTRACTED IN-NETWORK WITH A MANAGED CARE COMPANY

Many practitioners fear the process of filling out extensive applications to join managed care companies as contracted providers. It used to be that if you wanted to become an in-network provider, you had to complete a lengthy (sometimes up to 60 pages) application for each managed care organization. Certain states also had a state level addendum application that to be completed. While there are still some that require such an addendum, for the most part the paperwork is much less painful, and far less time consuming.

The Council for Affordable Quality Healthcare (CAQH, 2015), a non-profit organization established in 2000, launched a universal application database program that streamlined practitioner paperwork for application, credentialing, and re-credentialing processes. What does this means for you, the private practice owner? When you apply to be paneled with managed care, you only need to complete one secure, online application that CAQH holds for the entirety of your practice career. A much more seamless and less hassled process; once completed, you only need to update it a few times per year.

FIGURE 5.1 | Sample Invoice

Howard Baumgarten LPC, LLC
90 Street Blvd., Suite 100
Anytown, USA 00000
Tax ID: 70-XXXXXXX

INVOICE

October 5, 2016

Client's Name
DOB—04/27/1980
800 S. Michigan Way
Anytown, USA 80001
DX: 296.31 (F33.0)

Invoice Number: 10052015

DATE	DESCRIPTION	COST
09/15/2016	**90837—60-minute follow up counseling session**	125
10/05/2016	**Payment VISA ******3224**	-125
	This is NOT a bill. This is a receipt for services rendered that should be submitted for out-of-network insurance reimbursement to the client. Client accepts assignment for reimbursement by insurance as all services were paid in full.	
	TOTAL DUE	**$0.00**

Sample invoice to a client for submission for out-of-network reimbursement to client. Client date of birth, diagnosis, and Common Procedural Technology (CPT) must be on the form.

Before completion of the managed care application process on CAQH, you must first be invited to join a managed care organization's provider panel. It is almost unheard of for a managed care organization to extend an invitation to join out of the blue. When this occurs, it usually is because that organization sees a rapid increase in members in your geographic area, or they see a need for more providers for some other reason. If you wait for a managed care organization to cold call you and invite you join, you might be waiting for a long time! You must, therefore, outreach the provider relations representative or apply through the insurer's provider website portal.

You can create a letter of interest and send it to the various insurance companies with whom you'd like to contract. In the letter, clearly state you are asking whether there are current openings for a contracted provider in your geographic area. If you want to increase your chances of being invited into the network, it helps to be bilingual, add your unique training/specialties/certifications, and be willing to locate your offices in a more rural or hard to reach area of your town. It's important to be honorable about what you put into a letter of interest. Remember, you aren't stretching the truth. You are seeking professional membership with an insurer. Highlight your experience, and let the provider relations representative you work with get to know you so, should there be any future openings if there aren't any currently, you can continue to try and get on that organization's panel.

If you have never been on any managed care panel as an in-network provider, here are the steps you should take with the very first insurer:

1. Contact the provider relations department at the insurance company. Usually this occurs electronically through the insurer's "providers" drop down/page. There, look for information specific to how to become a participating provider in that insurer's network. Some sites have an online questionnaire, while others require a "letter of interest" sent by email. The methods for requesting participation differ for each insurance panel, and they change often. If you aren't sure how to proceed, just contact the provider relations department to inquire the best method for requesting panel participation.

2. Once the insurer gives you permission to join their network, if this is your very first participation on an insurance panel, you need to let them know you have not yet completed the CAQH application and a unique CAQH access code/identification number to create your profile is required. This latter point is very important as your first insurer should provide a CAQH access code which allows you to unlock and complete your profile, and in turn other insurers can gain access to your completed CAQH application. Thus your credentialing processes with other insurers is seamless, and without effort.

3. If you already completed your CAQH profile, you can skip this step by logging into your profile and allowing the insurer access to your information. If you haven't completed your CAQH provider application, once you have the access code/ID number, complete the entire CAQH application. Though it's a lengthy process, you can save your work and do it incrementally. Just make sure you complete it thoroughly and timely. Please note CAQH emails you approximately 2 to 4 times annually to update your profile. Make certain you are paying attention to these email requests for updating by keeping the information on your profile current so that you remain in good standing with your panel participation with each managed care organization.

    After you complete the CAQH, your next step involves managing and monitoring the credentialing process. Credentialing is the process of evaluating, vetting, and loading your information into the insurers massive system. That system consists of a background check, provider profile listings for referrals, claims and billing, contract finalization, and any other administration. This process usually takes three to six months. Some insurers allow you to begin seeing clients even before you are fully credentialed.

4. During or just before the credentialing process, you should receive your contract. Read the entire contract because once signed, you agree to exactly what the contract stipulates. If there are any changes or change requests on your part, make sure you offer those changes before signing your contract. I recommend you consult with your attorney, asking for recommendations or suggestions after you read it yourself. Make sure, once you are credentialed and effective on the panel, that you possess a fully executed copy of your contract, signed by both you and the insurer. Keep this contract in a safe place for future reference.

FIGURE 5.2 | Quick Steps for Becoming an In-Network Provider on Managed Care

1. Contact Provider Relations
2. Obtain Information on Applying
3. Obtain CAQH ID
4. Fill out CAQH
5. Review, Change & Sign Contract
6. Become Fully Credentialed

RENEGOTIATING YOUR RATES

Did you know you can renegotiate your reimbursement rates? Most practitioners accept the rates offered and never enter into contract renegotiation, even after long-term participation and loyalty with a particular managed care company. I successfully executed renegotiation of my rates with numerous insurers, which allowed me to increase my overall practice revenue.

There are optimal times to ask for new contracted rates. I recommend renegotiation of rates after your first five years of service on a given managed care panel. Then revisit the rate structure approximately every 4 to 7 years. As you continue to remain contracted with a given company, you are building loyalty and thereby increasing your equity with the organization. Thus, you can use the length of your relationship as a selling point for asking for higher reimbursement rates. Here are some other important pointers when asking for higher rates:

- Re-negotiate rates approximately each 5 years
- Be reasonable about your request
- Put the request in writing
- Discuss general fiscal rationale
- Highlight growth in professional experience
- Be extremely professional in writing your request
- Continue to follow-up
- Get rates signed under a contract modification

Take a look at the following sample letter. I used the bullet point ideas mentioned above by creating a letter that gives facts, which leveraged my position for obtaining a rate increase:

FIGURE 5.3 | Sample Rate Increase Proposal Letter

Date

Provider Relations [Company Name]

Re: Request for rate negotiation
Howard Baumgarten LPC
Tax ID: 72-xxxxxxx

To Whom It May Concern:

In follow up to my recent conversation with a Provider Relations Representative at [Company Name] I am sending this request for a rate negotiation in my clinical practice.

I have been in clinical practice for over 12 years and with [Name] as an in-network provider for just over six of the last 12 years. A seasoned practitioner, loyal to managed care, and extremely loyal to [Company Name], I am respectfully requesting a rate increase.

The current rate structure is at the same place it was when I became a provider in 2006. The cost of living has raised an average of 2.73% per year over the past 7 years (http://www.ssa.gov/cola/automatic-cola.htm). As such, based solely on a cost of living increase, my original starting and current clinician rate of $65 for CPT 90806 would theoretically be approximately $77.42 at present. Additionally, the current rate for CPT 90801 of $104 should be $123.86 according to today's cost of living increases. These changes don't take into account the lost years with no incremental increase, or the growth of my clinical experience.

While I enjoy a great working relationship with [Company Name] and think highly of its employees, and especially its members, the fact is that my current reimbursement rates are on the low end of the scale when compared with all the managed care companies with whom I affiliate. The average managed care rate for CPT 90806 is currently $76.26, for CPT 90847 is $79.09, and for 90801 is $110.82.

With the reasons and rationale for my request stated above, please consider my request for the following new rate structure for these CPT codes:

90791–$115
90834–$80
90847–$80

I am hopeful that in addition to the points above, you will also research and consider the fact that because I serve on numerous managed care panels, my caseload of [# of clients]clients is not large, and therefore should not be a fiscal burden. On average I bill around 5 sessions per month. That number fluctuates from time to time, and I don't anticipate any major jump in session numbers as I continue to be well diversified on managed care panels, as well as in my other fieldwork.

I appreciate and value my work with your members and look forward to continuing to support [Company Name] important mission as one of its providers.

My current practice address and contact information is as follows:

Howard Baumgarten, LPC, LLC
912 Wadsworth Blvd., Suite 102
Lakewood, Colorado 80214
Phone: (303) 333-2132
FAX: (303) 969-4435

Thank you for your consideration of my request. I look forward to hearing from you soon.

Sincerely,

Howard I. Baumgarten, LPC
Colorado License #2xxx

This proposal was an actual proposal written in 2013, modified and sent to various insurers. Half of the insurers awarded an increase in reimbursement. Remember that actual numbers were representative of the year 2013, when this letter was originally written. Be sure to do your research and use proper citation in your proposal.

What should you do when a managed care company denies your request for a rate increase? Here's what I did. I respectfully and repeatedly requested a rate reimbursement increase and eventually chose to terminate my relationship with a few insurance companies, because after over ten years of not getting a raise, being loyal to their membership, increasing my experience and expertise, I began to question the insurers' integrity, ethics, and my own professional belief in the value of services I provide.

While we must draw healthy boundaries, we cannot be foolish about terminating managed care contacts in good standing when we don't know of the potential referral and financial consequences. For this reason, it becomes important to recognize how much current business would be lost by terminating a managed care contract, as well as what you are risking in terms of future referrals when you are not on a given panel. Most importantly, think about the current clients who use the insurance you are possibly terminating and what is in their best interest treatment-wise. Each time I elected to terminate a contract, I made sure I could cover potential short-term financial losses, retain a good referral flow, and help existing clients who could not use their insurance any longer without financial barriers. When considering leaving a managed care contract (for any reason), the following steps should take place:

1. Refrain from accepting new referrals from the insurer in question as soon as you begin thinking you are going to possibly terminate your contract.

2. Consider the financial impacts of short-term losses of client referrals.

3. Never go off more than one insurance panel at a time.

4. Try not to terminate more than one contract in a 12-month period. (This gives you time to recalibrate your practice in terms of having enough client referrals).

5. Wind down your existing clients according to what's ethically responsible and contractually allowable. (In many cases, clients remained with my practice because it was clinically appropriate, they wanted to stay, and had the means to pay out of pocket. This unexpected development led to an almost automatic increase in revenue, even in situations when I offered discounts to my clients. I honored a sliding fee as well to those who needed it).

6. Finally, follow all termination expectations and procedures according to your contractual obligation. It's just not worth it to burn bridges and risk problems.

IN-NETWORK VERSUS OUT-OF-NETWORK

What makes the most sense? Should I join an insurance panel as in-network provider, or remain out-of-network? If I do join, how many insurance panels should I join? I receive questions like these often. The answer is not so cut and dry. There are definitely pros and cons to being in-network and the same holds true for out-of-network status.

In The Network

As an in-network provider, you agree to contracted rates, which are usually quite a bit lower than the rate you normally charge for your services. On the contrary, the likelihood of getting client referrals without any of your own marketing dollars or efforts is far greater than if you did no marketing on your own and did NOT participate on managed care panels. So, if you don't like marking for yourself, and/or you don't want to spend a lot of money on marketing your business, you may want to set all or most of your practice up contracting with managed care as an in-network provider. Remember, with this option, you are contracted with the organization and must abide by the terms of your contract. If you don't want to be tied to lengthy contractual arrangements with a third party payer, then serving in-network with insurance companies may NOT work for you.

Some believe that when working with managed care there is a lot of paperwork required. This claim used to hold true, however, due to many changes in the industry, there is now much less clinical authorization paperwork that is required when working with in-network insurers. Really the extra work when working in-network is the initial CAQH application for credentialing, keeping that application current, and filing insurance claims, and you can hire a medical biller to file the claim son your behalf. There remain a small number of insurers and/or insurance lines of business that require pre-authorization or ongoing intermittent authorization paperwork to be completed.

Very occasionally, you may be required to participate in a review of a patient's treatment with a "care manager" at an insurance company when working in-network. Insurers used to use this process of case management and member benefit management on almost all routine outpatient cases, especially those that were long-term. Now, the insurer typically reviews only clients they red flag through claims data as having a high amount of claims. In only a fraction of these cases does the insurance company request a review to make certain the treatment is appropriate, given the "high" usage of the client's benefit. Though these reviews are quite rare for most practitioners, it's entirely up to you to decide whether you are comfortable with this kind of experience, as this type of review process may be a deal breaker for your managed care participation. In many of these situations the clinical reviews are quite productive, albeit a little time consuming, in that the care manager, who possesses a clinical training background, serves as a second opinion in the case and may help keep you on track with the clinical process. If you benefit from a bit of oversight, especially with more complex clients, then the in-network arrangement may be a good fit for you.

Out Of The Network

Out-of-network participation is a good option if you want to work more on your own to obtain referrals, wish to have slightly less paperwork, and want to make more money per therapy session. This option is a good one if you are ready to wear your marketing and networking hat, something you should do even some of the time if you are in-network. Out-of-network practice owners spend more time on their own marketing and networking than in-network practitioners. Therefore, most out-of-network clinicians are seeing fewer clients per week. If this arrangement is a good balance for you, and you aren't afraid to "put yourself out there" then consider this option. There's less paperwork, no oversight, and no contracts when out of the network.

The Hybrid Model

Many private practice owners elect to build a Hybrid Model when it comes to working with insurance companies. With the hybrid method, the owner chooses a few insurance panels to join in-network, so that the challenge of getting referrals is not so insurmountable. The contracted insurers offer a little breathing room on the marketing and networking end, and help get clients through your door, even though your contracted rate is lower. This model of working with managed care suits practice owners who want some autonomy from managed care companies, yet still desire the experience and referral safety of working directly with insurers. Perhaps most important in this model is that you are employing a well-diversified process of for receiving client referrals.

The chart below shows a simple way to look at the three models from a financial and time breakdown perspective.

TABLE 5.4 | In-Network vs. Out-of-Network vs. Hybrid

IN/OUT/HYBRID	AVG. HOURLY RATE	# WEEKLY SESSIONS	TOTAL WEEKLY INCOME	NETWORKING MARKETING/ADMIN/ OTHER HOURS
In-Network	$60	35	$2,100	5
Out-of-Network	$95	23	$2,185	17
Hybrid (In/Out)	$75	29	$2,175	11

Based on a 40-hour workweek, this table shows a comparison break down of three different managed care practice models. The In-Network only model shows low hourly rates with the highest number of weekly client sessions, while the Out-of-Network only model shows the highest per-session dollar amount with the lowest number of weekly sessions and the most time for practitioner-related outside business activities such as marketing, networking, and administration. The Hybrid model of both suggests an approximate average of the two. The total weekly income is approximately the same in each of the three examples. Note that the dollar amounts in this table may not be accurate according to insurer, experience, and geography. It's important to check with each potential insurer for accuracy and run your own financial projections

MY MANAGED CARE EXPERIENCE

I began my private practice contracting 100% with managed care companies. Because I contracted through a group practice, my rates were slightly less than the contracted rate for in-network providers. Instead of earning $60 per client session, I was actually earning about $45. The other $15 per session went to billing, scheduling, website administration, and other expenses for the group. The group practice avoided the legal issue of "fee splitting" by structuring its contracts with providers in such a way that these costs were allocated as front and back end business fees paid into the group practice. In my first five years of practice, working both 100% under managed care contracts, and doing it through essentially a "middle-person" (the group practice), I counseled roughly 44 clients a week just to make $2,000 of revenue. I was working about 50–55 hours per week total, seeing around 40–45 clients a week. As a young clinician, seeing that many clients without doing ANY business-related work like marketing/networking, scheduling, or billing, was a great model. I spent 10 hours a week on writing clinical notes, and the rest of the time seeing patients, while working closely with a clinical supervisor. It was fast paced, and fun, something I enjoyed in my 30's when I had the energy. You might think seeing that many clients and working that many hours is too much. I thought I was lucky to be running my own practice and only working 55 hours a week. After all, I grew up with friends who became attorneys and were starting their law practice in firms that made them work 80 hours a week!

There was another benefit to working with the group and being a high-volume therapist in private practice. I quickly became known in the client community. **Successful intervention in helping your client change goes a long way toward getting future referrals.** Referrals coming by word of mouth, especially from current and former clients, are often a great compliment of your work and usually an excellent new client! During my time with the group, private pay clients found their way into my practice as well, which began creating a financial balance and slowly increased my average hourly reimbursement.

After an initial five years with the group, I realized that I had enough contacts in the community, a strong current client base, along with more experience and training. I desired fewer clients weekly for both personal and professional reasons. Personally, I had two small children with whom I wanted to spend more time. Professionally, I developed an interest in teaching, business consulting, wellness training, speaking and other areas outside my clinical practice.

After about 6 years with the group, (let's call it Phase I), I began ending my "middle-person" relationship and moved onto the insurance panels directly by switching from the group tax identification number to my company's tax id. I made this transition happen using appropriate channels, not violating any contractual agreements with managed care organizations or the group practice, and of course keeping the integrity of client care at a very high standard. By year 8 (2010) I ended my relationship entirely with the group, and on excellent terms.

Eight years into practice, I was totally on my own, still contracted with managed care organizations, about 10 of them, along with receiving roughly 5% of my business from private pay clients. At that time, I was teaching the curriculum I developed in the graduate program at the University of Colorado's counseling program, and doing wellness trainings for a large and reputable medical insurance firm. I was also counseling approximately 35 clients weekly, earning about $15 more per session after leaving the group. Seeing 10 fewer clients per week under this new model actually netted me approximately $1,200 more per month, and gave me 10 additional hours weekly to work on the other endeavors I mentioned. Those other endeavors padded my income more as well. Because I was already earning more money seeing fewer clients, it enabled me to spend many hours, unpaid of course, developing and teaching my curriculum on business building! I call this part of my private practice career "Phase II."

Phase III involved a major change in my insurance contracts, as the relationship I had directly with managed care companies was about to change. While my business grew, and more referrals came through word of mouth, rather than direct from insurers, as well as my building years of loyalty with each insurer and attending more training not to mention the overall experience growth, as mentioned earlier, I felt it appropriate to contact each insurer and request new updated rates commensurate with the current economy and my experience. I had success in these contract renegotiations about 50% of the time, and as each insurer turned down my request at least two times in a row over a period of two or more years, I began stopping taking new referrals from such companies, followed by phase IV, eventually starting to move away from contracts that wouldn't compensate me adequately based on experience, training and the current economy. With the increase of some rates from a few managed care organizations, as well as my getting more fee-for-service clients, I continued seeing about 30–35 clients weekly and saw my weekly revenue increase by about another $200 per week.

In phase IV, approximately 10 years after I began my private practice, I started terminating contracted in-network relationships with managed care companies that I felt didn't treat practitioners, including me, fairly. These were contracts that left me high and dry with regards to a raise during my entire 10 years in practice at the time. While I am not at liberty to say which companies wouldn't raise rates, you can send a message by writing a termination letter that states why you are terminating and "vote with your feet" by ending your contract. Now, I only recommend ending these contracts when there is a high likelihood that your bottom line will not be impacted by such changes. Please refer to the steps mentioned earlier under renegotiating rates when considering leaving managed care contracts.

As of this writing, nearly twenty years into private practice I am in-network with five managed care organizations, slightly less than half of the contracts I held within the first five years of clinical practice. I offer a sliding scale discount to those private pay clients who need a break, along with helping some clients with no-interest partial advances as long as it doesn't get in the way of clinical progress. I am able to see about 20 to 26 clients per week and earn slightly more revenue. About 70% of my business is now private pay and/or out-of-network, while 30% is through in-network insurance contracts. My caseload is in the average to slightly below average range of most full time clinicians, and I am able to work on other endeavors in my field, such as public speaking, writing, and training, while spending more time with my family. I also get to do pro-bono work in whatever way makes sense that isn't a liability to my practice.

Reading my process of development and change with managed care organizations should give you insight into a possible scenario of ramping up with in-network contracts, getting great experience doing high volume managed care work, then moving into a hybrid model, and eventually winding down most in-network contracts. My progression is one unique story, and if you ask other providers about their relationships with managed care organizations, you will get a different story for each person you ask! The cool part is that you get to try it the way you would like, and then modify as you go. Truly there is no perfect approach or only one way. There is a best way that fits you and I encourage you to make challenging choices and see what transpires. If you need further assistance with understanding the insurance process, a more comprehensive look at managed care for mental health providers can be found in Griswold (2015), *Navigating The Insurance Maze: The Therapist's Complete Guide to Working with Insurance—And Whether You Should.*

THIRD PARTY PAYERS

Aside from direct fee-for-service and managed care contracting, working with third party payers can provide further diversification in terms of options for getting paid. Some practice owners prefer not to work with third party contracts because of rates or contract limitations; however, there are numerous third party payer options, one or more that might suit you. In this discussion, the phrase "third party payer" refers to any organization or group that pays for your services outside direct fee-for-service and/or traditional private healthcare insurance companies. Let's discuss a couple examples of third party payers.

Employee Assistance Programs (EAP)

Programs that offer direct counseling services via an employer group, whether housed and managed by the private company whose employees it serves or managed by an outside company such as a managed care insurance company or other private firm, are known as Employee Assistance Programs (EAP). While EAPs started decades ago, they have seen many changes throughout their history. Today, most Employee Assistance Programs are housed inside managed care organizations, or operate as their own managed care company providing EAP packages to various employers. Some EAPs are owned and run by the employer itself. However, as the cost associated with providing these needed services increases, it's becoming more challenging for employers, even large ones, to staff and manage their own EAP.

Despite many EAPs existing inside managed care contracts, I talk about them as third party payers even when they are a part of a managed care contract, as you must still designate a willingness to accept EAP referrals and a special reimbursement rate, which is usually commensurate with most standard payment rates. Therefore, you are technically in a separate program/payer, and even in many cases a completely different contract.

EAP services differ for the consumer from a traditional health insurance plan. Employees who participate in their EAP are granted a limited number of free counseling sessions (free for them, though you are paid a contracted rated directly from the EAP), and receive other benefits as well. Over the years, EAPs listened to employee feedback and many now offer a wide array of services, including crisis intervention, counseling for family members, even free legal, financial and other helpful services. Some even sponsor large annual free healthcare screenings as well as full day health fairs right at their job site. Also, there are training opportunities available in some EAPs to offer wellness seminars to employer groups on a variety of topics. You may be interested in providing depression/anxiety or other mental health screenings at health fairs, or serving on professional speakers/training staff with a particular EAP. I provide training services for one EAP and counseling for several others and both together provide further diversification of payers, delivery systems and clientele.

Some EAPs require provider specialization, a certification known as Certified Employee Assistance Professional (CEAP). However, most organizations only prefer the credential along with a strong clinical background, an interest in EAP work, and perhaps prior experience that lends itself to working with an EAP. So where should you look for EAP opportunities? Here are three ideas for searching for an EAP opportunity in your community:

1. Ask about EAP opportunities within every insurer with whom you contract
2. Perform an Internet search typing in the words "Employee Assistance Program" and your zip code, municipality, county or state
3. Contact large private companies near you to inquire as to whether they house an EAP within their company and, if they don't, who do they use? If the latter is the case, then contact that EAP company

Don't forget, always respectfully inquire as to what their referral needs are in your office location area, how much they reimburse, what benefits they provide to their participants, how the contracting process works, and any other pertinent questions. Remember, your leverage is before you sign on the dotted line!

Government Programs

Medicare and Medicaid

Much like insurance panels, Medicare and Medicaid are social government-run insurance programs that offer private practice clinicians an opportunity to treat clients from diverse backgrounds. Medicare covers certain individuals who are disabled as well as Americans over the age of 65. Medicaid is a state- and federal-run program providing healthcare coverage for those with very low income, who cannot afford private insurance, and some individuals who have a disability.

Medicare and Medicaid provider rates are competitive with most provider rates offered by private insurers. While each state differs in provider reimbursement rates, my example in the next table shows most current rates as of this writing for both Medicare and Medicaid the state of Colorado:

TABLE 5.5 | Medicare and Medicaid Rates

CPT CODE & SERVICE DESCRIPTION	CURRENT MEDICARE RATE JAN. 2016	CURRENT MEDICAID RATE JAN. 2016
90791—Initial Intake	$128.72	$106.05
90834—45 Minute Follow-up	$85.56	$68.87
90837—60 Minute Follow-up	$128.72	$100.80
90847—Couple/Family	$107.50	$59.99

Medicare & Medicaid Rates for popular service types for state of Colorado.

Medicare

Are you interested in learning about Medicare reimbursement rates in your region before determining whether to join the Medicare panel? You can find provider fee schedules by CPT billing code and according to geographic location by accessing the Medicare Physician Fee Schedule (MPFS) search tool. Simply go to the CMS website (www.cms.gov) and use their search area to put in "MPFS search tool." Then click the top hit link within the site and the overview page of the tool appears. From there, you agree to terms and a page with several search criteria appears with drop down categories for specific CPT (called HCPCS) codes. When you specify by region, a drop down of different geographic areas by state and sometimes city will appear. When the search results appear, pay attention to the "non-facility" rate if you are in private practice. That number is your current reimbursement for that service code.

Currently, licensed Master's level counselors and marriage and family therapists are not permitted to serve as providers on the Medicare panel. Though numerous previously proposed bills failed to include this professional group, The Mental Health Access Improvement Act of 2015 (H.R. 2759) introduced in June 2015 in the 114th Congressional Session is currently in committee, and all predictions point toward this version not being enacted either.

A major reason these groups of providers are not allowed to serve on the Medicare panel is the simple fact that when laws were established that define who is a mental health provider, marriage and family therapists and professional counselors weren't in existence. It is absolutely essential that these groups of therapists be included, given the ever-increasing number of Medicare members, as well as a growing contingent of licensed service providers who legitimize the field of professional counseling and marriage and family therapy. If you are interested in getting more involved directly in helping this legislation pass, I recommend contacting your local congressperson and use www.govtrack.org to view and track the current bill, as well as contact your local congressional leader through this website, as I did recently.

If you are a licensed psychologist or social worker in private practice you are eligible to serve on the Medicare panel. The application form to complete is the 855i, Medicare Enrollment Application for Physicians and Non-Physician Practitioners, which can be found online at www.cms.gov. Once there, all you need to do is search "provider enrollment." Additionally, you can use their online application system known as PECOS, which stands for Provider Enrollment, Chain and Ownership System instead of the 855i paper application. You can access that system through the same web address.

Medicaid

Did you know Medicaid is the single largest payer of mental health service in the United States? In 2014, there were over 72.5 million Medicaid enrollees nationwide. Unlike Medicare, any licensed masters level or higher (Psy.D./Ph.D.) clinician, including professional counselors and marriage/family therapists may serve on the Medicaid provider list. Because Medicaid is managed through each individual state, in order to become a provider in your state, you must enroll through your state's enrollment process.

While provider enrollment is according to each state, you can search for your state's Medicaid website through the federal Medicaid site, www.medicaid.gov. Once there, view the categories on the menu. Click the category "Medicaid" and then from the drop down go to "By State" choice. A map of the United States should come up with the option of simply clicking your state or selecting your state from a drop down menu on the page. Once you select your state, a page pops up that gives you an analysis your state's Medicaid eligibility and enrollment data, along with a lot of other fun facts about recent Medicaid changes impacting your state. While I encourage you make time to peruse this page, it's not entirely relevant to the process of becoming a provider. Some of this data may be helpful to you in determining whether you'd like to be a provider on your state's Medicaid panel. Once you are on the state page in the federal site, you can navigate directly to your state's Medicaid information website as there's a click option on every state's page that says: "state of _____ website." Clicking that link will take you into your state's Medicaid website.

While each state's Medicaid website is different, it's important to locate a section geared toward providers. In most cases, state sites have "For Providers" on their menu, or a variation of wording that suggests there's information about becoming a provider. A few states make it more challenging to find provider enrollment information. If you practice in one such state, use your state's website search bar and type in "Provider Enrollment" or simply "Provider" to see if you can locate information. When all else fails and you can't find anything related to enrolling in your state as a Medicaid provider, simply contact your state's Medicaid office and ask for the department that handles helping providers get enrolled.

Children's Healthcare Insurance Program (CHIP)

The Children's Healthcare Insurance Program (CHIP) covers children through it's own separate program as well as under the Medicaid umbrella. In 2014, more than 8 million children were a part of this program nationwide. There's a strong need for providers to serve this often neglected and high-needs contingent. Medicaid providers are usually eligible to work with children covered by CHIP; however, it's important to inquire whether there is a separate application or even a provider panel for this program. In Colorado, for example, you can participate in a CHIP-related program called CHP+, which provides coverage for Colorado children whose families have strong financial need yet don't meet Medicaid eligibility requirements. Inquire in your state about unique opportunities to serve this population and whether there are specific insurers or other payers that offer provider contracting and reimbursement.

You may be wondering, "Did he mention private insurers related to CHIP?" Yes, I did! Some private insurance companies contract to provide "lines of business" through Medicare, Medicaid, and CHIP programs. So, it's always helpful to learn about these relationships either through your state government programs or the private insurers with whom you contract in your state.

Serving as a provider with one or more of these programs is an important part of creating success in your business. You definitely need to know about the programs themselves, including how services are accessed, whether there are significant referral portals or other networking possibilities within the ranks. While you will learn more about networking in the next chapter, one example of networking within your Medicaid population involves contacting your local community mental health centers and asking whether they have a need for outside contractors/clinicians to receive referrals. Learn your community mental health centers' needs so that you have something from your clinical practice to offer them. More on creating lasting networking relationships later. Let's move on to another popular government program, Tricare.

Tricare

Tricare is a comprehensive insurance coverage program for the military and their families. Herein lies opportunity as a private practitioner to serve those who serve our country (including their families) and are experiencing mental health problems. If you specialize in PTSD, grief and loss, substance abuse, depression and/or anxiety issues, as well as relationship/family therapy, or any combination of these issues, then participation with this plan is highly recommended. While these particular issues can be found in any given cohort, they are especially present within the military population.

The management of the Tricare system is currently broken into three geographic regions in the U.S.: North, South, and West. Each region has its own managing entity, known as the Managed Care Support Contractor (MCSC). For example, currently, a division of United Healthcare is the MCSC for the West region. Tricare provider enrollment offers two options. You can either be a "network provider" or a "non-network provider." Network providers are contracted, much like a contracted provider is with a managed care organization. As a network provider, you agree to accept beneficiaries' in-network co-pay and bill for the remaining contracted amount. If you elect to be a non-network provider, you do not need to file claims for the client, and are you agreeing to accept the maximum allowed by Tricare as you can charge your full usual and customary rate. However, you must still be certified by the MCSC in your region.

The Tricare website is not user friendly when it comes to searching for provider fee schedules. Here's my recommendation for learning about rates, provider enrollment procedures, and other relevant information relating to becoming a provider under Tricare:

Step 1: Go to www.tricare.mil

Step 2: Scroll to bottom of homepage

Step 3: Click on "For Providers" at the bottom of the homepage

Step 4: Scroll part way down, and under Managed Care Support Contractors, click on "TRICARE region"

Step 5: Find your region according to the U.S. map that is showing

Step 6: Using the contact information for your region, contact a provider relations representative

Step 7: Inquire about fee schedules, number of covered families in your area, and enrollment processes

Local Government Programs

As if Medicare, Medicaid, and Tricare weren't enough on the federal and state levels, did you know that you have a unique opportunity to serve local government contractors directly in your private practice? And, again, reimbursement rates are often comparable to private insurers, sometimes even higher. If you are looking to work with government agencies serving those in great need, and you don't want to contract with larger entities like the ones previously described, these programs and entities typically offer less intensive contracting/partnering processes. Because these programs/payers within agencies are smaller, they often have more flexibility, and routinely carry more opportunities to network for referrals with known individuals.

Examples of partnerships with local government agencies or programs include but, are not limited to, county probation departments, victims assistance programs, and courts that need referrals for specialized counseling areas such as parenting classes or drug and alcohol counseling or groups.

One of my interns developed a relationship with our county adult probation department and brought several of our office clinicians in to meet the probation officers. This meeting led to an understanding of that department's counseling needs. Subsequently, the intern was able to negotiate a reimbursement rate, along with both sides determining a seamless professional assessment and referral process as well as collaborative ongoing treatment updates. Over a year later, two clinicians in my office are now receiving referrals, and both individual and group counseling is offered to this underserved population.

To help you get started, consider this list of local government agencies and programs. Find their contact information in your community, and start building referral and reimbursement relationships:

1. County Probation Departments
2. Family Courts
3. Criminal Courts (Offense-Specific, Drug/Alcohol Issues)
4. Victims Assistance Programs in city, county, state jurisdictions
5. Department of Youth Corrections
6. County Social/Human Services Divisions
7. Government Job Assistance Centers/Programs

Non-Government Third Party Payers

While government programs offer a unique portal for client entry and payment, there are many other third party payer options right in your own community. In my practice development, sometimes by accident and occasionally very much purposefully, I found community agencies, partnerships, private and non-profit organizations that needed a private therapist to whom they could refer clients. And, some of them had budgets to pay directly for their client fees.

PROFILE OF A THIRD PARTY PAYER

To prove my point, a great example of one such non-profit agency in Colorado whose sole mission is to provide counseling services to teenagers at risk of suicide is Second Wind Fund (www.thesecondwindfund.org). It organized in 2002, just a year after I started my private practice, on the heels of four teenaged deaths all by suicide at one local public school within the same year. The impact of this tragedy was both widespread and deeply felt within the community and a short time later, it's founders, members of a local community church, started gathering donations to help pay for teenagers to receive counseling. Since then, over the past 14 years, the program has grown its services across much of Colorado, building a network of over 160 contracted therapists to serve the needs of children and teens who are at risk of suicide and can't afford services. Referrals come from schools and other outside mental health professionals. In addition, the program offers secure HIPAA compliant telephonic counseling for those referrals that come from rural areas where there's no face-to-face provider accessibility. The agency has referred over 4,000 children and teenagers at risk of suicide who experience barriers (of any sort) to treatment through alternative means. These individuals receive up to twelve counseling sessions that can be used any time up until the individual is 20 years of age at no cost to the client. Outcome studies suggest that completion of a course of treatment through this agency yields the consistent finding of a significant decrease in suicidal thinking during course of treatment.

When you find a third party payer with whom you may be interested in creating a partnership or referral relationship, make sure its mission aligns with your clinical experience, target population, issues/areas of interest, and that you know how and what you are being paid. Equally important, inquire about the agency's referral process including how many anticipated referrals you may receive on a monthly basis, as well as knowing what the actual referral process is like. Third party organizations are fun to partner with as long-lasting relationships often grow between practitioners and those serving such programs. If you don't have the good fortune to accidentally stumble upon such opportunities, search the Internet, talk with colleagues, contact local agencies you know that may have insight into other programs due to their partnerships. To get you started on your third party payer search, here are a few search ideas:

1. Contact local community health and mental health centers
2. Outreach public and private schools about partner organizations
3. Check with local hospital, long-term care facilities about grants/programs
4. Look directly for non-profit organizations in your community
5. Perform a web-search of organizations/programs in your area
6. Talk with colleagues about third party payers they know

THE AIRPLANE MODEL — PAYER DIVERSIFICATION

Now that you read this chapter, you should be clear about the numerous ways you can get paid while in private practice. And, this chapter only covered direct clinical work, one layer of your practice. While it's one layer of building a solid revenue stream, it's definitely the most important. The infrastructure of your business relies on diversification, both in time spent and financially! You read earlier about the hybrid model, as a way to think about building over time. As I shared my story of building and diversifying by contracting with numerous managed care organizations, other third party payers, and some cash-only clients, diversifying your revenue streams by contracting with numerous organizations that fit with your model of providing services is an extremely wise method for building your practice.

The next time you are flying the friendly skies, look around the airplane for an empty seat. There is rarely an empty seat on the plane, and almost never one right next to you. Bummer! Right? Well, maybe not. If I am an airline owner, I want every possible seat filled, because a filled seat means revenue. If the airline charged $500 for every seat, fewer people would book that flight, and there's more risk in making enough money to be able to cover the expense of flying. (Hint: that's the cash only practice model). Airlines need to guarantee bottom line revenues so that operating expenses are fully covered for each flight. That's why there are a few people who paid $110 for that seat, several who paid between $150 and $200 for their seat, some who paid about $250 for their seat, and a small number, the first/business class, who paid over $300. The fees vary, but the plane and destination are the same! The main success is that it's full and everyone paid something, enough for the airline to service its diverse array of customers while covering expenses and generating profit. Just like an airline, you need certainty that your bottom line revenue goals get met and your operating expenses are fully covered each month. Hands down, I choose the "airplane model" of practice building when it comes to bringing in referrals and getting paid. This model is a big reason why so many clinicians contract with managed care organizations and third party payers.

Moral and ethical reasoning play a vital role in this model of doing business. Wouldn't you rather serve an economically diverse population, some who have less availability of funds to pay for services, some who are mainstream insurance card-carrying clients, and some who prefer to pay out of pocket? I can honestly say that working with a socio-economically diverse population led me into working with diversity in other areas as well. Offering clinical "specialties" administered across religious, gender, cultural, and socio-economic lines makes for a better clinician, and human being. If all you do is cater to one type of person, such a view surely narrows your practice and filling your "airline" seats will certainly be far more challenging!

More and more clinicians in private practice are foregoing managed care and third party payers altogether, providing therapy to 100% cash-only clients. Those who choose this path seem able to sustain strong revenues for a given period of time. I often receive calls from fee-for-service clinicians asking for help in generating more revenue for their practice as they experience a high degree of anxiety due to short-term peaks and longer-term valleys of no referrals. If you are going to be 100% cash only, please know that you will need to be comfortable with lean referral periods, more extremes in financial volatility, and an extremely high amount of marketing and networking.

One of the greatest benefits of contracting with a managed care organization or any third party payer is, once contracted, you are automatically placed on referral listings of that company/organization, and these lists are often searched online by members/customers. In a way, you are creating a seamless, effortless marketing/networking portal for your client referrals by contracting in-network with these entities. This helps cut down on outside marketing costs and networking time. Cutting down doesn't mean not doing any of these activities. In fact, you still need a marketing and networking plan that is well planned and executed on a consistent basis!

CHAPTER SIX |
BRING CLIENTS THROUGH YOUR DOOR!

Did you ever wish you knew the secret to attracting the clients you want while building life-long community referrals and relationships? Not only will this chapter show you how, you'll discover it's a lot less work than you ever imagined. In this chapter, I explain how to navigate the ever-expanding Internet so your target client can find you at the right time. Finally, you need to know how to make referral-generating mechanisms grow without much work and in a manner that is integrative, practice-efficient, and clinically sensible.

Now that you set up the infrastructure of your business and engaged your primary work sources, it's vital to improve your existing base with a solid, well-defined networking and marketing plan. When you work in the world of managed care and third party payers, it's always important to keep your profile updated with each payer, and to contact these organizations from time to time to let them know when you currently have openings. Beyond that, the information found throughout this chapter discusses what many providers don't know and/or never even try.

Let's dive in by redefining networking and marketing with an understanding of the concepts of "Specialized Networks" and "Smart Marketing!"

SPECIALIZED NETWORKS

A "specialized network" is my fancy term for creating person-to-person and business-to-business relationships unique and specialized to suit your practice referral and collaboration needs as well as some of the needs of the other providers and agencies to whom you will refer. Creating strong collaboration and referral networks are a critical part of creating, growing and sustaining a successful practice. Here's the best part! You are not paying a lot of money to get you noticed; the opposite in the case of advertising.

Setting up these networks is an investment in your time. You must commit to "putting yourself out there." As an experienced public speaker, putting myself in situations in which I am vulnerable with others, talking about wellness, business, relationships or whatever the topic, many say, "Howard, speaking comes so easy for you! You are a natural, extroverted and experienced! What about those of us with little or no experience and especially the droves of practitioners who enter private practice in part because we are introverts and just want to hang out in our offices treating clients?" I also hear, "I am too different, not outgoing enough, nervous, and afraid of looking like a fool."

While I enjoy talking, sharing, and connecting (as my wife and kids often remind me), this doesn't mean speaking publicly, providing trainings, or even starting networking discussions are easy tasks. Even extroverts experience fear and anxiety when it comes to creating professional connection. Whether you are more or less outgoing than others, the recipe for reducing your networking anxiety is exactly the same. Practice, practice, practice! It's just that easy. As a clinical behaviorist intervenes with a client, telling their client to habituate to a certain positive behavior in order to develop or hone a skill, so too am I offering you a system of networking that forces you to "get out there" not just once, but often, again and again, creating new connections, and sustaining older ones.

Early in the book I mentioned that perspiration leads to inspiration, which results in reaching your aspirations. This philosophy applies to your networking activities. "Getting out there" doesn't occur in just one form. There are many platforms for networking, some of which are less intimidating than others. Whether you provide trainings in front of hundreds or are an online blogging maniac, your consistent and thoughtful networking efforts pay many dividends. These dividends come in the form of creating referrals, clinically-collaborative relationships, professional education and training opportunities, and other benefits to your private practice.

People, Places, and Connections

If you are asking one or more of these questions, you are very much on the right track when it comes to setting up and maintaining your networks: Who are the people I should connect with in order to get referrals? Where shall I go to meet these people? How do I maintain these referral connections over time? All three of these points are extremely important. While the possibilities are endless, the list below helps you get started thinking about your "people, places, and connections!"

3 General Methods for Getting Client Referrals:

- Face-to-Face Meetings
- Provide Workshops/Seminars/Trainings
- Attend Conferences

EXAMPLE 6.1 | Three Methods for Getting Referrals

Face to Face:

1. Ask my colleague Bob out for lunch to talk about how we might mutually refer to one another.

2. Contact the physician's office down the street to see if we can do a meet and greet, and information sharing session to learn whether a cross-referral relationship is mutually beneficial.

Workshops/Seminars/Trainings:

1. Apply to provide a workshop at this year's state mental health conference—topic of my professional interest, and one that's popular right now.

2. Provide a free seminar in my community resource center or local public library to generate interest in my practice.

Attend Conferences:

1. State conference in April

2. At least one PESI training on trauma

EXERCISE 6.1 | My Networking Ideas

In each of the three general areas write two ideas for each category. Use this information and add more for the next exercise in this chapter.

Face-to-Face Meetings:

1. _____

_____

_____

2. _____

_____

_____

Workshops/Seminars/Trainings:

1. _____

_____

_____

2. _____

_____

_____

Attend Conferences:

1. _____

_____

_____

2. _____

_____

_____

Bear in mind that while networking can be pursued from a well-researched, planned out mode, so too can it be natural, organic, and instinctual. While you create opportunity by planning ahead, keep an open mind about starting professional conversations regarding what you do in a very natural way. Many experts suggest you create a 30-second "elevator" speech, just enough time to share who you are and what you do for a living in the time it takes to ride with someone up or down in an elevator.

My 30-Second Sound Bite

Use the elevator talk as your introduction to securing "networking time" such as training others or having coffee. Most people aren't going to remember a few moments just meeting you and hearing what you do in a 30-second sound bite. People remember real experience, such as an hour over coffee sharing interests, or a 30-minute training on an area of your expertise. Creating networking opportunities may be serendipitous, or planned out. While you have good ideas brewing about the people, places, and connections you want, specific and proper strategies and tools are essential.

Let's begin with the golden rule of networking, which is: DO NOT talk about yourself right away until asked and ONLY after you learn a bit about others. Growing up, this was the principle of politeness. Polite meant showing a GENUINE interest in others, caring about people and their purpose, and of course helping whenever possible. When networking for referrals, your best strategy, simply put, is mere politeness. In every networking relationship it's crucial that you show interest in the person or people on the other side of the table, whether it's one person at a coffee meeting, or 100 people in a training.

This networking protocol is counter to what many business experts suggest. An aggressive approach in our field is a huge turn off. Instead, take an interest in the other person/people and find out first exactly how YOU can assist THEM in your relationship. Lead with GENUINE interest and humility. Then, as the conversation moves further into connection and trust builds, usually what can be done for YOU by the other(s) in front of you comes in line. When the time is right briefly, but thoroughly, share your interest area(s), clinical focus, intake and referral process, and any other pertinent but brief information. When you aren't asked directly about your work, then offer an open-ended opportunity for the conversation to move toward interest in your work by politely asking whether there is a need for or interest in your practice/work. If not, let them know it's absolutely okay and that you will still try to refer to them when there's a fit. You never know when another professional's or group of professional's needs to refer out might change and actually fit your practice.

EXERCISE 6.2 | 30-Second Sound Bite

Take a moment or two now to develop a few quick lines about who you are and what you do. Remember to make it short and sweet. You may want to make two or three versions to fit a few different things you do or ways of saying what you do.

_____

_____

_____

_____

_____

You also need tools to help cement relationships with those you meet and spend time. Tools come in many forms. Maybe you offer a Power Point presentation as a giveaway during a training you provide that leaves a lasting impression on your trainees, who may become clients themselves or refer others to you. Your calling card is not only a well-designed business card. It's every practical tool at your fingertip that allows others to remember you and what you offer.

SMART MARKETING

"Smart marketing" is my simple term for the actual tools that help in obtaining referrals and is an adjunct to your networking. The use of intelligent tools allowing you to create and sustain your relevant networks is what smart marketing is all about. Marketing is passive in that you manufacture the "sales" material and let it do the "talking" for you before, during, after and at times instead of networking events. Yes, you can and should use marketing in conjunction with your networking. For example, many clinicians have "leave behinds" such as pens with a logo or flyers with information to contact you after you give presentations designed to create a referral relationship. Your materials should appeal to the feelings and thoughts of your potential clients, while providing enough information about you and your clinical specialties. There are many examples of marketing materials. Below is a list of actual materials you can create to help your business bring in referrals, and keep people interested in your practice.

Sample Marketing Ideas

- Publications (Books/Articles/Chapters)
- Business Cards
- Brochures/Flyers
- Gadget Giveaways (Pens, Calendars, Tape Measures)
- Creative Logo
- Dynamic Business Name
- Local Advertising
- Certifications
- Website/Blog
- Social Media Presence
- Internet Directory Listings

Remember marketing materials should be creative, thoughtful, targeted to your desired client(s), and extremely well written, free from spelling, grammar, and punctuation errors. There's nothing worse than having a well-written blog with punctuation and other routine errors. When developing your materials, always proofread your copy and get a second set of eyes on your work before it goes to your target population. Your marketing materials are public. You want to be noticed in a positive and professional light.

MARKET RESEARCH

In order to reach your target population, both with networking and marketing, you must perform your market research. Ask yourself, "What is it that I wish to be doing service-wise?" The first and perhaps most important step in doing research is defining your clinical interest. If you don't have well-defined service emphases in terms of population, issues, interventions, etc., you aren't going to ask the right questions, and target the right people for your business.

Many practice development business coaches talk about building marketing and networking strategies around your "ideal client." This philosophy limits you because there is really no *one* ideal client. Yes, you want to be working with clients who fit your area of expertise and respond well to your interventions. Instead of focusing on your "ideal client," focus on defining what you do best, and knowing how you best do it. Describing an ideal client limits your ability to create a business that accepts a variety of referral types and treatable issues within your training competencies. Instead, develop and highlight clinical specialties in your networking and marketing materials.

"What is it I do well? How do I do it well?" That's just the first simple step! You need to learn the needs of your community. There are various ways to learn about your community's needs. First, you may already reside where you have an office and therefore know much about the needs just by the places you frequent, the people you know, and the organizations within your geographic area. This strategy alone, however, is not enough. Talk with those who you know, and actually go to organizations and learn more about who they are and what they need. Here's a list of methods for learning the needs of your community:

- Word of mouth
- Meetings/Conferences
- Surveys
- Feedback Forms
- Paying attention to community news outlets
- Attending professional events in your community
- Looking for articles online that support what you do

It's crucial that you write down information about your research, trying different methods at different times. When you are diligent about writing down whom you talk with, what you ask, and what the stated needs are, you more accurately predict the fit for your practice and target your offerings with better precision, increasing the probability of more quality client referrals. In addition, continuously evaluate your progress by measuring where each referral is coming from.

Create a chart or keep a notebook that houses this important information. You will reflect on it occasionally as a way of helping make key marketing and networking decisions. I always ask new and potentially new clients, where they heard about my practice? I then document on a spreadsheet the date of the referral and where the referral came from. When a referral comes directly from another individual or agency, I send a note of thanks in one form or another. This practice is important as it sustains healthy referral networks.

THE REFERRAL WHEEL

The primary purpose for smart marketing and creating specialized networks involves establishing an ongoing flow of quality referrals coming into your practice. Consistent flow cannot be achieved without proper market research, and developing solid and diverse marketing materials, while going out and networking with others. When you engage in all three of these activities in an integrated and routine manner, you establish an excellent flow of referrals to your practice. Results can come at the cost of numerous unsuccessful attempts. The most important piece of advice I offer when it comes to bringing clients through your door is *don't panic when clients aren't coming through your door.* Instead, remember that by doing these three important things in succession (Market Research, Marketing, Networking), over and over again, eventually the clients you desire find their way right through your door. I call this three-part process your "Referral Wheel":

Here's my referral wheel in action:

My Market Research

- Identified Clinical Interest Areas: Child/Adolescent Therapy, Parent Training, Couples/Relationship Work, Men's Work, Trauma & Grief, Business Development, Work/Life Balance

- Therapist Demographic Research: (Online Search Engine, Insurance Companies, and Word of Mouth data collection). Result: High need for male therapist in general, and highest need for male therapist who treats children/adolescents

- Other Community Needs: Identified need for business development support to other service providers (discovered by word of mouth, dialoging, networking and free trainings)

Marketing Materials

- Business Cards: (Separated Business Coaching from Clinical as an experiment)

- Website(s): BuildChangeGrow.com & SmartPracticeCentral.com

- Branding: Logo for Business Consulting, Program Design for Specialties, Speaker Bio, Curriculum Vitae

- Authoring Book: Business Development

- Trainings: EAP Clinical/Business & Business Training Through PESI

- Insurance Company Participation: Clinical

- Social Media: Mild on Clinical, Medium on Business Development

- Future Ideas: Reposition website and branding, increased commitment to social media, creation of blog

Networking Ideas

- Dr. Offices near my office, target pediatric doctors, contact for free lunch presentation on topic of their choice

- In-house consultation group, meet every 6 weeks, and bring in a speaker for information and referrals (This is VERY successful)

- Attend regional conferences in my interest areas

- Present at conferences

- Participate with some managed care

- Network on LinkedIn and other social media (Need to improve)

For the purpose of this book, I considerably shaved down many of my networking/marketing activities to a few important ones. After nearly twenty years in private practice you can well imagine the numerous activities that can be construed as networking and plentiful marketing strategy attempts. As you might

EXERCISE 6.3 | My Referral Wheel

Now it's your turn to create your own referral wheel. Take time to write out your ideas of how you see your referral wheel. Use your previous work in the chapter to help you complete your wheel. Add to it as you discover new needs that you can fill in your community, new ways to network, and innovative new strategies to market your services. Re-visit your referral wheel every so often and evaluate what's working and what isn't. Take necessary action to make the changes you desire.

MARKET RESEARCH   MARKETING

NETWORKING

My Market Research:

_____

_____

_____

_____

My Marketing Materials:

_____

_____

_____

_____

My Networking Ideas:

_____

_____

_____

_____

imagine, I have old business cards, program flyers and other materials from attempts at offering trainings that never came to fruition, along with memories of countless uncomfortable moments in which I thought my networking strategies were solid and landing in the right place, only to discover that was not the case. I failed during my journey and you will fail at times too. When failure is looming, and it's all you know, that's when you go back to your process and re-invent your referral wheel.

How will plugging away cause success to eventually find you? In his book *Outliers: The Story of Success* (2011), Malcom Gladwell shares the secret of success of the extremely outrageously successful people in many different fields. There is one salient point that Mr. Gladwell reveals which appears to be the answer for such enormous successes as Bill Gates' monstrous impact on technology, the world's alarming infatuation with a little known foursome from Liverpool known as the Beatles, and countless other ultra-successfuls. The answer? 10,000 hours of time and mastery! Literally, these people became aware of their surroundings, taking advantage of the tools and helpful people around them, and perspired and perspired even more, especially when failure occurred. In other words, successful people put in the time to persevere and practice over and over again until what was not "right," became "right enough."

As you embark upon the unknown, researching, planning, marketing, and networking, remember you must continue to examine and when necessary re-invent your referral wheel. Make the appropriate tweaks. When you discover that something isn't working well, give yourself permission to modify it or drop it. Keep what is working well, and perhaps replicate in other areas. It never hurts to try new ways of doing things. Get others whom you trust to critique your efforts. Consider their feedback with relevance to your overall growth process, and be resourceful. Be your own guide to opening up doors!

GET ME ONLINE

Your marketing materials no doubt take on many forms, the most popular these days being a hearty online presence. Creating and sustaining an online presence may be daunting, especially if you struggle with technology. Even if you are a tech-savvy individual, you did not obtain an advanced clinical degree to spend hours a day creating and maintaining your online professional profiles.

Let's agree on one important point. In today's market, you MUST have an online presence of some kind, and it's becoming more apparent that clinicians who develop a strong online existence get noticed more, obtain referrals more frequently, and seem to be more well respected by colleagues. Those who don't create and maintain an online presence are now thought of as not serious about business. At the very least, get your information on some therapist directories, and create a business website.

REVIEWS & TESTIMONIALS

Before we discuss your online presence in greater detail, let me make an extremely important point. The use of client reviews and/or testimonials on any platform online, even when they are anonymous, is never a good idea. Anonymous testimonials that are entered on your site submitted from your client's IP address may contain information that is privileged, and if it's coming from your IP address, someone may believe it to be fictitious. If it's coming from the client's IP address, such as uploading a statement on a "comment" part of your site, their IP address is then the identified originator. This technically may be a violation of the Health Insurance Portability & Accountability Act (HIPAA).

If you are providing a clinical health-related service, your responsibility to each client is in the protection of privacy. Don't allow clients to review your services or provide a testimonial in writing, online or in print. If a client asks whether they can write a review/testimonial, say the following, "Thank you for the offer. I don't put client reviews/testimonials on my website or in print to protect my clients' privacy. Rather than write a testimonial, be a walking breathing testimony of success by always honoring and maintaining the hard work you put into your therapy." Also, do not ask for a referral in lieu of a testimonial. It's simply tacky to do so.

Have you ever "Googled" your name online? What if you stumbled upon an unsolicited negative review or testimonial on a third party site? There are many third party review/testimonial sites that list you. Without your permission, these sites allow others to make public comments under your listing. Online healthcare review sites are extremely dangerous and unethical in that they invite current and former clients/patients to share reviews of their experience with a provider. The provider's hands are tied with an inability to respond to reviews due to HIPAA laws, and therefore the provider never gets to tell their side of the story. If you ever come across a negative online review on a health-review site, I strongly urge you to contact the site's owner, and respectfully demand that they take the review down.

Zur (2015) offers several solid tips on how to handle negative online reviews. In his groundbreaking online article he discusses many sensible strategies about this growing problem. What I like most is that he too questions the legal and ethical issues that arise out of clients identifying you as their therapist. It's also helpful to practice owners to learn that receiving a poor review is not the end of one's career.

A good solution to not posting client reviews or testimonials is to ask colleagues that know you and the quality of your work to write a testimonial or review and post it on your website. Also, ask participants of any trainings who are NOT clients to review your program and training style. In this way, you have good information from others who know your work posted online without running into ethical or legal implications of actual client reviews. I recommend only posting on your website or your social media platforms, and not on third party review sites when it comes the online environment. Use those third party online review sites for retail, restaurants, hotels, automobiles, and other non-privacy industries and not your clinical practice.

WEBSITES

The Truth About Websites

It's very important to have a website, and to be effective it needs be a good one. What makes for a good website? There are several aspects to consider. First, you need to create a domain that reflects who you are and/or what you do. Over time add new information to the site, changing information frequently. A good website is rich in features. Write about the services you provide, develop downloadable initial forms, create a blog within, and make certain you have your accessibility visible and written on nearly every web page on your site. You want to be sure you are pointing social media to your site. The more hits you receive, the higher your search ranking goes. There are other features to consider, such as placing a short video and/or headshot of you somewhere on the site. The sky is the limit! Here's your quick list summary of smart ideas for your site:

1. **Creative domain about you/your work—(Examples below)**

    a. ZenCounseling.com—for a mindful based counselor
    b. LosingYourLoveTherapy.com—for a grief counselor
    c. ParentWithPride.com—for a parenting counselor
    d. CounselingConnection.org—for a general group practice

2. **Change & add new information often to help with freshness**

    a. Create a blog where you post new information

3. **Put your initial paperwork on your site for new patients to download**

4. **Make your contact information visible and accessible**

5. **Point social media to and from your site**

6. **Include a short video**

7. **Take headshots professionally and put one on your site**

8. **Consider using an online scheduling widget placed within your site**

Website Design and Development Methods

What's the most effective way to make your website? There are many options for creating a good helping profession website. Let me save you the trouble of searching by breaking down website development and hosting into three main categories:

Category 1: "Do It Yourself"—Creating your own website on WordPress, Wix, or Square Space, for example can be a good option if you are on a very low budget, and have lot's of free time. Wix and Square Space offer free hosting, but they come with advertisements and it seriously reduces the professional look and feel of your site. You will need to upgrade and pay monthly (approximately $15 to $30 a month, depending on your needs). If you go with this option, plan on spending a lot of time working independently. Using this option may cut into your clinical or personal time.

Category 2: "Hire a Webmaster"—Hiring a professional Webmaster, who creates, manages, and hosts your site, is an excellent choice when you have the funds to pay for these higher end services. A trusted Webmaster can be an individual or a company and works with you offering an hourly rate, a flat package rate, or a combination. The overall financial cost will be high, as you should expect to pay up to about $3,500 per year on average with higher amounts upfront for design and build.

Category 3: "Sites Designed for Helping Professions"—Design and hosting in this category is paid through a recurring flat monthly fee. This is usually a reasonable fee, a bit more than the first category, but significantly less than the cost mentioned in category 2. This option is a good method because it has all the nuts and bolts of what professional helpers want and need, with built in site customization tools that make your site stand out. Good companies who provide this service understand the online needs of therapists, and find innovative ways of packaging design, hosting, and technical assistance at very reasonable rates.

Regardless which category you pick, getting your professional services online via your own website is extremely important. Listings on therapist directories typically won't bring you enough referrals. You must diversify your web presence. For specific solutions to help you get your website going see Appendix I—Website Design and Online Presence for Therapists.

Your Ultimate Website

Regardless of the way in which you design and build your site, your ultimate website is not it's best without exclusive advice from one of the world's leaders in designing and building websites for counselors/mental health practitioners. (The following information will also apply if you are in a "specialist" service practice of any kind, including but not limited to Occupational Therapy, Physical Therapy, Massage Therapy, or other ancillary health-related practices.)

Becky DeGrossa (2016), founder and CEO of CounselingWise.com, a company dedicated to helping therapists effectively market their private practices online, revolutionized the online therapy website building process. After spending 20 years in the corporate world, Becky pursued her master's in psychology and became a successful therapist. Now she combines her technical, marketing, and psychology backgrounds to serve the private practice community, helping therapists fill, stabilize, and grow their practices by building awesome websites.

With the help of my assistant, Veronica Tunis, we interviewed Becky to get hands-on advice about building your "Ultimate Website." What follows are excerpts from our interview:

1. **Why is it important in the helping field, in this "tech" culture, and time to have a website?**

    *   People search online for everything these days, including therapists. Even if a potential client has been referred to you by a very trusted source, they will still look you up online to get a better feel for you, see where you are located, see your office hours, your fees, get your phone number, making sure you are credible.

    *   If you don't have an online presence, OR if your online presence is shoddy, or not within their expectations based on the recommendation they received, they will not call you, and instead will search to find another provider.

    *   If the person is searching for help with, say, depression (as opposed to looking for your name because they were referred to you), then being VISIBLE in Google is the best way to be found.

2. **How do I determine what content in my website will lead to the highest amount and most accurate referrals?**

    *   This questions encompasses several questions, actually—

        1) **WHAT** content you should have (i.e., the topics covered),
        2) **HOW MUCH** content you should have, and
        3) **WHAT IS THE QUALITY** of the content you need?

    *   I'll stress this again, determining your audience and making sure there is a demand for **WHAT** you offer is first and foremost. There is obvious demand for depression treatment, anxiety treatment, couples counseling, etc. There is less demand for help with the psychological impacts of living with diabetes. This does not mean that you can't get some clients looking for that, but it will be harder to build a full practice that way. Therefore, content that appeals to a market that exists and is searching for help is key. So the **WHAT** question could be content covering Depression Treatment/ Counseling / Therapy—specifically.

    *   Second, the **QUANTITY** of your content matters, a lot. If you work with Depression and have a specific page on Depression, that page should be a minimum of 1000 words (according to recent studies). And, having **many more pages** on your site (blog posts, usually) that cover more specific issues encountered by people suffering from depression will also significantly help your visibility. Examples of these more specific pages of content (or blog posts) are: Will you need to take depression medication? Or, How to get to work when you have no energy. Or, nighttime rituals to ensure better sleep, etc.

    *   Third, the **QUALITY** of the content must be high. Your page on Depression Treatment/Counseling/ Therapy should be written in a way that builds rapport with the potential client. Just listing symptoms and statistics is not effective. Your website copy must enable the reader to feel seen, to feel hope that you can help them, to instill confidence in the process of therapy. It must answer their fears and doubts about taking the first step. It must make you stand out as unique and better than the hundreds or thousands of other therapists in your city who work with depression. There are specific, proven ways of doing this. But you first need to know that it's important.

3. **What should I budget monthly/annually for ongoing maintenance of the site?**

- Websites are never completely done, but are an ongoing work-in-progress. They need hosting, standard maintenance, AND ongoing content building. I would budget at least $300/month. Remember, you are running a business. No real business runs without ongoing marketing costs.

4. **How do I make my website stand out from other therapists?**

- If you focus on site structure (having specialty pages, rather than general pages), write high-quality pages, and have plenty of other content where potential clients can see their specific issues reflected back to them (like the blog post examples mentioned above), then you will stand out as a very knowledgeable, experienced helper. Most therapists aren't doing these things, so if you treat your website seriously in this way, you will be in the minority.

5. **How do I get my website seen above and before others?**

- If you OPTIMIZE your website pages, then you will most likely rank highly in search engines. Optimization is the shorthand phrase for SEO (search engine optimization). In very competitive cities (New York, Los Angeles, etc.) you may also need to have paid advertising via Google Adwords to be visible.

6. **How do websites for therapists differ from other websites?**

- Therapy is a sensitive business (ha!). But what I mean is that as opposed to an e-commerce site that might be selling a tech gadget people are rabid for, a person considering therapy to address an emotional issue is in a very different place. They are typically quite scared. They often feel ashamed that they have an issue in the first place. Rather than attempting to convince them to buy a gadget, which is very straightforward, therapists are asking potential clients to engage in a very personal, risky, self-confronting and exposing process. Therefore, this "sale" usually takes much more skill and time. Credibility and trust must be established.

- One of the best things that therapists can do, that most therapists do not do, is to build a mailing list of folks who are "shopping" for help. If they come to your depression page, have them take a quiz or opt-in for an email series on how to deal with depression. If you have the email of a person who is searching for a solution for their depression, you can provide them information over time. This is the best way to build trust and credibility.

7. **What do you suggest for someone who's intimidated by the process?**

- The biggest mistake I see therapists make is to just throw up a cheap website, based on guesses as to what it should contain and how it should work. If you don't know what actually works in marketing therapy online, then get help. Get educated.

- If you are intimidated by the technical pieces, go with a company that will not only do those pieces for you, but educate you in the process.

8. **How do I determine what is right for my budget and business plan? I am just starting out and can't afford a "fancy" website.**

- The best thing you can do, if money is tight, is to learn what you ultimately want from your online success, and then start it with a barebones website. You can add content yourself without spending money. It is best to have the right framework in place, and then do all the other work yourself, rather than to create the wrong framework, and have to re-do it later.

- Get the right framework in place, and build upon it toward the dream website. Simple is better than nothing. You can get fancy with design, later. Potential clients are most interested in good INFORMATION. A site with great design and graphics that lacks solid, helpful information will not stack up to a simply-designed site with good information.

9. How do I integrate my specialties into my website and cater to what potential clients seek?

- Some of the most successful and fulfilled therapists out there have found the intersection of where their passions and love of working with a certain client/population meet with the demand of why people are seeking help. When thinking about the populations you want to work with and the type of services you want to provide to these populations here are some general guidelines: have three to five areas in which you specialize, (too many and you give the appearance of being a catch-all therapist).

- When building your website have each of your specialties on a separate page. These pages will increase your visibility because the bigger your website the better you will be ranked by search engines like Google.

- Choose multiple areas of clinical focus that are in demand and for each of those do niche marketing; for example if "teen counseling" is one of your demand areas then niche marketing for that area might include social issues, depression, ADHD, and school challenges.

- Your website is where you talk to your clients and what you say is very important. As a clinician, you are probably aware of taking a client-centered approach; in a similar way, you want to use this approach when developing the content of your website. What does your client need? What is going to capture their attention? What is valuable to them? When writing to the client you want to place yourself in the position of the seeker and look at their journey. What are they doing? How are they feeling? What are they thinking about? I've developed an exercise for therapists to use when writing the content of their website called the "The Dig Deep Exercise." This is a valuable tool to help you get into the mindset of your client and write in such a way that they feel heard, and understood, and will hopefully then reach out to seek your support.

EXERCISE 6.4 | Becky De Grossa's Dig Deep Exercise

How To Really Get To Know Your Potential Clients So That You Can Reach Them

Note: Each marketing message is specific to one issue or population you work with.

In order to write a strong marketing message, you need to crawl into the skin of your potential client. The more specific your message is and the more spot on it is about what your potential client is feeling, the more they will perk up and pay attention to what you're saying.

IDENTIFYING THE CLIENT

The following questions are for you to better understand your target, client(s) and to determine for whom the message will be written—see question 2.

1. Who are these clients?

   ○ Individual adults   ○ Children   ○ Couples   ○ Families   ○ _____

2. Is the client you seek a person who will be contacting you directly for your services? If not, who will? *Note—the rest of the questions need to focus on the person looking for the coach or therapist . . . This is your prospect and this is the person you need to be thinking of.*

   _____

   _____

3. What is the relationship status of this person (the person shopping for a coach or therapist)?

   ○ Single   ○ Partnered   ○ Married   ○ Divorced   ○ _____

4. Who does this person live with? _____

   _____

5. What does this person do for a living? _____

   _____

6. Gender?

   ○ Female   ○ Male

7. Age range? _____

IDENTIFYING THE PAIN/PROBLEM

The following questions help define the challenges your desired potential client(s) are facing so they can see that you understand their situation and what they are going through.

8. What keeps them awake at night, worrying, dissatisfied/unfulfilled, in pain, or just frustrated, lying in bed, eyes open, staring at the ceiling?

    _____

    _____

9. What is their single biggest problem (related to this issue) that causes them the most pain or frustration?

    _____

    _____

10. TAKE TIME WITH THIS ONE: What do they secretly, privately desire most? Become your potential client and finish this sentence.

    "If I could just _____

    _____."

11. Describe a typical day for your potential client as it relates to their problem.

    _____

    _____

NORMALIZING THE ISSUE/NEED

Why is it common (or uncommon)? Give specific examples of issues in our culture or your community that may contribute to these issues. You can give stats. This is your opportunity to "normalize" the experience and make it less intimidating to seek help.

12. How common is this issue?

    _____

13. Are there common reasons individuals struggle with or respond to challenges as your client is currently struggling? *e.g.,—relationship issues may be commonly tied to communication challenges, patterns of behavior formed in previous relationships, cultural or societal pressures.*

    _____

    _____

OFFERING SOLUTIONS, HOPE AND HOW/WHY YOU CAN HELP

What is your approach and why is it so effective in helping clients? Here you can go into more detail on your specific approach/methodologies, skills you teach, how sessions work and what clients can take away from therapy.

14. How effective is coaching/therapy in helping people through this issue and why?

_____

_____

15. What may a client expect to experience, better understand, learn and apply through sessions with you?

_____

_____

16. How do you approach your practice? Are you problem-oriented; is it a safe, compassionate environment? Do you emphasize accountability and real-world application? Do you offer tips, techniques, and strategies? Are they tailor-made?

_____

_____

17. What would you say to a potential client to provide them with hope about this issue? With help and support, what is possible?

_____

_____

18. How long have you been working with clients on this issue?

_____

Take a moment to consider the following two questions. You may or may not wish to incorporate these answers into this specialty page, and these responses may fit better in your About Me or How I Work pages.

19. What is your educational/professional experience specifically as it relates to this issue?

_____

20. Do you have any personal or life experience that is relevant to your client's problem?

_____

Review of Becky's Website Basics

While you might be inclined to go with a cheap site when first starting out to save yourself some money, you might as well spend it up front and have a good working website. In the end, it is most often the case that you won't save much money going cheap at all. Sometimes spending more money up front to build a solid website that works for you and has all the basics you need for it be successful at bringing you clients is much better.

Here are a few basics that will maximize your website's effectiveness:

- Your website should have a built in blog and it would be beneficial to make blogging part of your routine marketing/networking/reaching out to clients practice. The more blog posts you have, the stronger your entire site will be in terms of SEO.

- Make sure your website has the ability to perform good SEO. This has to do with choosing a platform that allows you to optimize all of your website even your blog posts.

- If you decide to choose a company to help build your website be sure to do some research and find a company that educates you about online marketing in the process of building your website so that down the road you know how to make changes and updates to your site on your own. In this process you want to learn what works, what doesn't work and why.

- Treat the marketing part of your business with as much energy, effort, time, and importance as you do the clinical knowledge you bring to your practice. In much the same way you attend trainings, read books, increase your knowledge and skill set about a certain treatment modality or therapeutic intervention to maintain a certain degree of excellence in your clinical knowledge, your marketing and business parts of your practice require the same attention.

INTERNET MARKETING AND SEO TESTIMONIAL — A CASE STUDY OF SUCCESS

Now that you heard advice from a seasoned and very highly respected expert on website building and management, and you heard a little more detail about improving your online views through search engine optimization, here's a story of true success.

Shortly after going into practice, in one of the most saturated therapist markets in the country (Denver, Colorado), Lori Johnson LPC, LAC, worked hard to get her online presence to Google Search page #1. Now, she has a thriving full-time fee-for-service practice just two years graduated and into the field! Lori identifies six key Internet marketing and SEO strategies for all private practice owners as well as some vital "do's and do not's" when managing your online presence.

Lori Johnson's 6 Key Internet Marketing and SEO Strategies

1. **Branding** ties everything together. Before clients even recognize your name they will recognize your brand. Your brand is instrumental to your marketing. When thinking about your brand, you want to be sure to have consistency in everything from the colors, images, and font to how you talk about yourself, your practice, and your niche market.

2. **Consistency**. When choosing how you are going to market yourself and what you are doing through social media whether blogging, sharing brief posts, or creating newsletters, be consistent because your audience will be expecting your next installment, and will notice when you aren't showing up.

3. **Authenticity**. In whatever you choose to do in terms of online marketing, branding, building your practice and your online presence be your true and genuine self. While this might be challenging at times because we keep parts of ourselves contained for the better interests of our clients, there is a significant part of us that enters the room and finding the right balance for you is key.

4. **Know your desired client.** Target your online marketing materials and content to client types you want. By knowing your client you are speaking to their needs and giving them the right information so they feel empowered and encouraged to make the call and get into your office.

5. **Know your skill set.** Know what you have to offer from a technical/clinical perspective and what you bring to your session personally in terms of your personality and temperament. Knowing your professional and personal attributes/experience allows you to bridge the gap between what your client is seeking and what you have to offer. Your skill set helps you identify key words to use in SEO and improve your chances of getting found online by the right client for you.

6. **Take the client's perspective.** Getting discovered online is about learning what your client is searching for when looking for their ideal provider. When developing key words, think about words your perspective client would type into Google to find you. Remember that articles, blog posts, video blogs, photos, quotes, hash tags, keywords and key phrases should be talking to the client who is looking for you. Your website and online presence is a way for your client and potential clients to find you without having to be vulnerable or leave the comfort of their own home.

DO'S AND DON'TS OF MARKETING AND MANAGING YOUR ONLINE PRESENCE

DO'S	DON'TS
• Always be professional. Be mindful and intentional about what you are posting and how that message can be perceived.	• Be cautious when considering a third party vendor. If it sounds too good to be true, it is likely the case. Many companies are not aware of the regulations and ethics of your particular field.
• Protect your privacy. Know what is personal versus business and make sure you are following your professional organization's code of ethics.	• Don't underestimate that what you are putting out there might not matter or have influence.
• Pay attention to your profile picture. Your photo matters and is a reflection of you and your business. Professional headshots are a good investment.	• Don't give advice. This can be challenging because we often give tips and suggestions. Be mindful of your language and stay away from telling your audience exactly what or what not to do.
• Always credit your sources.	• Don't slack off on maintaining your online presence, as it will begin to impact your ranking. Take care to maintain the hard work you have already put in. Remember clients and other professionals are seeking you out online.
• Be relevant and helpful with the information you are offering online.	

DO'S	DON'TS
• Give it time and patience. It typically will take 6–8 weeks to see results from changes made to your marketing or networking strategies. • Track search behavior using Google Analytics. It is important to know how people are finding you online.	• Don't be afraid to put yourself out of recruiting a client. Rather than being overly cautious and reluctant about sharing helpful information online, it is okay to provide resources and encouragement. • Don't be afraid of your competition. Rather than approaching this with a mindset of scarcity, embrace a mindset of abundance and encourage yourself to stay connected with your colleagues and share what others are doing. • Don't compare yourself to what your colleagues are doing. You have our own unique character, skills and experience that you bring to the field. Be true to yourself and focus on what you need to do for your clients. Don't feel like you have to follow what others are doing. Remember you can't cater to everyone. You have specialties for a reason.

CLINICAL EXCELLENCE AS A MARKETING TOOL

While your online presence is extremely necessary for building your practice, and person-to-person networking is vital, perhaps the most crucial selling point that not only brings you quality referrals but ultimately becomes the number one most relevant definition of your business is whether you are awesome at your job. Be the best clinician you possibly can, fulfilling your potential and beyond, and your referral growth will eventually occur, especially the right kind of referrals. Personally, I find that as my clinical skills improve, word of mouth from satisfied clients reaches other individuals seeking therapy, and even professionals somehow learn about your clinical excellence.

By the way, the best testimonial/review (gift) from a current or former client is an unsolicited word of mouth referral. Just remember when a new client is referred by your current or former client and tells you who referred them, never acknowledge that you actually are seeing or used to see that person making the referral. You wouldn't want to violate privacy laws. Also, for obvious reasons, never schedule a referred client from a current client back to back in your schedule.

CLIENT RETENTION PRACTICES

Most everything in this chapter is about creating referrals. But you also need to keep the clients you want, and do so in a way that is ethically responsible and highly clinically relevant. When you think about the phrase "client retention," be careful not to assume that you should keep clients beyond the time that is necessary for clinical recovery. You have a legal, ethical and moral obligation to discharge a client when the client no longer benefits from your intervention or makes a recovery.

Suppose for a moment that you are seeing a therapist to help you change something in your life. While that therapist may specialize in the problem for which you seek help, you come to realize that this professional can in fact help you in ways that you did not expect prior to engaging this relationship. In fact, as you continue to work with your therapist, you find that the connection grows and your confidence in your therapist's ability to help you change grows as well. You discover that you'd like to continue to seek help from this person even for issues for which they are not especially trained, yet certainly competent to provide help.

This process is no different than you desiring to keep an excellent physician as your doctor for as long as you can because you like the way they work with you, that doctor really knows you, and is competent to treat or refer to specialists when necessary.

So, how do you "retain" the clients who like working with you, and who may not need service any longer for what was originally presented? In all my years as a clinician, I never became quite comfortable with this notion of terminating the relationship with my client, unless of course my client preferred to leave the practice for good and wanted a termination process. If you learned in graduate school to "terminate" with your client after the initial problem is solved, then I ask you question this teaching. Termination is a relevant part of the process of any therapy course, and it's good you learned how to process the end of the relationship. In many counseling offices, however, termination of relationship occurs far less and termination of issue is a much more common occurrence that is more clinically apropos, and quite business-wise.

It's useful to break the therapeutic process into three phases:

- Phase 1: Evaluation & Treatment
- Phase 2: Change Management & Maintenance
- Phase 3: Prevention & Growth

Each phase has a certain frequency and duration of sessions based on the clinical presentation, and the client needs. As you might imagine evaluation and treatment has the most frequency, and prevention and growth has the least.

Many practice owners only use the first phase with their clients and then "terminate" with them, sending them off with extra resources for their management and prevention processes. If you are doing this practice, consider changing it. Why would you give away an opportunity to offer your client ongoing contact at less frequency when doing better, and still checking in. After all, you never want to have to see your doctor for invasive routine medical treatment, but you are sure glad to see your doctor for an annual check-up to make sure everything is functioning just fine.

So here's a typical treatment protocol.

EXAMPLE 6.2 | Sample Session Frequencies During 3 Treatment Phases: A Model for Mental Health Wellness, Prevention, and Growth

Bob, a 56-year-old male, presents in my office with clinical depression and anxiety after a recent caree-ending job loss.

PHASE 1 (Weekly Sessions—8–12 Weeks)

- Discovery of further triggers, history of depression/anxiety gathered, and other relevant information for intensive treatment
- Treatment included positive responses to cognitive restructuring and change occurred evidenced by client report and data points of lowered anxiety and depression

PHASE 2 (Tapering to Bi-monthly, and once per month—over 6-month period)

- Termination of depression and anxiety issues into tapering toward bi-monthly at week 10
- Development of management/maintenance tools during this phase
- Moved to once per month at 20 weeks

PHASE 3 (Prevention & Growth—Quarterly for 12 months, then tri-annual check-ups)

- Prevention and growth opportunities explored
- Routine check-in regarding medication compliance and fit
- Outside individual resources engaged
- Four quarterly appointments attended for checking depression/anxiety levels
- Tri-annual (3) visits over following 2 years recommended for routine check-up

In this example, Bob's symptoms mostly went away within 3 months. However, his overall counseling course led him well into 4 years by phase three, and now he chooses to come in once a year for his annual mental health check-up. Bob, like many other clients, appreciates this multi-phase approach because he appreciates that his provider knows him well, and for a long time. Insurance companies and other third party payers like this protocol because there's less utilization over a longer period of time. Without tapering and routine well checks, there is a greater likelihood that the client will not return on their own should a secondary course of intensive treatment be needed. Often, that secondary course is detected sooner when the client is still engaged in the counseling process at later phases and therefore less intensive treatment or less frequency may be warranted. Also, when clients aren't engaged in those later phases, and a serious crisis occurs, sometimes the client is hesitant to return after being "done" with treatment, and the crisis then leads to hospitalization. On average, a mental health hospitalization costs more than 5 clients seeing you quarterly (20 times total) in one year! Tapering and check-ups save cost, client pain and more importantly lives. That's why this multi-phase approach is clinically, ethically and morally the right thing to do.

From a business perspective, this three-phase model is a great way to keep your practice thriving. It is a strategy that is beneficial to you as a businessperson and as an individual seeking balance in work. As a professional managing your business, you won't need as many clients as you would if you only performed the required amount of treatment necessitated to get the patient's symptoms under control. And, by practicing in this manner you are always seeing a few clients who are gaining or have gained mental health and are just checking in for maintenance and prevention, or they are working quite independently now and are simply there for progress check-ups. You are therefore more balanced in your professional work because of the diverse levels of wellness you treat, rather than risking burn out from seeing only depressed clients who, as soon as they get better enough, leave and the next deeply depressed client walks through your door.

It's important to note that throughout this retention process, I am constantly reminding my client (and myself as well) that their choice to come and do work is theirs alone, and that while I might recommend a certain protocol of counseling, they are always free to end the counseling relationship or take a break from counseling at any time they wish. Some prefer to end counseling before phase 1 is even complete. Some want to be done seeing me after phase 1. Others stop in the middle of phase 2 or 3. Find the right integration of meeting your client where they are in terms of what they think is right for them, while making recommendations that are clinically appropriate. Adding this multiphase approach to your counseling process offers a greater more abundant way for your clients to engage in your help, and in turn for you to assist your clients, along with a more solid and diversified way to treat the business of your practice.

BEING DIFFERENT AND MAKING A DIFFERENCE

Earlier, I mentioned Gladwell's *Outliers* and the 10,000 hours it takes to make successfuls into superstars. You don't need to be a superstar in this field to enjoy career fulfillment. You only need to be successful enough to make your practice thrive. If being an outlier isn't your cup of tea, try just being different. Private practice consultant for the American Counseling Association, Anthony Centore (2016), believes in counselors pouring more of their energy into being different, otherwise one won't have a practice to make a difference in the lives of others. While he shocks his readers with the possibility of practice failure among the droves of successful practices, he basically asserts in his recent article that one's practice will be relegated to mediocrity at best when one is not thinking out of the box and doing some things differently than other practitioners.

Making a difference is about being different! That's why I challenge you to think differently not just with your business ideas, also with regards to your clinical approach and its impact on your business. Marketing and networking will often be sour and no fun when you aren't doing things differently from other practitioners. While some routine similar behaviors that all counselors do can't be avoided, dare to be different at times. Think creatively, act differently, and experience more success.

Don't just perform stress management therapy. Be the "stress reductionist" known for creative stress management groups, writing blogs on stress prevention and management, and who develops a mobile app that reminds clients of a beneficial daily breathing exercise, which becomes a clinical tool for clients and an amazing marketing technique and calling card.

EXERCISE 6.5 | Being Different

In the space below, write about how your approach to conducting therapy is unique. How do you stand out? What creative ideas and different approaches might create further success in your practice. You may find this exercise a useful prelude to your work in Chapter 7.

_____

_____

_____

_____

_____

_____

_____

_____

_____

DYNAMIC PROGRAMS

You now understand that getting referrals is really a multilayered, diversified and consistent process by which you are putting in effort and energy to bring about a stream of referrals that are a true fit for your practice. Your referral wheel is perhaps the most important framework for this part of your business. We discussed specific strategies and many ideas for building both online presence and face-to-face relationships that not only get you referrals, they help make your practice more relevant. A great "sales approach" helps create a memorable product, which exemplifies your hard work and brands you as a competent and successful professional.

With everything you just learned in this chapter, I hope you believe as I do that marketing and networking are still not enough. Once you master the art and science of smart marketing and intelligent networking, and you are well on your way to getting "practice full" with the right kind of clients you like, you should hopefully be hungry for more success.

Learning more and continuing to grow personally and professionally is what this journey's all about. In her book *Daring Greatly*, Brown (2012) shares, "We crave purpose, and we have a deep desire to create and contribute. We want to take risks, embrace our vulnerabilities, and be courageous (p. 212)." There's no better way to add purpose than to create new contributions by diversifying yourself and your work further beyond just seeing clients.

CHAPTER SEVEN |
DIVERSIFICATION & GROWTH: SERVICES, PROGRAMS, ROLES, PRODUCTS

> *"It is sort of boring to stay in the same spot. You know, I didn't set out to become the first to do this, the first to do that. It was just that my interests were so diversified."*
>
> —*Barbara Streisand*

The secret to Barbara Streisand's ultimate success may be found in how she diversified her interests throughout her career becoming extremely well known as a singer, songwriter, actress, filmmaker and philanthropist. She managed to diversify in other areas, too, working in genres such as Broadway, jazz, traditional pop, and disco. While we can't all be successful performers like Barbara, her example shows that you can be successful doing one thing really well. What is more, diversifying *how* you do that one activity is essential to professional success and your personal satisfaction with your practice.

In this chapter, you'll learn how to diversify your specialties in delivering your expertise across many mediums—in unique ways, using conventional and non-conventional (yet appropriate) methods that are proven to create value, revenue streams, and overall business sustainability. You will learn how other clinicians, myself included, diversified and developed their business ideas. Finally, you'll be introduced to a few extremely successful professionals in the mental health/wellness field who, while not as well known as Barbara Streisand, are certainly at the top of their game.

The one thing you strive to do well is provide therapy or professional services as a healthcare practitioner. Remember in Chapter Two I talked about concentric circles in specified clinical areas? Your few specialty areas, and diverse outer circles of interests serve as one important manner in which you diversify for success, within your interest areas. Now you are going to put to use these specialty areas not simply as a practitioner providing therapy or a service professional providing clinical services. As an expert within your community and as far reaching outside your community as possible, you can diversify your offerings by creating unique methods designed to reach those who aren't benefitting from your direct counseling/professional routine care services.

"COUPLES CONNECT"— A MODEL PROGRAM FOR MAKING YOUR SPECIALTY PRACTICE WORK WELL

I want to share a story that actually occurred in my practice back in 2008. As we often do, clinicians are inclined to take study courses or attend trainings to keep up with the latest and greatest interventions, studies, and/or healthcare developments in the field. I am no different, and up until 2008 though I attended many trainings before, never would I experience the therapeutic "aha moment" more than when I attended a couples training from a leading expert and relative newcomer at the time in the couples counseling field.

Just after starting my private practice, I fell in love with doing couples work (and thankfully still enjoy working with couples immensely). Early in my practice I had a couples supervisor as well as a group of other clinicians with whom I routinely met to discuss cases, many of which were couples. Though I thoroughly enjoyed the work, I found myself feeling frustrated by many of the parameters placed on clinicians regarding patient care and billing for services under managed care contracts with regard to couples work. I found the 45-minute hour far too short as a process session with more than one person in the room. I kept feeling just when I am getting some "session momentum," disappointingly the time was up and I couldn't help my couple work far enough through their issue during the "short" session. I couldn't get very far with couples even during a 60-minute time frame. Weekly sessions became cumbersome for many as often both partners worked and drove from long distances just to get to their appointment. Back then, my average length of treatment for couples work using this format was around 15 to 18 months. At the time I thought "either I am a poor couples therapist, or there's something wrong with my couples therapy model."

So, let's go back to the 2008 professional training. After this couples training, I became inspired to shake things up. I decided to move away from a "managed care model" way of providing relationship counseling (no longer one week at a time for a short amount of time, only allowed by the billable codes provided by managed care). **Honestly, I realized that couples or relational work is non-reimbursable by insurance, even when insurance allows it to be billed. It's non-reimbursable because one cannot provide a mental health diagnosis for a relationship issue**. And, "Partner Relationship Problem" is a diagnosis that is most often not reimbursed when billed to insurers. While managed care provides for couples billable coding, the hour is too short, and the clinician must provide a diagnosis of one the partners in the couple in most cases. As if the couple didn't already have enough problems! Now one partner is or has "the real problem" and the other is just fine. And, trust me this theme played out even when I kept diagnosis confidential from the couple. If you treat couples then you know what I am talking about.

For ethical reasons, reasons regarding the limits of managed care, and the information I learned at the training, I shook things up by providing longer session time and more time apart for couples to practice what they learn in my new 90-minute session length. I developed a treatment philosophy based in large part from my experience with couples. That treatment philosophy became the blueprint model for my then newly branded "Couples Connect" program, which has a defined framework for helping couples gain and practice techniques for healing in a shorter period of overall treatment time. I managed to reduce my rate of relationship improvement overall, as couples starting getting healthier in about 4 to 6 months, as opposed to 15 to 18 months.

With this new way of delivering help to my couples, since the program didn't fit within the managed care design, I charged my usual and customary out-of-pocket fee for service for the couples treatment program, and while the couple incurred a larger expense over the 3 to 6 months of treatment, on average they paid about the same for their shorter term, longer lasting, quicker change therapy program as they would in long-term weekly therapy paying insurance deductibles and/or co-pays.

Under my current couples therapy program, the couple has a greater incentive for changing faster. Not only do they have the leverage of their presumed failing relationship, they are now paying a therapist out of pocket to learn how to change. That is a major reason why my couples experience the "sink or swim" phenomena very quickly when it comes accountability and change process.

In addition to changing the framework of delivery, my theory about couples and the struggles that occur in relationships became more refined. Between the numerous couples experts whose trainings I attended over the years, and the surprising consistency of relational dynamic issues seen across couples in my practice, I began forming a unique treatment approach that utilizes proven methods from a variety of relationship counseling intervention models, which I tweaked to fit into a program revolving around communication, intimacy, and trust in relationships. In essence, I branded my relationship therapy into a well-defined couples therapy program that I simply call *"Couples Connect."*

This development and diversification provides a triple benefit. Perhaps the most significant benefit is the couple gets healthier much quicker, and for about the same dollar amount. Secondly, healthcare costs don't get driven upward due to managed care payouts to clinicians for issues that really should not be reimbursed by a "medical model." And, thirdly, the clinician is paid a fair specialist rate for his/her specialty service. Any good couples and family counselor knows that working with relationship dynamics in session is often far more challenging and harder work than providing individual treatment in most cases.

The experience of moving my couples work into a well-defined, easily explained, professional program created a more diverse practice and currently helps me work more effectively with couples seeking change. Many couples note at the end of treatment that they are surprised by the efficacy of the therapy and that they didn't think that they could or would work as hard. On the other hand, several couples left the program early in appreciation realizing that either one or both weren't ready and decided on their own whether to wait and try again when both were ready, or end their relationship.

In almost every situation in which a couples referral comes my way, I always offer to that couple an opportunity to use their insurance for this work with a provider who sees couples under insurance. I am happy to refer them to a qualified licensed couples practitioner who is in-network with their insurance. For that reason, numerous couples don't enter my practice, and I get to gift these cases to my colleagues who in turn send me people who don't fit their practice. Upon occasion, some will come back to me after experiencing no or limited success with the couples therapist they saw under their insurance.

If you are a couples therapist, you may not want to create a program that is outside the confines of managed care. You may choose not to adopt this specific kind of diversification of your services. That is okay! **My purpose for describing this process and development of how I changed my service orientation is more about teaching you a manner in which you can begin to think outside of the box in a way that is in your clients' best interests, and in a manner that protects, preserves, and grows your business.**

FROM ONE-TO-MANY

Private practice business expert, David Steele (2012), emphasizes the importance of business building by moving from a "one-to-one" business practice model to a "one-to-many" practice. He claims that such a transition in his own business helped him bring his powerful message and experience to more people more often, and make it easier to enroll paying clients in his business. In fact, many of his practice changes allowed him to provide more free trainings and information to numerous people, while allowing for the enrollment in more formal paid group trainings, along with continuing individual work. This model of diversification is extremely business wise, as it benefits your target populations, while allowing for more business opportunity.

As you think about expanding your business, start with the idea of how to move from one-to-one into some one-to-many situations. There are many ways you can provide help in a one-to-many format. You can develop a "one-to-many" stream both with online and live in-person programs, services, or trainings.

SEIZE THE OPPORTUNITY

Over the course of my practice development, I found numerous opportunities for expansion into a one-to-many framework of providing my message, some paid and some unpaid. All brought me success in the form of more clients and increased the meaning of what I do and more importantly my reach in distance, across culture, class, and other diverse categories within our population.

Successful business ventures in private practice don't occur overnight, and certainly don't manifest without your keen awareness, recognition of opportunity and powerful creativity. Once you have your base, your "bread and butter" of individual clients, and you've perfected your practice machine through a great flow of referrals, a deep commitment to your clients, and an administrative system that works well, it's time to start thinking about new ideas and to work on ideas that you may have previously shelved because you weren't ready to try them. Most great ideas become shelved because either there is a lack of time, infrastructure or foundation in your business, which makes trying something new more risky, or owners are simply insecure or otherwise uncertain.

Now is the time to get these expansion ideas written down. Make your list of your top three ideas, even if you never actually intend on working on them, or think you don't have the time to do so. Seeing these ideas will help make the process real. You aren't just dreaming up ways to be successful. You are in fact creating prospects for new ways of delivering your services that are more meaningful, beneficial to your clients, and helpful to business sustainability.

EXERCISE 7.1 | My Top Three Ideas for Diversifying Delivery of Services and Expanding

Try making at least one of these ideas a "one-to-many" idea.

1. _____

_____

_____

2. _____

_____

_____

3. _____

_____

_____

FROM OPPORTUNITY TO REALITY

Discovering an opportunity for expansion is the first step toward creating more success in your practice. This requires astuteness toward seeing every collegial relationship you know, and the ones you are yet to make, as an opportunity. When I finished graduate school, I maintained a close connection to a few esteemed professors. Of course, these professors were those whose courses I enjoyed most during my training, and the ones who, quite frankly pushed me the hardest. Over the next few years while training to complete licensure I remained in touch, from time to time letting them know how my clinical training progressed. When I opened my clinical practice in 2000, they invited me to give a talk about my experience of starting private practice. These talks, given to the local honors society gratis, eventually led to my developing an entire curriculum on private practice building, the first of its kind in a fully credentialed graduate program in counseling in the country!

Pioneering such study was actually easy and fun, as I saw an opportunity and kept discussions warm with the people I knew well and who could help get the curriculum launched. The experience involved a lot of design, development, and delivery over many years of actually teaching the curriculum. This endeavor for me was not about making money, though I did earn some (quite a bit less than what my hourly rate is for private practice). It was more about giving back to the profession and offering expertise and experience to those coming into the field. I found that in my training back in the 1990's, there were absolutely no formal courses on how to start and develop a private practice. The lack of resources for building a practice, along with an interest in business development, really led to my developing this curriculum.

The literature on practice development available outside of academia at the time was in its infancy. Lynn Grodski (2000) broke ground on private practice coaching books with her initial volume on practice building. She's gone on to write numerous books on practice building and coaching, along with others like Chris Stout, a Midwestern psychologist and consultant who co-wrote a fantastic practice building book in 2005, along with an updated edited volume of chapters written by practice consulting experts and successful practitioners (Stout, 2012). I used many of these texts in the curriculum I developed and taught for over nearly fifteen at the University of Colorado.

AWARENESS OF INTERESTS

Being aware of your own interests in the field guides you toward special pursuits that may become profitable in earnings, professional growth, and recognition. My awareness of business interests early in my private practice led me to acquiring a provider management and marketing role with a small group practice located in the western suburbs of Denver. During my 6-year administrative role (while continuing to see clients in my own clinical practice) I grew the private company from 5 providers to over 40 throughout metro Denver, and from 3 managed care group contracts to more than 12. At one point it became the largest mental health group practice in Colorado, with Medicare as one of the payers, and I was able to recruit several prescribing mental health experts to collaborate with the mental health counseling providers. I am proud to say that I built the foundation of this company, thanks to the generosity and hands-off approach of its owners. Upon reflection on this experience, it's amazing to me how awareness of interests creates business opportunities that turn into reality when risked.

POPPING THE TOP

Have you ever thought about renovating your home by "popping the top" and building a second story? Your house has a great foundation and now you want to build something on top of an already great home. Much the way homeowners "pop their top" on their house, to improve upon their investment and live even better, I recommend you "pop your top" in your practice and improve upon what you already built at the right time.

I popped my top by using the foundation of who and what I knew to create more opportunities. How did I end up developing trainings on the business of practice through PESI? I had a year in which my course didn't fill, and instead of becoming distraught over not teaching that fall, I used the extra time I would normally be running my course to develop a proposal to train professionals in the field on the concepts of ethical practice building using good business principles, essentially taking my graduate curriculum and morphing it into a solid one day professional training. Two months after submitting my proposal, it was accepted into PESI's speaker/trainer program and I realized that I had just begun "popping the top" on my own business "house!"

That was back in 2012, just a year after my mother died of ovarian cancer at the age of 69, too young for any person to leave, and particularly one with so much energy. I share this personal note because I believe her life being cut short led to my leaning toward risks and activities that I had previously only mulled over in my head. A personal event in your life (doesn't have to be a death) can often lead to moving forward with something that advances your business. Have you experienced something deep and personal, something profound and relevant personally that led you to "pop the top" on your business?

EXERCISE 7.2 | Personal Experiences

Write down personal experiences in your life that might be a catalyst to your creative professional pursuits. You can use parts of your story from Chapter One if you'd like to help get you started.

1. _____

_____

2. _____

_____

3. _____

_____

4. _____

_____

5. _____

_____

As you build from personal experience to professional pursuits, eventually you will begin creating a multitude of professional experiences, some you enjoy and others you don't, though many that you can draw from to turn into further experiences that build your credibility, expertise, and success.

Designing and teaching my course at the graduate program in a university setting built my credibility and led to creating day-long training programs which were delivered to professionals in private practice or starting a practice throughout the country over a two-year period, which eventually led to my being asked to write this very book you are reading!

Another personal example of popping the top was how my clinician's role within a group practice led to taking on an administrative and leadership role, which ultimately built enough credibility and trust with the group practice's owner that he highly recommended me to an insurance executive who heads up an EAP speakers division. Working hard for this owner and our trusting relationship resulted in the opportunity for me to provide wellness seminars throughout the Rocky Mountain Region to private companies and public organizations, something I have been doing on an off for nearly ten years.

My many experiences with business development and training generated an awareness that led me to open a second business alongside my clinical counseling practice. That business is a small consulting business, helping practitioners in any helping profession start and/or build their private practice. The secondary business is conducted in person with local clients, and over the phone with clients from all over the country. I keep it small only because I like to hand pick practitioners who are interested and ready to build, and because I am still enjoying my clinical practice immensely. So, I determine how much business I want in each of these interest areas.

None of this happened overnight, as developing credibility and expertise are two important factors in the diversifying and building of your success over time. And believe me, for every one of these successes ,there were many more ideas and experiences that simply didn't work. So, when you fail to hit the mark, keep learning and trying and eventually you will succeed.

EXERCISE 7.3 | My Expansion Ideas

Make a list of your unique ideas for expanding your practice from one-to-many, and in diverse ways that are creative and sustainable. Fill in the boxes below with your unique ideas of expansion programs, services, or even products that might make your business more diversified, meaningful, and sustainable.

While it's not easy to determine the right moment to begin expansion, you should pay close attention to the foundation underneath your business, your comfort level with risk, and any other factor(s) that might be getting in your way. You might be surprised to learn that even if you are just beginning your practice, you still have some foundation. You may have money in your bank to be able to start one of your programs, or be able to secure enough funding for a program you want to launch while launching your clinical practice. The important piece is that you must accurately assess what makes up your foundation at present, and list your current concerns.

EXERCISE 7.4 | My Foundation for Expansion

In this exercise, write down what makes up your current foundation. Similar to your 4C's area of "Capability," add what makes your foundation "strong," For example, your foundation may consist of having enough clients to meet your current business expenses, (met the break even point consistently for 6 months). Or you may put something in there like meeting your minimum revenue goals for a year. Or, include how you are on 5 insurance panels and readily receiving referrals. You may want to put other aspects that make your foundation such as my spouse has a full time job in an agency that can help offset future risk.

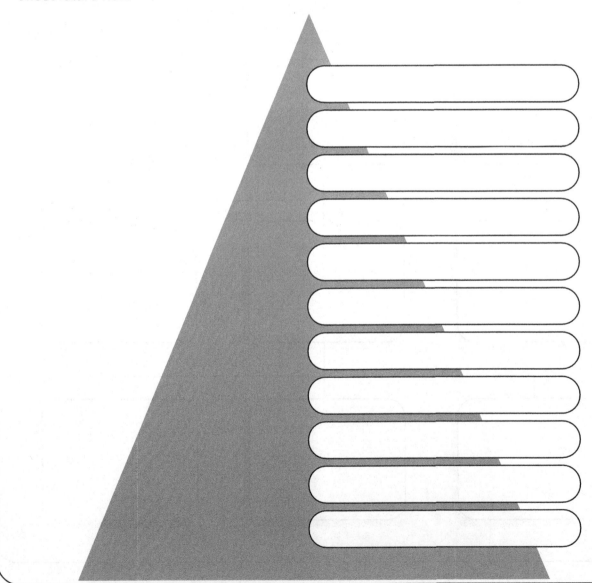

EXERCISE 7.5 | My Concerns About Expansion

This exercise is really part two of the previous exercise. In this part, take a moment and fill in any personal challenges that concern you related to risking practice expansion. For example, you might see a lack of funding for your project as a barrier. Or, you may note that there isn't adequate physical space to provide your seminar at your office. These can be barriers that might make you think twice about starting your new idea. Writing them down helps you to address them directly.

REVISITING AN OLD FRIEND

Sometimes, the ultimate experience of combining something very personal with business credibility and expertise might be personally gratifying even if not financially rewarding. Remember my personal story in Chapter One? The part about the impact my summer camp experience had on shaping my interest and eventual choice to become a professional counselor is most significant here.

About four years ago, I revisited an old camp friend who connected me with the current director of the camp I once attended. We had lunch one afternoon and talked about the changing needs of overnight summer camps as more children are coming to camp with mental health issues, on medication, and in treatment during the school year. A brief homesickness was no longer the only mental health crisis campers shared at camp. For the past 4 years while my own children enjoy the benefits of being campers there (yes, it's their turn), each summer I return as the Camp Consultant. This position, jointly created by the camp director and myself, allows me to mentor camp counselors and senior staff, help campers and their parents adjust to the camp experience, and provide availability for urgent and emergent consultation. For the development of this position, I went so far as to contact the regulatory board to discuss the parameters of consultation and where the line is between a true counseling relationship and professional consultation. This job is very meaningful and a value to the camp community. I am blessed to give back to an old friend, my camp, which was an experience that gave so much to me for so many summers of my youth.

Revisit your old friends, your past experiences, anything and anyone that helped shape who you are. I guarantee success will eventually find you, almost as if by accident. Others before me leaned into their roots, and risked their interests. Terrence Real (1997) shares some of his motivation for writing his best selling book, *I Don't Want to Talk About It,* as he writes about his own difficult relationship with his father. In it he humbly describes the personal pain and empowerment that helped lead him into a personally healthy place and toward his own relationship theory. Now, many years later, he's thought of as an expert in gender, relationships, and intimacy. Irvin Yalom combined a love of providing therapy with writing, and became an extremely respected and well-known existential psychiatrist, psychology trainer and storyteller. John Gottman developed The Gottman Institute and wrote many books about marriage and relationships after establishing credibility through his research laboratory and work at University of Washington, building success through building credibility over time.

REVISITING YOUR CONCENTRIC CIRCLES

Go back now to your services plan. Revisit your concentric circles and insert into those circles specific plans to diversify by developing your ideas for expansion.

EXERCISE 7.6 | Practice Expansion Planning

Take one or more of your expansion ideas in this chapter, and actually write out program goals, including objectives that are realistic and reachable within each goal, as well as methods or techniques you may use to achieve those goals. The program should have realistic clinical goals and objectives, financial goals/objectives/methods, and marketing goals/objectives/methods.

Set a timeline for program implementation and create an honest evaluation portion so that you can modify as you go. A program that works then becomes a stable part of your concentric circles of services you provide. (You may wish to use the "Program Goals/ Timeline Template in Appendix A for this exercise.)

SMART DIVERSIFICATION

The smartest part of diversifying and developing unique programs and products, and creative roles is simply not giving up after your first fail. In fact, smart and successful business owners fail often and sometimes miserably. I once tried to develop a mobile phone application for mental health practitioners that failed. Luckily I didn't put money into the investment, just time. And, while the idea was original, it wasn't meant to be for a variety of reasons. Other failures like this one lurk all over my experience map. Smart diversifiers never lose sight of their passion nor their mission. Smart diversifiers understand the delicate integration of growing a diversified client population with one or more niche areas, along with unique and diverse marketing and networking strategies, and a diverse program development plan.

Part III

SECURE YOUR FUTURE

By now you know that building your foundation and creating diversification systems throughout your practice is essential to your success. Hopefully at this point in the book at a minimum you are writing ideas down and completing sections of your business plan in Appendix A, testing your ideas using practical action as a private practice business owner and clinician.

The last part of this book focuses on three highly relevant general areas of importance to your future. You'll gain an understanding of healthcare reform through ongoing legislative awareness, and advocacy as a professional ambassador of mental health in the overall healthcare industry. Next, you will learn about how to secure your future financially through financial savings, growth, and a revisiting of protection strategies. Finally, we'll bring it all together by exploring professional development, creating and sustaining work/ life balance, and learning how to avoid burnout and compassion fatigue while embracing growth and change over the long haul.

CHAPTER EIGHT |
HEALTH CARE REFORM & ADVOCACY

In his message to Congress over 50 years ago, on February 5, 1963, President John F. Kennedy uttered these words:

> *". . . . mental illness and mental retardation are among our most critical health problems. They occur more frequently, affect more people, require more prolonged treatment, cause more suffering by the families of the afflicted, waste more of our human resources, and constitute more financial drain upon both the public treasury and the personal finances of the individual families than any other single condition."*

Approximately eight years prior, Congress established the Joint Commission on Mental Illness and Health, which addressed the quality of care and inadequacy in patient access to care in large state and county psychiatric facilities. It is the first time a federal body considered managing the allocation of resources for the mentally ill. In his first message to Congress, Kennedy supported the commission's recommendations, which included shifting resources from inpatient state and county psychiatric hospitals to outpatient treatment centers.

Are you wondering what the historical nature of government legislation has to do with starting and running your practice? After all, today's world is different, and what matters is what happens today. The role of government legislation in mental health and healthcare in general throughout history and today is crucial to understanding how your private practice model fits. It provides a legal framework for practicing within federal, state, and local laws. Knowing the history of government involvement by becoming well informed and actively involved in advocating for what's in the best interests of our profession is crucial to practice success.

While you are a "change agent" to your clients, you are also an ambassador to your helping profession. You have the honorable responsibility to be involved in any way possible in the advocacy of further advancement. There are many ways to advocate, and we shall discuss those later in the chapter.

So, "Why should I worry about the history of the mental health field?" Your knowledge about the shaping of mental health (or your helping field) gives you an edge over other practitioners. Seeking out and learning historical trends provides clues to where the field is headed. Such unique, well thought out perspectives often create glimpses of what you can do to stay ahead in your business planning. This notion is especially important when you see a trend toward something that hasn't yet occurred and looks like it might happen.

For example, the birth of managed care organizations occurred largely out of the need to control costs. Mental health was particularly challenging because it was and still is extremely difficult to estimate treatment costs. For this reason, "carve out" behavioral health companies that were stand-alone organizations were formed to specialize in cost control measures for mental health treatment and reimbursement. The legislation leading to privatizing health essentially caused separate mental health payers to emerge, which further legitimized the profession. Providers coming into practice in the 1980's and 90's didn't like these "carve-outs" because they often over-managed the care, creating cumbersome paperwork for practice owners to complete for treatment authorization of their patients and even cut provider reimbursement rates as well. New clinicians starting in the late 90's and early 2000's didn't know any better and signed up for lower rates and a lot of paperwork. The trend shifted when the economic crisis of 2007/08 hit. Layoffs at managed care companies occurred, and for that reason and others the practice of intermittent authorization paperwork gradually went away. And, after a few managed care organizations lowered or froze their reimbursement rate, some began increasing rates after about 2010.

Understanding the financial and political climate during these times helped clinicians make informed decisions about how to weather the financial storm and it's impact on the professional care industry. The history of managed care helped me make effective decisions around what companies I wanted to remain with under contract and which ones I did not. Some seasoned clinicians moved entirely away from a managed care model when rates were frozen and reduced thus becoming "Fee for Service" or "Cash Only" providers in their practice. And, because managed care organizations largely stopped accepting new providers between approximately 2004 and 2011 (some panels are still closed to new providers), many practice start-ups during that period of time happened without managed care and either fee-for-service only or 3rd party payments or a combination of both.

One of the historical trends I theorize occurred between 2004 and 2012 as a result of lower insurance reimbursement, more paperwork, and practice owners not able to contract in network with insurance panels, is the incredible surge of the coaching industry! Whether it be life coaching, relationship coaching, business coaching, or any other form of coaching, the notion of counseling for non-clinical purpose, outside of medical/mental health rehabilitation model has become a very popular business and way of getting consumer interest in counseling without stigma of mental health issues. Further, this option eliminated "the middle person" of insurance. I know many trained clinicians who are now providing "wellness care" even though they aren't calling their service a "coaching" practice.

History matters. Landmark legislation and its impact on mental health are critical components to practice success. Let's take a look more closely at some of this historic legislation and its impact on your bottom-line.

HEALTH INSURANCE PORTABILITY AND ACCOUNTABILITY ACT

In 1996, the Kennedy-Kassenbaum Act, which became formally known as the Health Insurance Portability and Accountability Act (HIPAA) was passed and signed into law by President Bill Clinton. In addition to creating patient privacy protections, the aim of the legislation was to reduce and hopefully eliminate fraud, waste and abuse in the healthcare profession, help make healthcare coverage more portable and improve continuity of care, encourage use of medical savings accounts, and other provisions.

Two significant outcomes relating to mental health practice resulted from this legislation. First, while it took a while to catch on, the use of Health Savings Accounts (HSA) and Flexible Spending Accounts (FSA) provided consumers with a tax savings option for payment of services. Practitioners don't even need to be participating in-network with a managed care company to accept some of these benefit cards. Knowing more about Medical Savings Accounts as a provider helps you educate your client about methods of payment and possible tax savings while attending therapy in your office.

Second, the mcre endorsement of patient privacy put a huge stamp of approval on an already highly privatized and specialized industry of mental healthcare. Mental health clinicians have a long history of practicing strong patient privacy behavior revolving around confidentiality. New HIPAA regulations only created further endorsement of this practice and provided a more standardized guideline revolving around protection of patient privacies. As such, when consulting with third parties, you must provide a written release of information signed by your client, dated, and with proper language outlined by the federal statute. A sample copy of the HIPAA-compliant release of information form can be found in Appendix B.

Compliance with privacy policy and utilization of the Release of Information (ROI) form is essential every time you need to have conversations outside of direct client communications. And, it is entirely up to the patient as to whether they wish to allow you, the practitioner, access to discuss their treatment with other parties, with exceptions for dangerousness to self or others, or in the case of child abuse reporting as required by law.

Finally, as a matter of practice in every third party letter I write, such as to a probation officer or a court, not only am I making sure the patient signs a legally binding written release of information, I also make sure to state at the beginning of the letter that the patient has signed a legally executed written release of information and that said release is on file. Then, I document in the notes that a letter was sent and that proper written release of information was obtained and is on file. This administrative practice meets professional and legislative requirements and is an essential business practice that clinically safeguards your confidentiality agreement and the patient's privacy in general.

MENTAL HEALTH PARITY

In 1996, Senators Paul Wellstone (D) and Pete Domenici (R) reached across the aisle and collaborated to write legislation that initially passed on a small scale. After Wellstone died in a plane crash, the bill eventually passed with the help of other bipartisan leadership as The Mental Health Parity and Addiction Equity Act of 2008. The passing of this act further expanded upon the initial passing of parity legislation back in 1996, disallowing insurers from putting greater dollar limits on mental health coverage, such as lower maximums, higher co-pays or deductibles. It also labeled more mental health diagnoses, such as substance abuse, most clinical depressions, and anxiety-related disorders as major medical conditions. It ensured that individuals dealing with these issues would receive the same insurance benefit as they would for a standard physical medical condition.

Just five years later, clarifications made by the Obama administration in 2013 led to further enforcement of the original legislation, which closed loopholes that insurers were using to bypass the law. These clarifications include that large company group plans of over 100 employees may elect to offer mental health coverage and if they do, they must offer it at the same rates as medical coverage. All small plans must now offer mental health coverage, and comparable rates as well. All costs for mental health must be no different than regular medical or surgical rates. Also, hospitalization rules are the same for mental health hospitalization as with other inpatient conditions.

This law and its recent clarifications and enforcements further legitimized mental health as a medical practice. Utilization of insurance by consumers is dramatically on the rise, creating more demand for outpatient practitioners, especially those in private practice wishing to participate with managed care insurance companies.

Katherine C. Nordal, PhD, Executive Director of Professional Practice for the American Psychological Association, stated in an NPR interview (Varney, 2013) that a likely result of the mental health parity clarifications is those private practice owners who band together to create multidisciplinary outpatient mental health practitioner groups may have greater bargaining power with insurers setting reimbursement rates. In other words, groups made up of practitioners who provide the full-range of mental health services from medication evaluation and management to psychotherapy to family and couple therapy to child/adolescent therapy will benefit more in terms of financial positioning. I agree with Dr. Nordal and believe that diversified specialty areas in these groups will help build a solid practice foundation and increase better positioning with insurers and other third party payers. Further, Nordal stated that practitioners would also start providing services from within primary care physician offices and other general medical practices, providing a new line of private practice possibility.

In the Varney (2013) story, Linda Rosenberg, President and CEO of the National Council for Behavioral Health, suggested that in our monopoly economy, the solo practitioner might eventually go away, replaced by large group practices and corporations. Her assertion that individual practice owners will become employees of larger systems may in fact already be happening as many frustrated and failing practice owners are already shutting their doors because they can't adjust their business model to fit the changes of our time. Additionally, some are electing to leave their practice for other reasons such as isolation and a desire to work within a team environment, among other colleagues in practice. Other opportunities are emerging in our field as outpatient and inpatient addiction treatment centers are emerging at a fast rate, taking the place of a traditional hospital setting, and specializing in one or a few areas of treatment. These are examples of the larger systems and moving away from solo practice that Rosenberg predicted.

While Rosenberg seemed correct in her predictions about moving away from the solo practice, other trends are emerging as well. In Colorado alone, numerous multidisciplinary provider groups and networks emerged in the last few years. Some are set up as networks of independent providers who share clients and collaborate on a routine basis for patient continuity of care, and others are in-house groups where clinicians are contract or full employees of the group. This trend may not be the only result from increasing bargaining power and offering consumers more from one group or network. It also appears to be more attractive to the provider going into practice from a safety standpoint. With more healthcare regulation, increased administrative upkeep, and a crackdown on fraud, waste and abuse of healthcare systems, individuals seem more reticent to hang a shingle alone because they want to feel safer among their peers. Provider groups offer access to accountability, supervision, and the physical presence of other professionals like them.

Still solo practices won't likely go away entirely. There will be smaller bands of practitioners who are able to set up, manage, and grow a practice individually. If you are one of these practice owners, remember all private practice owners, regardless of setting or structure of business, need colleagues with whom they can collaborate. Make sure you have some systems set up for professional collaboration and consultation to help your solo practice flourish.

EXERCISE 8.1 | Practice Type

Take out your "private practice notebook" or work in the space below. Describe the type of practice you are in or would like to be in. Explain whether it's solo or group. If a group, how large is the group and who are the professionals in it? How are you paid? What type of setting are you practicing in? Is it a small office building or large clinic? If it's a group, what value do you get by working within this group, and what are you giving up? If you are solo, what value do you gain from being solo, and what are you giving up?

_____

_____

_____

_____

_____

_____

EXERCISE 8.2 | Supervision, Collaboration, Consultation Options

Write down the colleagues and/or groups of professionals who supervise you, collaborate or consult with you. If you are just getting started, research groups of professionals in your area that meet regularly or write the names of colleagues you trust to supervise you, collaborate, and or consult with you. You can always use professional support.

NAME OF GROUP, INDIVIDUAL	CONTACT INFORMATION

AFFORDABLE CARE ACT

Healthcare reform in America saw large scale multilayered changes brought about by The Affordable Care Act (2010). Now, with a new administration taking steps to repeal and replace the legislation, there is chaos and uncertainty among consumers and providers alike. All the more reason that it's extremely vital to study this landmark legislation, empowering you, the practice owner, to advocate for proper changes. So, without hesitation, let me walk you through the finer points of what former President Obama's healthcare legislation sought to do for the industry and in particular, for mental health.

Enacted in 2010, and implemented over ten plus years through and beyond 2020, the Affordable Care Act brought about sweeping change and the start of what I call the healthcare delivery system revolution. Are we embarking on an experiment of systemic change that will doom our healthcare industry or perhaps pull it out of the "dark ages" and into innovation and proper representation? The challenges ahead are great and answers to these questions too early in the game. Perhaps we'll always ask these questions, whether healthcare improves or not. For now, America's healthcare delivery system is in flux, and its constant change brings about hope and despair, conflict, debate, worry and for some a certain new security that may soon be taken away.

The volatility and unknown consequences during these sweeping changes can only translate to new outcomes and impacts in private practice business. Republicans vow to repeal the Affordable Care Act and now attempts to change the current health care act are in the works as America's government goes through yet another shift. Still, the Affordable Care Act already impacts millions of Americans with greater access to Medicaid, more insured lives, and improved coverage for children. Moreover, it's a hope of mine that the positive impacts on healthcare consumers and providers are kept in place, while new initiatives help our health care system grow in a positive direction. For, now, the ACA is what's in place, and you as a provider must understand its impacts.

Let's take a look at this landmark legislation, how it may be impacting the mental health industry, and specifically how it may affect your business model.

While the Affordable Care Act was signed into law on March 23, 2010, it wasn't until June 28, 2012 that the Supreme Court upheld the law following challenges that the law is unconstitutional. The Supreme Court's decision to uphold the largest healthcare reform policy in America's history is landmark. This law written, enacted, challenged, and upheld involved all three branches of government working together to reform a system that saw per capita costs double in the first decade of the twenty first century. As an industry, healthcare in the U.S. ranks higher in cost, at 16% of GDP, than in any other country in the world. You can imagine from a fiscal perspective why this legislation needed to occur. The lack of accessibility of care by families from lower socio-economic status, along with a history of fraud, waste, and abuse on a systemic level were other important issues needing to be addressed in the healthcare system. The passing of this legislation addresses these large-scale issues.

The Affordable Care Act is divided into two main parts: (1) the Patient Protection and Affordable Care Act and (2) the Healthcare and Education Reconciliation Act. In addition to protecting patient rights and creating more accessibility for consumers seeking care, the law aims to reduce and eliminate problems in the healthcare insurance industry, cutting down on wasteful spending and fraudulent activity, improve inpatient care facilities, hold providers more accountable for their work, and provide rural communities with more services. These changes and provisions are outlined in the 10 Titles of the law, which are broken in to Subtitles, Parts, and Sections. For a complete read of the law itself, you can access it through the following link: http://housedocs.house.gov/energycommerce/ppacacon.pdf.

TITLE I— AFFORDABLE CARE FOR ALL — THE INDIVIDUAL MANDATE

The Individual Mandate is perhaps the most recognizable term resulting from the Affordable Care Act, as it's what many consumers care about. It's also a portion of the law that was and still is highly opposed by non-backers of the legislation. This part of the legislation basically says every American citizen must carry medical insurance in one form or another. This mandate can be found in Title I as this title deals largely with improving accessibility, affordability, and availability of coverage, while ensuring high quality, and lower overall costs.

Title I—Business Impacts on Private Practices: This title in particular brings change that is undoubtedly already affecting the world of private practice. More availability and accessibility means more people insured, higher rates of utilization overall, and an increasing demand for private practice owners who accept insurance for payment.

TITLE II— PUBLIC PROGRAM CHANGES

Under the new legislation in Title II, beginning in 2014, Medicaid programs expanded to include more impoverished individuals and families that are not eligible for Medicare. The fiscal limits on Medicaid eligibility are now at 133% of Federal Poverty Level (FPL), 33% higher than prior to the Affordable Care Act enactment, which allows many individuals and families who were previously in the gap between Medicaid ineligible and uninsurable, to now be eligible to get coverage through Medicaid.

In addition to the new eligibility requirements, Medicaid coverage must now provide mental health services coverage at actuarial equivalence. As well, former foster care children under the age of 25 are now automatically Medicaid eligible for six months. Other sweeping changes in the public programs include helping impoverished children through increased support in the Children's Health Insurance Plan (CHIP). Long-term care programs now have more options including removing barriers to providing home- and community-based services. Medicaid expansion is also allowing for coverage of certain mental health related prescriptions drugs like smoking cessation medication and benzodiazepines.

Quality improvement overall in the Medicaid program is another aim of the legislation, and this improvement is two tiered, aimed to help both patients and providers. For example, in the interest of helping patients better, and improving provider accountability and care delivery, there are provisions for "demonstration projects" that involve bundling payment with performance standards backed by ethical accountability measures. Another project outlined in the law is aimed at holding inpatient medical facilities accountable for improving emergent psychiatric stabilization processes. These examples are research studies outlined in the law that may impact future reform of this law.

Finally, relevant to mental health practitioners, public program changes are occurring in maternal and child health services. Reduction of infant mortality rates are helped through expanding home visitation programs for expecting mothers, infants and early childhood development. More support is also becoming available for women suffering from post-partum depression. And, more funding is now available and earmarked for personal responsibility education around topics like teen pregnancy and sexually transmitted diseases.

Title II—Business Impacts on Private Practice: If you have never thought about providing Medicaid services as a private practice owner, now may be the most opportune moment to consider becoming a Medicaid provider. Medicaid is expanding overall, and specific changes outlined above that make programs for children, teenagers, aging adults, mothers-to-be and moms more resourceful and plentiful provide for outpatient practitioner opportunities that never previously existed.

Each state differs with respect to what services and programs are available, and what reimbursement rates are offered. It's important to contact your state's Medicaid service provider and discuss reimbursement, provider eligibility, paperwork load, credentialing process, and number of people on Medicaid in your geographic catchment area. Providing Medicaid services in your practice may, in fact, become another way to diversify your business. I diversified by providing services with a Medicaid payer for a long-term outpatient care client and it's been helpful to my business and it feels personally gratifying providing services to a family and individual who have high financial, medical, and mental health needs with few resources.

TITLE III— QUALITY AND EFFICIENCY IMPROVEMENT

The manner in which services are provided to healthcare patients must improve. This issue is exemplified in the Medicare program when it comes to the new legislation. Value-based pay is being introduced into the Medicare payment system, which basically means that physician fee schedules will more and more be based on value to patient, including outcomes-based research programs that evaluate value in services provided. While this system sees the change occurring in hospitals and agencies primarily, one must deduce that systemic change will eventually hit the world of outpatient care and even private practice. By linking payment to quality outcomes, one can see that there may be client outcome surveys coming soon from an insurer near you. Changes within the Medicare program can only mean that the insurance industry is not far behind.

Quality measurement, data collection, and public reporting processes resulting from this part of the legislation are being put into place in the Medicare program. Seventy-five million dollars over a five-year period is allocated for developing these quality measures through Centers for Medicare and Medicaid Services (CMS) and the Agency for Healthcare and Research Quality (AHRQ).

The development of new patient care models, including shared savings programs through Medicare, a national pilot program with bundled payment models for groups of providers, home-based care programs for the chronically ill, hospital re-admission reduction programs, and community-based care transition programs, all aim to improve healthcare efficiency while reducing costs.

Access to physicians and other health services for Medicare recipients has been a problem. Changes aimed at improving access to providers under Medicare, especially in rural areas, are occurring. In order to create more access to providers in rural areas, more providers must be recruited to establish services in these rural markets. And, since many are unwilling to go, the Affordable Care Act creates incentive through increased pay models for those practitioners willing to locate their services in rural areas. There's even a provision in the law to increase mental health add-on psychiatrist pay by 5%, most likely because of high demand for psychiatric services. Finally, due to inefficiencies in the Medicare payment system, the new legislation aims to improve payment accuracy to its providers.

Title III—Business Impacts on Private Practice: While this title deals mostly with public programs such as Medicare and Medicaid, I suspect that the privatized healthcare insurance industry will adopt some of the successful efficiencies and quality assurance models. Whether or not private companies adopt and/or use modified models based on the outcomes in the public healthcare programs, you can expect that further legislation will require private insurers to make changes that require greater efficiency and quality improvement.

Linking payment to performance is an interesting notion in healthcare. In the old days of managed care in the 1980's and 90's, mental health insurers tried something similar, managing costs by authorizing outpatient care sessions in small increments, suggesting that providers must be good enough to complete their patients' treatment within certain session limits. This model failed because there is really no way to predict ahead of time what the patient really needs in terms of the number of outpatient visits. It is equally concerning that outcome measurement in mental health is likely to be extremely subjective, and therefore when "pay for performance" hits the mental health world, and particularly private practitioners, it will become a highly debated topic, and one with which I truly hope many private practice owners become very involved. Advocacy becomes important when rate determination and pay models are threatened to be changed dramatically.

Finally, the trend in this title seems to suggest a move further away from costly inpatient care, and toward a more community-based model. Community-based treatment programs, centers, and agencies are becoming more prevalent. Private practices that are built to include partnerships with inpatient programs, public programs such as Medicare, Medicaid, Tricare, and CHIP, nursing and long-term care facilities, and other in-patient and partial hospital programs will benefit with a stronger referral base and a practice that is representative of our changing mental health delivery system.

TITLE IV — CHRONIC DISEASE PREVENTION AND PUBLIC HEALTH IMPROVEMENTS

The aim of this section of the Affordable Care Act is to modernize the prevention of disease by improving overall public health through expanding clinical and community prevention services and creating an education and outreach campaign around preventive benefits. Community prevention services such as tobacco cessation and physical activity programs are examples of raising long-term health awareness over the lifespan. Coupled with the actual increase in services will be outreach and education programs in these areas and others like obesity screening and counseling for children and adults. Under this provision, the Secretary of Health and Human Services is charged with creating a national media campaign on health promotion and disease prevention focusing on smoking cessation, nutrition and physical activity, and is based on scientific social research.

Increases in prevention translate to coverage for wellness visits and creating incentives in the form of grants given to states that address chronic disease prevention through the development of weight loss, smoking cessation, and diabetes prevention programs that also address co-morbidities like clinical depression. Speaking of weight loss, under the new legislation there is a large amount of money allocated for reducing rates of childhood obesity. Finally, grant programs are being established in the interest of helping healthcare providers better understand, assess, and treat pain appropriately.

Title IV—Business Impacts on Private Practice: While chronic disease prevention and public health improvements are primarily changing within public government-run programs, as with many other changes resulting from this legislation, expect to see implementation lead into private agencies and hospitals, and then eventually into the private outpatient care world.

With inside knowledge of these changes, you can actually be proactive and innovate in your private practice what others aren't doing because they are simply not aware. The impact of new thinking about prevention may lead to more opportunity for private practitioners to create psycho-educational "quit smoking" programs, or "the mental health benefits of exercise." When you begin developing such groups and trainings, and offering them in your community, suddenly you are in line with the new construct of healthcare, and you are out in front diversifying your practice in a manner that is in line with legal direction of the healthcare industry as a whole.

Remember our discussion in Chapter Six about the three phases of treatment? Phase three had to do with "prevention and growth" by engaging in routine check-ups following a course of treatment. The implementation of wellness check-ups and prevention screenings in Affordable Care Act is one outcome of the legislation I am most excited about when it comes to impacting private practice.

From the moment I started my clinical practice, I worked with clients around the belief that once the client is well from his/her presenting issue(s), the client should follow up with mental health "wellness and prevention" check-ups at various intervals. In Colorado and other states, where there are 4 very distinct seasons and major shifts in temperature/climate, and daylight, I recommend about 3 to 4 brief well visits annually. That is once every three to four months. I recommend this frequency in all U.S. communities that have such variances in climate and daylight. Also, our traditional holiday season and summer break make for a good set up of seeing clients for well checks in the following months: Jan/May/September or Feb/June/October. The well check prevention outpatient therapy model is no different than seeing your dentist for a teeth cleaning twice a year, or your primary care physician once a year for your annual physical. If individuals checked in with a mental healthcare provider approximately three times a year, the financial savings in prevention from hospital stays and long-term outpatient mental healthcare would likely be huge. More importantly, people would feel better more of the time, instead of waiting for a crisis to present in therapy offices.

TITLE V — WORK FORCE CHANGES

As more previously uninsured lives attain coverage through the Medicaid eligibility changes and the individual mandate, and as the new healthcare programs and prevention models take effect, you can imagine a growing demand for healthcare providers nationally. Using this basic model of economics, the next ten years and well beyond will see large-scale growth in the overall healthcare workforce.

Title V in the Affordable Care Act calls for increases in the supply of healthcare workers in the workforce. It doesn't stop there. Specific sections of the title were created to give incentives in the form of loan repayment programs to mental health providers who work in a health professional shortage area, medically underserved area, or with a medically underserved population.

Enhancements to education and training in the workforce were also developed under this title. Schools that offer specific emphasis in child/adolescent development in mental health within their graduate level curricula and in paraprofessional training programs will be awarded grants for these trainings.

Cultural competency, prevention, improved training to help individuals with disabilities and nurse education, training and retention grants are all focused on changing how our healthcare workforce is trained for the future. For example, changes in the diversity of our population require a more culturally aware and diverse population of professional providers. As such, under this title, scholarships are provided for disadvantaged students who commit to working in medically-underserved areas. Work diversity grants for nurses and increased funding toward community-based education and training grants are a part of this provision.

Title V—Business Impacts on Private Practice: More workers in the workforce to meet a growing demand for services means more competition, right? You may look at it as such, or you can see more practitioners as an opportunity for a greater impact when using your business relationships for collaborations and referrals, all in the interest of the patients you treat. I suspect that private practice models will change, not necessarily toward more group practice models. There will almost certainly be a return to group practices on some level. However, I think the mental health field will see more private practice owners who partner with other non-mental health providers in multi-disciplinary networks. For example, you may see group practices constructed of one or two mental health providers alongside a nutritionist, an acupuncture professional, a massage professional, a life coach, and so on. These new alternative and holistic practices are already becoming established and many are thriving.

Consider that many new practitioners coming into the field possess more opportunity and increased incentive to establish practices in rural and underserved areas, with populations that up to now didn't have access to proper care. With the grants and loan repayment program incentives put in place, healthcare professionals will relocate and recalibrate their practice models and business philosophies.

Additionally, practice owners will have a greater opportunity to provide services outside their office in the community, offering trainings, education, and support services. Because there will be a surge in graduate level professionals entering the field over the next 10 to 20 years, opportunities to provide clinical supervision and/or continuing education master trainings should be plentiful.

Finally, and perhaps most impactful, this title begins to address the growing cultural diversity within our country. Practice owners who are "difference" sensitive and who work with populations that are socio-economically, culturally, and religiously diverse thrive. Those who don't set up practices that are inclusive and thus hold rigid boundaries, only looking for a certain "type" of client, ultimately fail. Failure in these cases may come from a lack of referrals, and/or lack of fulfillment in treating the same type of person/people all the time. My practice is filled with diverse cultural backgrounds, gender, socio-economic levels, religions and other differences. Such diversity keeps me interested and inspired! I am pushed to learn more about culture and other differences outside my practice so I can bring that education back in and be effective and helpful to my clients.

When you look at changes in the workforce and see abundance and opportunity rather than scarcity and competition, then you are thinking along the right lines when it comes to impacts of changes in the workforce resulting from the Affordable Care Act. Ask yourself, "what trainings and services to other professionals can I offer, who can I partner with, where can I deliver my unique services, and in what type of practice would I like to work?"

EXERCISE 8.3 | Planning and Delivering a Professional Training

In this exercise, write down a topic of interest and experience that you'd like to offer as a professional training, helping other professionals learn about your unique findings as a practicing clinician. Consider presenting at a conference live, or providing an online webcast about your topic:

Area of Clinical Interest:

_____

_____

Name of Training Program:

_____

_____

Goal(s) of Training:

_____

_____

TITLE VI — TRANSPARENCY AND INTEGRITY

Aimed at reducing and eliminating fraud, waste and abuse, this title deals with creating greater integrity by raising standards of healthcare in public health programs, insurance companies, and providers through transparencies and accountability measures. In the media, you are aware of the high number of reported cases of abuse by dementia patients toward professionals in facilities. Perhaps you know of such instances firsthand having worked with dementia patients. One example of integrity improvement is the allocation and implementation of dementia abuse prevention education to help professionals better serve this often misunderstood and behaviorally unpredictable population.

Another major change under this title is the patient-centered outcomes research program designed to better understand treatment efficacy and help shape good treatment in the future. Under this provision, outcomes are not permitted to dictate treatment guidelines, nor are they to be used to determine insurance benefits for treatment, or for any discriminatory purposes against the patient.

Public programs, including Medicare, will have more screening and disclosure requirements for providers wanting to serve on its panel. There will also be compliance measures put in place to assure that good providers continue to serve on public program panels and poor ones are banned from providing care under those panels. Medicaid, Medicare, and CHIP are beginning to share information about providers through an integrated data repository, keeping providers who are not competent to provide care out of its system. In addition, the National Provider Identifier (NPI) system was put into place to help assure payment accuracies and find inaccuracies more efficiently.

Many other provisions to Medicare and Medicaid aimed at reducing and eliminating fraud, waste and abuse are established in this title including allowing Civil Monetary Penalties (CMP) against those who make false statements on applications to participate with a Federal program, or even for practitioners who don't return payment on overpayments by Federal programs. Other public program provisions include timely filing for Medicare claims, waste and abuse risk reporting for providers, and enhanced penalties for non-cooperation.

Insurance companies that have plans deemed fraudulent and/or create a serious threat to the public can be ordered to "cease and desist" until hearings are completed. Also practice providers who are under investigation for wrongdoing are subject to accessibility of privileged communications when such information is part of the evidence or investigation. Finally, there is mention of finding alternative methods to resolving fraud, waste, and abuse in the system, reducing large litigation costs by keeping such issues out of the courtroom and addressing them preventatively as much as possible.

Title VI—Business Impacts on Private Practice: The impacts of this title are all about your ethical integrity as a business owner in private practice. While graduate training programs focus on forming trusting and ethical relationships with your patients, not much is mentioned about building strong ethical relationships with other parties such as insurance companies, government programs, administrative support people, and so on.

A successful 21st century practice is one that doesn't cut corners inside or outside the therapy office. Over my career, I met far too many practice owners who while showing ethical integrity directly with their patients, would do things like not report income to the IRS, not make an effort to return overpayments by insurers or government programs, fail to pay quarterly taxes on time, and operate outside the definitions of their managed care contracts. It is my belief that one's integrity as a business professional and a person hinges on these relationships. It's imperative to correct honest mistakes, provide transparencies where appropriate, and behave in all business endeavors ethically and responsibly.

In summary, as a result of the "Transparency and Integrity" provisions, private practice owners may see more state and federal regulation of practices. You should see an increase in the regulation of insurance companies, including policies and procedures that insurers require of its providers resulting from the legislation. More regulation of providers and provider groups is already occurring, and will continue in that same direction. Finally, outcome-based research implications are currently unknown. It is hoped that outcome study results will truly be used in the best interests of the mental health and medical professions, helping providers better patients and assisting patients in a more improved manner.

AFFORDABLE CARE ACT— SUMMARIZED

While there are four other titles (VII—X) not discussed, the information is important, though somewhat less in line with direct impacts on private practice for specialists. Many other provisions have to do with revenue, reauthorization of the Indian Healthcare Improvement Act, improvements to access to innovative medical programs/therapies, and greater community living assistance and support services.

Unfortunately, the legislation falls short of addressing the long-standing issue of licensed counselors and marriage and family therapists not able to serve on Medicare panels. While numerous attempts to pass legislation separate from ACA have failed, you would think that with the large increase in need for more practitioners due to an increase in Medicare recipients and provisions to the Medicare program, the inclusion of these licensed providers would be imminent. Instead, this legislation is stuck in committee as mentioned earlier in Chapter Four.

While the Affordable Care Act was enacted in 2010, upheld in 2012, and will complete its implementation in 2022, its impact will be far reaching beyond 2022. You can expect more reform on top of this reform , and now even the possibility of repeal and replacement. Whether you work with private managed care insurance companies, public programs or neither, in some way your practice will be impacted. Some practitioners will decide to sever ties with insurers and/or go off of public program panels to not be as impacted. Remember, when you choose not to participate with third party payers, you may experience less frustration with regulation and administration and an increased challenge when seeking referrals for out-of-pocket fee for service only clients.

What is perhaps most surprising about this legislation is the number of times and manner in which mental healthcare is addressed. When I combed through the pages of legislation and noted specific mention of pilot programs, federal grants, more research, and money given to mental health-related treatment and issues, I realized how mental healthcare is primed to become a more mainstream, less stigmatized form of care. I was once again reminded of Kennedy's words to congress over fifty years ago emphasizing the relevance of mental healthcare in our society. It is up to you as a provider and practice owner to help continue Kennedy's message, the endorsements of mental health by the Affordable Care Act, and other relevant mental health legislation, regardless of how our healthcare system is reshaped.

PROFESSIONAL ADVOCACY

In addition to your role as a clinical specialist and business owner, you must consider becoming an advocate for your profession. Good business owners run successful practices. Excellent business owners run successful practices and take on a role advocating for what is relevant to their business, care specialty and most importantly, their clients. In order to advocate properly, you must become knowledgeable about trends in the industry, including what is happening in legislative circles, and business and industry circles that connect to your specific area(s) and broader areas, and you have to GET INVOLVED. The table below shows a list of helpful websites to keep you well informed.

TABLE 8.1 | Professional Advocacy Websites

List of websites to assist with gathering legislative and business information for purposes of professional advocacy.

Kaiser Family Foundation
www.kff.org

U.S. Department of Health and Human Services
www.HHS.gov

Centers for Medicaid and Medicare Services
https://www.cms.gov/

Obamacare Facts
http://obamacarefacts.com/obamacare-facts/

Pychotherapy Finances
http://www.psyfin.com/

Tracking the U.S. Congress
https://www.govtrack.us/

Another way to advocate for your business and the profession as a whole is to join and support your professional organization nationally and within your state. Participation with your professional organization(s) is a key to keeping up with ongoing changes in your nearby community and throughout the country. Each professional organization typically has a legislative and pubic policy division or committee that researches, documents, and discusses information about current legislation nationally, and locally within your state's organization. In addition to finding great information through your professional association, there are ample opportunities to serve on advocacy committees, in appointed or elected board positions, providing for a leadership role that can help immensely with creating legislative progress in the professional care industry.

FIGURE 8.1 | Healthcare Change Implementation Plan

A way of summarizing the chapter and to help you put thoughts into action in creating a 6-point plan that helps you fortify a solid practice and responds effectively to large-scale changes in the healthcare system over time.

THE 6-POINTS DEFINED

1. **Systemic Organization**—How you organize your systems of business in ways that make sense for delivery of your craft. Examples include billing, scheduling, storage of records, etc. Make certain these systems are in full compliance with local, state, and federal laws, that they are ethical, and that someone trusted you know has access to know these systems should anything happen to you.

2. **Continuity of Care**—What plans do you have to create healthy continuity of care? Who do you consult with on a regular basis? How are you creating continuity of care now? Examples:

   • Create a separate 3rd party contact form, in addition to a written release, so that when I talk to a 3rd party it's easy to document and find in the patient chart.

   • Make a point to call the patient's doctor within the first month of treatment.

   • Get a list of all patient providers and discuss who needs to be contacted.

3. **Diversification**—Remaining diversified in your endeavors helps safeguard a positive adaptation to healthcare reform changes. How well are you diversified in what you do? What do you need to do now to diversify?

4. **Transparency**—Certain transparencies in what we do become important. When it comes to healthcare reform, how transparent do you want to be? How about business matters? Does it make sense to talk about your relationships with managed care or Medicare with your patients? Write down your ideas.

5. **Development**—Professional development is an ongoing process that increases your clinical knowledge and helps you stay at the top of your game. What professional development topics or trainings interest you?

6. **Advocacy**—In your new role of advocate, how will you educate others and advocate for what is important in your field? Remember advocacy empowers change and professional growth, both individually, and in the greater community.

EXERCISE 8.4 | Healthcare Change Implementation Plan

Now it's your turn. Use the chart below and fill in ideas on how you plan to address these 6 areas of your practice in order to help you and your business be resilient and achieve success through change.

SYSTEMIC ORGANIZATION	
CONTINUITY OF CARE	
DIVERSIFICATION	
TRANSPARENCY	
DEVELOPMENT	
ADVOCACY	

This Healthcare Change Implementation Plan is now an emphasis area in your overall business plan. Change and update it as you see fit, always watching what is happening with legislative updates in your profession. Remember, the more you get involved, the easier the accessibility of this information, and the more power you gain to help create large-scale changes in your field. Remember, the grandfather of Existential Psychology, Viktor Frankl (1984), once said, "When we are no longer able to change a situation, we are challenged to change ourselves" (p. 116).

CHAPTER NINE |
FINANCIAL MANAGEMENT AND GROWTH

When teaching the course on practice building to my graduate students, on the first day of class I'd ask each student to share something they are excited about and something they fear about private practice ownership and development. By a landslide the most consistent comment that permeated the introductions was "I am terrified of dealing with money," and "I handle finances very poorly" or "I don't know anything about the financial side of building a business." Equally, there were comments like, "I can't wait to learn about how to do the money part," or "Learning about money is why I took this class." Over the years, variations of these comments on both ends of the spectrum led me to understand that most, not all, practitioners are ill-equipped to manage the financial end of practice building and management. Many learn as they go, finding new ways to maximize profit, and minimize financial loss through trial and error, sometimes experiencing success, and many times failure. **This chapter will help overcome fears and provide a grasp on how to build a solid financial foundation.**

Klontz, Klontz, and Kahler (2009) discussed how our early developmental wiring regarding wealth has much to do with future beliefs and practices regarding money and money management. Financial influences, beliefs, and practices you experienced in your home, as well as the state of the world economy during your formative years wired your brain into practices and beliefs that are a reflection of that history. Before or while in practice I recommend you explore that history much the way you would introspect and examine your social and emotional history to prepare you professionally to be an effective clinician.

A further complication is the notion that most practitioners enter this field with a strong desire and passion for helping, not an altruistic interest in earning money doing so. Often, a formulation of what I call the "business guilt complex" occurs, enabling the practice owner to develop poor financial habits such as charging less than they are worth, failing to budget money on the business and/or personal side of the ledger, forgetting to set aside money to pay routine business taxes, not caring to protect assets legally, or other financial errors that bring about costly consequences. Thus, in addition to exploring the financial history and shaping of your money values, so too should you make efforts to examine your "business guilt complex." When you struggle with certain money matters that you cannot seem to get through, I recommend you work with a practice consultant who can strategically find ways to set up healthy and ethical financial systems that work well for your practice.

The most important advice about managing your finances well while building a solid practice is that there is no one way to do it. How deliberate in your methods, and how frequent and careful you become about looking at your inflow, outflow and savings is what is most important. For example, the financial stability of my practice withstands the test of time—despite changes in healthcare, the economic downturns of post 9/11, and the bank/housing failures in 2007/08—because of a multi-faceted 5-step system that I teach throughout this chapter. This system doesn't have to be followed to the letter. It comes with a flexibility "knob" that you can turn to your liking so that you fine-tune your financial "music." In other words, as long as you include these essential elements in your business model for financial management and growth, you own the freedom to move within these safeguards/pathways to meet your financial goals.

Your Protection and Growth of Assets (PGA) hinge on these 5-Steps:

1. Legal Protection of Financials
2. Insurance Protections
3. Banking/Financial Management Practice
4. Tax Savings Strategy
5. Growth & Investment Strategy & Practice

For the rest of this chapter we will focus on these five areas. The best part is you already learned about the first two steps earlier in Chapter Three when I discussed legal protections and insurance policies at length. Keeping in mind that these first two steps are an important part of the 5-step system, let's review these two steps briefly first.

PROTECTING YOURSELF AND YOUR FINANCES

Your best asset isn't the number of clients you bring into your practice. It's not how well you market or network. It's not even your graduate degree. **It's actually YOU!** Who you are includes the valuable traits mentioned above, and much more. Being a humble professional care provider, all too often you aren't thinking much about protecting yourself. What you earn financially also helps determine your value as a professional in the field. How well you manage your finances, protect your money, and grow your wealth are important areas that must be taken seriously and given more attention than you think. The protection pieces are the first two layers of your foundation.

STEP 1: LEGAL PROTECTION — REVIEW

TABLE 9.1 | Legal Entity Options

LLC	Limited Liability Company
LLP	Limited Liability Partnership
PC	Professional Corporation
S-Corp	Subchapter S-Corporation

Generally, these legal entity options are the most popular. Remember, states have varying fees for these entities, and some entity types may differ slightly from state to state. The LLC/LLP option operates as a "pass through" entity, which means that you are federally taxed on a Schedule C form. If you elect to be an S-Corporation, you must file a separate federal business tax return. The above entity types provide legal protection of your assets provided that you create an operating agreement, as well as any other legal documents necessary, and operate in exactly the manner in which your entity is set up as recommended by your corporate attorney. Be careful when selecting the right entity for you from a taxation perspective. In addition to consulting an attorney about the best legal protection, consider consulting your accountant regarding options suitable from a taxation perspective.

STEP 2: INSURANCE PROTECTIONS — REVIEW

Though I already discussed the importance of protecting yourself with numerous types of insurance coverage, for the purpose of our discussion about financial protections, remember to purchase the following insurance policies and be sure that you have the proper coverage:

TABLE 9.2 | Insurance Protections

Insurance coverage protections that protect you financially should dire circumstances dictate. The insurance policies listed are crucial to the financial solvency and protection of your assets. Note that the information about insurance policies is not a recommendation for what exact coverage(s) you need. When determining your coverage, consult with insurance agents and other knowledgeable professionals who are credentialed in helping with the purchase and attainment of your protections.

PROFESSIONAL LIABILITY	BUSINESS KEY POLICY	DISABILITY POLICY	LIFE INSURANCE	UMBRELLA POLICY
Malpractice 1 Million Occurance 3 Million Aggregate A must have for all mental health practitioners!	Theft Provision Slip and Fall Coverage (Also called Premises Coverage)	Proper income replacement amounts are key! Make sure head injury and other brain disorders are covered injuries	Term Life Policy is usually best 20 Year Term is Good Make sure you are in good health when applying	Coverage after other policies have met their maximums Premiums should not be very expensive Make sure you know what it will and will not cover

STEP 3: BANKING AND FINANCIAL MANAGEMENT STRATEGY

Recall that we talked about "flow through entity" in Chapter Three when I described the importance of depositing all business revenue into one "business account" that your money "flows through." In this step, I show you what to do with that money and exactly how to do it.

One of the first actions you will take before ever seeing your first client, and once you have your Federal Employer Identification Number (F.E.I.N.) is opening your business checking account. There are numerous advantages to using the same bank for all your personal and business banking needs. First, it's much easier to transfer money from one account to another. Online banking makes these transactions extremely simple. The ease of moving money is a factor of time, a valuable commodity you need to free up for seeing clients, or use in some other needed area of life. Second, by having all your accounts at one bank, you automatically bring higher value to the banking relationship. Banks are hungry for your business because you are using multiple accounts, and you are a small business owner. You help the bank's mission because you are holding money in their safety, which gives them more power to invest, and they are able to better serve you the more business you give your bank. For this reason I highly recommend that no matter which bank you choose, go to a smaller branch near you and develop a relationship directly with that branch. They then know you by name, build trust with you, and do more for you than the average customer because they need your business more than the larger branches do. I use this strategy and reap the benefits of knowing a few people in the banking industry closely and now they are my "go to" people for banking advice, products, and services I need.

My Bank Is Earning Me Over a Half Million Dollars, with NO Investment!

Let me share a true story of how my local bank helped me save nearly $5,000.00 per year over the last five years. By car, my local branch is a 45-minute round trip, which is exactly the same time a routine outpatient visit lasts in my practice. Once a week, I would get in my car, drive to my branch to make my business deposit and drive back to the office. I did this for many years while developing my practice. It was actually a nice break from clients and got me out of the office. That said, there were days that I was so busy, I wish I didn't have to make the trip over to make a deposit. I was too lazy to mail in deposits, and I don't like using ATM's for depositing/withdrawing money. On the busiest of weeks, when I had clients on overflow, I wished I could use the time for an extra client, and on days I wasn't busy with clients, I thought it might be nice not to have to go to the bank and instead use the time for home projects, hobbies, or lunching with friends or family.

One day, about five years ago, I was talking with my banker at the local branch, asking when there might be a branch built closer to my office. He kept promising me that corporate was "looking into it" for years. This time, I noticed that they had just rolled out a new product called "remote deposit." He explained that the bank actually gives you a real teller machine, trains you how to use it and then you deposit large batches of checks right from your office or home in minutes. I know you may be wondering why not just use mobile applications now that most banks have them? Five years ago my bank didn't use mobile deposit technology, and even today, given the large number of co-pay checks to deposit, it's not so worth it to use the mobile application for business checks. I now use it to deposit personal checks all the time. But, for business, my remote deposit machine saves me a 45-minute round trip to and from the bank every week.

At an average of $100 per 45-minute session, I now can fill my calendar with a client every week, instead of going to the bank. That's about $5,000 per year, for the past 5 years. Imagine that you are in practice for 35 years. That's a savings of $175,000. Now let's say you invested 100% of that money, leaving the rest of your earnings for paying bills and short term investments. At an average annual return of 5% can you guess how much you'd have in the bank after 35 years of just that $100 a week client session? You'd put in about $175K. If that's what you guessed, you are wrong, because at 5% compounded over time, while putting the money in monthly, in 35 years you'd earn $502,141.05. In short, my bank saved me time. I used that time to see one extra client a week. I earned an extra $5K per year that I put into a 5% yield investment monthly over 35 years, and soon I will have a half a million dollars. Well, I am only 5 years into it. I am getting ahead of myself! And, if you are confused about compounding interest and figures I just mentioned, don't worry. I will explain further when we talk about saving for retirement. This true story is just an example of how doing something very small like consistently saving time, and then seeing an extra client, and putting that money away can yield very high dividends over time.

Tips for Finding the Right Bank

Let's resume our banking discussion. Below are a few tips for finding the right banking situation.
- Bank at a smaller local branch and get to know at least one bank professional there
- Put all your accounts at one bank, if possible
- Save time and bank online
- Make sure to bank with a bank that offers truly FREE banking

To this last point, when you are bringing a bank a high amount of business, find out what it takes to get extra banking fees waived that aren't necessary. Many banks charge for number of items deposited, online transactions/banking, monthly statements, and most banks charge for over-drafted accounts. In many cases banks will waive the latter fees when you don't have too many in one year, and you are good about keeping balances in the black most of the time. On numerous occasions, I obtained refunds for overdraft fees because of my relationship with the branch and my established history with the bank. Of course, I recommend ahead of time setting up overdraft protection accounts so that when you go under a $0 balance, you are covered, usually at a very nominal charge much less than the normal overdraft fees. There are many strategies that banks use to get you into truly FREE banking, and most small business owners never think to ask.

Revenue Distribution Strategy

How you distribute your revenues among accounts is extremely important for making finances run smoothly. In addition to your business checking account, I recommend a general personal savings account and personal checking account. Recall that once revenue flows into the business account bucket, you can move money from the business account to either of your personal accounts. Additionally, you can move money into a personal savings account as much as you like. However moving money out of personal savings to your personal checking carries a monthly limit. Ask your banker how many savings account transfers and withdrawals are allowed per month.

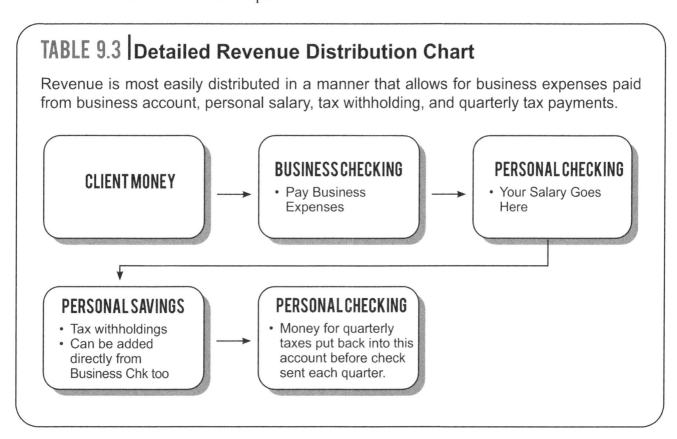

TABLE 9.3 | Detailed Revenue Distribution Chart

Revenue is most easily distributed in a manner that allows for business expenses paid from business account, personal salary, tax withholding, and quarterly tax payments.

CLIENT MONEY

BUSINESS CHECKING
- Pay Business Expenses

PERSONAL CHECKING
- Your Salary Goes Here

PERSONAL SAVINGS
- Tax withholdings
- Can be added directly from Business Chk too

PERSONAL CHECKING
- Money for quarterly taxes put back into this account before check sent each quarter.

Deposit client checks as soon after you receive them as possible. Depositing checks once a week is a smart process for clients paying with a personal check. Some providers automatically generate a receipt for every client payment, while others elect to only provide receipts when requested by the client. Clients who seek reimbursement for medical expenses through their Health Savings Account (HSA) may request a more detailed invoice. There are a few free invoicing programs available online, or if you purchase online practice tools, usually an invoice template comes standard.

Once your money is safely in the business account, be sure to budget for business expenses, and pay all business expenses directly from your business account, or a business credit card that can be paid off directly from your business checking account on a monthly basis. Obtaining and using a business credit card is an excellent idea for fixed monthly business expenses, and only when you know you can pay your card's balance in full every month without accruing interest charges. I enjoy the benefits of my business credit card, including points for travel and other rewards and the purchase protection that goes with it. When you travel around the country giving talks, attending conferences, or doing other business related activity, the convenience of the card is always helpful. One very important note is that every receipt you obtain from your business purchases should be saved for at least 7 years. Many accountants insist you write a note on the receipt regarding the business purpose of the purchase.

It's a good idea to leave enough money in your business account to cover expenses plus a small base. But, remember, if you have a lot of money in the business account and you are sued, that money is subject to a monetary judgment against you, whereas money that is outside the business account is more protected, provided you operate your business account under proper liability protection, such as the Limited Liability Company (LLC). I usually keep a few thousand dollars in the LLC business account and the rest is transferred to the personal accounts pretty quickly for the financial protection.

Merchant Services

Creating the ability to accept credit and debit cards in your practice is a must. It took me several years before I decided to accept plastic money. Once I started using merchant services, my practice revenues diversified, and my business grew more. Being a merchant offers many benefits. Probably most significant, clients are able to use health savings debit cards. An increasing number of clients ask me if they can use their Health Savings Account (HSA) card, as it's extremely convenient for them. Being a merchant pulls in money on a more frequent basis, and even though there's a small cost per transaction, it's well worth it. Some practice owners charge a small fee to offset their merchant account expense.

At this time, I do not operate my practice with an extra charge for use of credit/debit cards. It's a choice that is entirely up to you. Shop for good merchant rates, and make certain that you and your merchant are Payment Card Industry (PCI) compliant. You may want to use your bank as your merchant service provider, even if your bank's rate might be a bit higher. Use of your bank for this service establishes that "monopoly" of services you are using with them and benefits you in other areas. Once you select your merchant services provider, they help you get the right credit card machine, making sure you get one with a chip reader. The service provider will also help you link your account directly to your business checking account so that at the end of each day you will have direct deposits of the day's transactions put into your business checking account.

Finally, whether you use a traditional credit card machine, or an Internet application for your merchant service, here are a few important reminders:

1. You and the merchant servicer (e.g., your bank, Square, PayPal) must be Payment Card Industry (PCI) compliant. (Brief annual assessments apply)
2. Shop rates and get the best rate possible.
3. Know that different card issuers and card types (Visa, MC, Discover, AMEX, and Debit VS. Credit) charge different rates, so inquire about ALL rates.
4. Let the merchant servicer know you are a healthcare provider and ask whether they can set you up to take Health Savings Account debit cards.

Staying within Budget

Keeping within your budget is critical from the start. Establish a needs based budget that is conservative in the beginning, even if you are starting your practice with a large amount of savings equity. Get out of the starting gates with good money practice, by making a sensible budget and sticking to it.

TABLE 9.4 │Sample Budget

Below is a sample monthly budget for your business. You may refer to Table 4.2 to review start up costs for your office. The budget depicted here is for routine monthly expenses. Some expenses are paid once per year and broken into 12 equal parts. These numbers are for sample purposes only and do not reflect your actual cost.

MONTHLY EXPENSE ITEM	MONTHLY EXPENSE CATEGORY	MONTHLY COST
Office Rent	Office	$500
Land Phone/FAX/Internet	Utility	$65
Office Cell Phone	Utility	$125
Website Hosting	Marketing	$39
Office Supplies	Office	$50
Professional Association Dues	Professional Fees	$25
Continuing Education	Professional Fees	$125
Clinical Supervision	Professional Fees	$200
Accountant	Contracted Services	$45
Billing Specialist	Contracted Services	$125
Professional Licensing	Professional Fees	$10
Professional Online Listings	Marketing	$25
Professional Liability Insurance	Insurance	$28
Business Key Policy	Insurance	$35
	TOTAL	$1,397

Based on the model above, you need about $1,400 per month of revenue to break even. You now have a budget to make some relevant projections. Let's do some math. Ask yourself, how many client sessions would I need to have in one month to break even? Project your average per client fee based on what you charge, including your discounts. If you charge $80 per session, and expect to earn on average $60 per visit, then you would need 24 client visits during the month to break even. That's an average of 6 sessions per week. The remaining sessions' revenue would be pre-tax gross revenue, meaning you just need to pay taxes based on the remaining money you earn after expenses, which account for about 28% of the remaining money you earn. We will talk more about taxes in a moment.

Think you can't get 6 clients weekly within a few months? Are you wondering how to stay out of the red and be in the black with expenses starting out high considering you have no clients? Take a look for a moment at the highest expense on the list. Yes, you got it. It's your rent. Starting with your highest expense, figure out how you can pragmatically reduce your highest expense. You may be thinking, "But I have to rent an office, and $500 is even a pretty low number in my geographic area." Well, why not look for a rental space one or two days a week at half that cost until you build to your first "break even" point, and then expand? Or you could even find office space by the hour, and then your rental commitment is even less risk. Manipulating your budget in smart and sensible ways is how it works best, as long as you make it work. You must follow through on your commitment to stay within your budget or financial comfort zone.

Now it's time to complete your budget chart. Using the chart below, make a list of your budget items, expense category, and monthly associated costs. Then, in exercise 9.2 right after, determine your break-even point.

EXERCISE 9.1 | My Monthly Budget

List the items, categories, and projected or actual cost in your monthly budget. Total your figures and that amount becomes your projected monthly expense.

MONTHLY EXPENSE ITEM	MONTHLY EXPENSE CATEGORY	MONTHLY COST
		TOTAL

EXERCISE 9.2 | Breaking Even Exercise

Determine your expected average per session (EAS) revenue. Divide the monthly expense total from the previous exercise by your EAS number and your result shows how many sessions you need per month to go out of the red and into black.

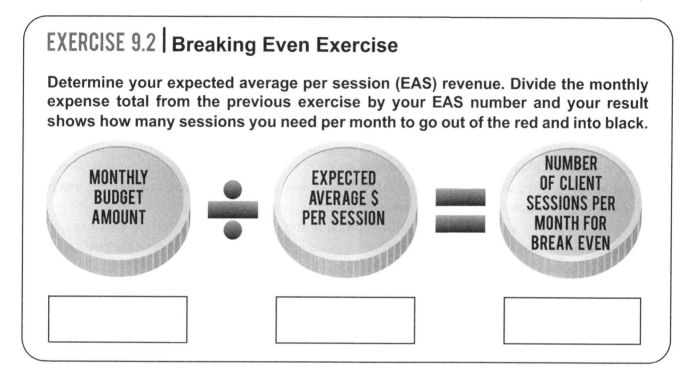

STEP 4 : TAX SAVING STRATEGY

What's your best tax strategy in the most simple of terms? **Pay your taxes, and always pay on time.** If you always pay your taxes in sufficient amount and pay by the deadline throughout the ownership and operation of your business, you are reducing the likelihood of audits by the Internal Revenue Service (IRS), and you will never owe the government in arrears with interest. Each issue, an audit and owing the government back taxes with interest, causes nightmares for small business owners. And yet, you'd be surprised at the number of private practice owners who don't pay their taxes using the quarterly estimated system or even on time on an annual basis. Make a good plan to always file your annual returns on time, without requesting extensions. While extensions are sometimes unavoidable, the more you file routinely on time the better. You want to show the government that you are a trustworthy, reliable, and extremely consistent payer.

My first year in business, I had no idea how much to save for taxes and didn't put nearly enough in my savings account, only to be surprised by a rather large tax bill with little tax money in my savings budget. In order for you to be cash positive and to have enough to pay your taxes, set aside 30% of your post-business expense revenue on a routine basis.

Here's a great savings strategy that helps with tax dollar allocation:

1. Pay your expenses from the business account and keep a minimum of $2,500 and a maximum of $7,500 in your business checking account
2. Transfer weekly amounts from business checking to personal checking (these transfers are called "draws").
3. Further, transfer 30% of each draw from personal checking to personal savings. This is your tax savings money.

Estimated Tax Payments

Each fiscal year (January 1–December 31) you will make four quarterly payments to the IRS and to your state department of revenue. Total payments should equal approximately 110% of last year's federal and state tax, broken into four equal parts. Make these estimated payments when you are set up as a "pass through entity" taxation-wise. This means file a Schedule C along with your personal annual return. Your estimated payments are due on **April 15, June 15, September 15, and January 15** (of the next year for the current year). You can contact your state's revenue department to obtain mailing coupons for the state quarterly tax. For federal payments, visit the federal IRS website, www.irs.gov and search "self-employed individuals tax center" which takes you to an information page that will show you how to use the electronic payment system and obtain federal tax payment coupons if you are using the mail-in method. If you use a tax preparation service or accountant, that individual should be able to tell you exactly how much you owe for quarterly payments each year and can get you the payment coupons.

At some point, you may elect a tax filing status of sub-chapter S-Corporation (S-Corp). Some accountants believe that the S-Corp filing status provides a lower employer tax because you can claim a "reasonable" salary and the dividends that you draw are not currently subjected to the employer tax rate. In this case you still have to pay personal tax on all your earnings. The down side with filing as an S-Corp is that you must file a separate business tax return, and pay monthly taxes broken into Federal Withholding, Social Security, and Medicare, all on the employer side of your business. Quarterly estimated taxes continue as well on the personal side of your ledger. In order for this status and strategy to pay off financially, you need to be earning approximately a 6-figure revenue stream annually or more. When you hit these earnings, discuss your federal filing status with a tax preparation expert with specific emphasis on the pros and cons of changing your filing status to subchapter S-Corporation.

Paying your estimated quarterly tax is easy. The table below shows exactly how to allocate the funds through your banking practices and then pay in your quarterly installments.

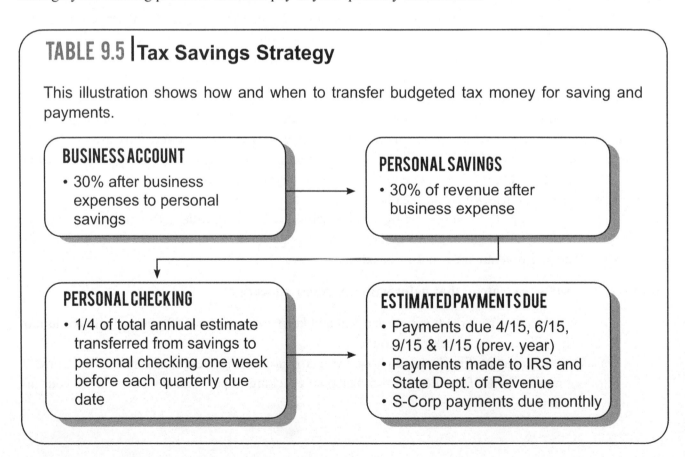

TABLE 9.5 | Tax Savings Strategy

This illustration shows how and when to transfer budgeted tax money for saving and payments.

BUSINESS ACCOUNT
- 30% after business expenses to personal savings

PERSONAL SAVINGS
- 30% of revenue after business expense

PERSONAL CHECKING
- 1/4 of total annual estimate transferred from savings to personal checking one week before each quarterly due date

ESTIMATED PAYMENTS DUE
- Payments due 4/15, 6/15, 9/15 & 1/15 (prev. year)
- Payments made to IRS and State Dept. of Revenue
- S-Corp payments due monthly

Accounting Software

Some practice owners may elect to use software programs such as TurboTax for tax preparation. I did my own taxes for the first few years in practice. Moving to a professional tax preparer is a personal decision of course. When I decided to switch, I realized that the cost of professional preparation was well worth it when considering the value to my practice. A professional tax preparer not only helps save you time. My tax advisor and preparation expert helps reduce further the likelihood of an audit, gives me peace of mind knowing that if audited, I have a professional in the field to rely on for back up, and lessens my time spent on the preparation itself.

Find Your Ultimate Tax Expert

A final and critical key to managing your taxes, other than paying on time, is making certain that your relationship with your tax preparer is one that fits well. I fired two accountants/preparers before finding an individual who understands the values of a small business owner in the professional care field, and who works efficiently, thoroughly, and with honesty and integrity.

STEP 5 : GROWTH THROUGH INVESTMENTS

Imagine you have a dollar bill in your hand. It's a dollar you earned from working with one of your clients. You worked very hard for that dollar. What would happen to that dollar if you spent it on going to the movies? It would be gone, with no value (other than you hopefully watched a great movie). Imagine now you decided to hold that dollar and not spend it. You set it on your bedroom dresser and there it sits for months, even years. What is the value of that dollar after many months or even years as the dollar sits there on your dresser? If you guessed less than a dollar, then you are right. If you guessed that it's still shrinking, you are even smarter. That's right, a dollar spent is a dollar gone. A dollar saved at home is shrinking in value.

Now, what if you took that dollar and put it into a 2% compound interest savings account for 10 years. Certainly, you would have more than $1. Still, based on average rates of inflation, the result is a slightly shrinking "actual value" despite earning more than a dollar. So, what's the rub? Not only do you need to think about investing a portion of your earnings, you need to find the highest yield investments possible, and in a way that hopefully lowers your current tax rate. A great method for achieving both ends is in developing your retirement investment strategy.

Let me first say that I am not an investment banker, or any kind of professional investment counselor. So, any advice provided does not guarantee return on your investment as there are always assumed risks on your part when making any type of investment purchase. I am a practice owner like you, who consulted with many different financial people over the years, read numerous financial planning and investing books, and mostly strategized on my own how to effectively use investing as a vehicle for solidifying a stronger financial foundation in my personal wealth as well as my professional practice. That said, I am about to give you my two cents worth (no pun intended) of advice on investing strategy for the private practice owner.

Debt Reduction and Consolidation

Before making any actual investments, first look at any and all current debt you own. Make a list of all debt starting with the highest interest rate down to the lowest. Even if you have higher amounts of debt at a lower interest rate, your interest rate is a key factor in extra money you pay on top of the money you borrowed. Even though you are listing all your debt, for some of it, such as student loan debt, you won't change a thing since this kind of debt is generally fixed with tax-deductible interest. Debt that carries a variable interest rate and/or the fixed rate is quite high is "bad" debt. Try quickly addressing effective ways to either pay off "bad" debt sooner, and/or move your "bad" debt into "good" debt by consolidating or asking your bank to lower your interest rate.

The table below should help with getting a clear picture of types of debt and how to list each debt. What follows is your exercise of listing your own debt, and creating your own consolidation plan.

TABLE 9.6 | Sample Debt Reduction and Consolidation Plan

ITEM	OUTSTANDING BALANCE	INTEREST RATE	VARIABLE/ FIXED	YRS	ACTION PLAN
Credit Card	$3,500	18%	Variable	N/A	Pay off using savings over 3 mos. Call CC company and ask for lower interest rate
Student Loan	$28,000	6.5%	Fixed	20	No Action (or consolidate with new refinance of home at lower rate)
Home Mortgage	$250,000	3.5%	Fixed	29	No Action

EXERCISE 9.3 | Debt Reduction and Consolidation Plan

Write down your list, beginning with highest rates of interest, and make an action plan for how to reduce and/or consolidate your debt.

ITEM	OUTSTANDING BALANCE	INTEREST RATE	VARIABLE/ FIXED	YRS	ACTION PLAN

Retirement Planning

Now that you created a secure plan for your debt, it's time to focus on a money growth plan that works for you personally and professionally. One of the very best methods for growing your money is through your retirement account. There are many advantages to using a retirement planning and investing strategy as your first and most important financial growth vehicle.

First, at some point, as much as you enjoy performing the good hard work you offer, eventually you come to a point in life when it is time to retire. At that point, you want enough money in your asset portfolio to live from ONLY the annual interest your principal holding produces and your Social Security Income (SSI). This ideal financial situation means your aim is to avoid a "dip into" principal savings as much as possible. Your principal money is hopefully maintained and passed on to surviving family and/or charity.

Second, many retirement accounts are tax free on the front end, and taxed at the time of withdrawal. This method is a benefit to your current business as it lowers your tax rate each year you contribute to your pre-tax plan. Alternatively, there are accounts, such as the ROTH-IRA, which allow you to grow money after tax, and the growth of those contributions is tax-free and payouts after retirement are tax-free as well. It's important to consult with your financial planning specialist to determine which retirement strategy is best for you.

In the beginning of practice development you may be hard pressed to find a dime to save, much less contribute to your retirement account. I certainly didn't begin my retirement contributions in the first year of practice. Still, sooner is better than later and a small contribution consistently made early on is a smart way to grow your money. The younger you are and the earlier you start contributing the better.

I recommend starting a ROTH-IRA and either a Simplified-Employment Pension Plan (SEP) or Individual 401K. You don't need much to start these accounts and can contribute what you like on a routine basis. There are maximum annual contribution limits. Checking with a financial expert or tax adviser on the annual maximums and other retirement strategies is wise. However, you don't actually need a full time wealth manager to engage and contribute to these accounts. You can go online and open your account through a relationship manager through your bank or at a brokerage that specializes in retirement accounts.

To illustrate my point about starting early, even if it's just a small amount, take a look at the figure below:

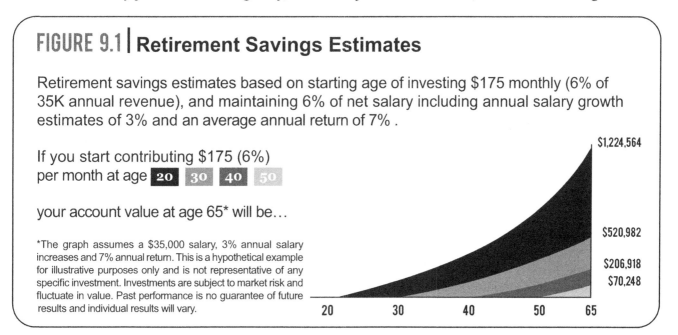

FIGURE 9.1 | Retirement Savings Estimates

Retirement savings estimates based on starting age of investing $175 monthly (6% of 35K annual revenue), and maintaining 6% of net salary including annual salary growth estimates of 3% and an average annual return of 7% .

If you start contributing $175 (6%)
per month at age 20 30 40 50

your account value at age 65* will be…

*The graph assumes a $35,000 salary, 3% annual salary increases and 7% annual return. This is a hypothetical example for illustrative purposes only and is not representative of any specific investment. Investments are subject to market risk and fluctuate in value. Past performance is no guarantee of future results and individual results will vary.

$1,224,564

$520,982

$206,918
$70,248

I currently contribute the maximum allowed annually based on my salary. It took me about 10 years to get to that annual maximum, as I gradually grew my contributions while also eliminating bad debts.

The 50/50 Game

What is this 50/50 game? Well, it's not really a game. It's actually more like a 50/50 challenge. In order to eventually reach your goal of maxing out your annual retirement contributions, I developed this 50/50 concept. Most retirement advisers used to suggest an annual contribution of about 10% of yearly income to make it financially viable to retire. This figure when paired with your Social Security Income (SSI) was thought to be enough up until recently. Today, many advisers are suggesting contributions up to 20% of annual income. So, if you earn $50,000 after business expenses, you would contribute $10,000 annually. In this case your taxable income is about $40,000 provided you contribute to a tax-deferred retirement account. Remember earlier I mentioned saving 30% of your net for taxes. 30% of 40K is $12,000. Adding the tax amount and the retirement contribution, 10K (retirement) + 12K (Taxes) = $22,000, which is close to 50% of your $50,000 net after business expenses. So, if you aim to put into your savings holding account $25,000 based on this example, you'll build a growing cushion of $3,000 annually in short-term savings, while still being able to pay your taxes and contribute to your retirement at 20%. This 50% savings can be directly deposited from your business account to your savings or be passed through your personal checking to your savings account. You can then transfer money back to your personal checking account when you need to access it for tax payments or retirement fund contributions. Here's how it works:

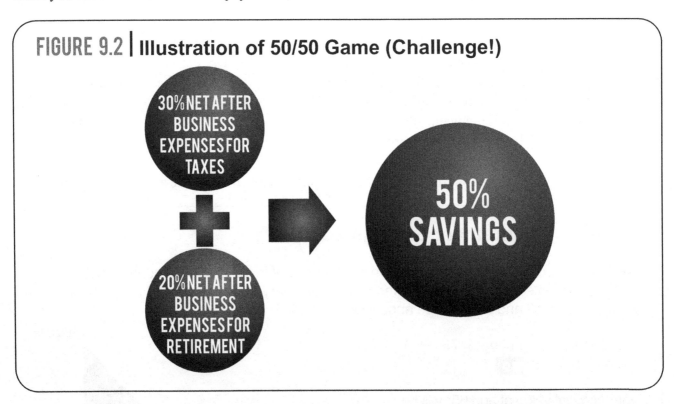

FIGURE 9.2 | Illustration of 50/50 Game (Challenge!)

The other side of the 50/50 game lies in the challenge of funding your personal needs and wants with the remaining 50%. I understand that most people can't live on $25,000 annually in terms of monthly expenses. After all, that's about $2,000 a month, and we both know most monthly rent/mortgage payments alone are close to that amount or more. It's much easier to get to 50% of net revenue for living expenses when you hit 6-figures, or if you have a household partner with a full-time salary. Look at your budget, talk with your family, and plan accordingly.

Other Investments

Small contributions to start, along with decreasing your bad debt are just the beginning. Building to maximum annual retirement contribution is a next goal. And, for some, there's a further step. If you are fortunate enough to be in a situation where you can max your retirement, and have income left over, then you may think about other investment vehicles. There are many options beyond retirement accounts to safely invest money. Some people purchase bonds, mutual funds, stocks, or whole life insurance plans with a defined benefit. Others prefer to collect rare art. Some like to collect antiques. Regardless of where you put your investment dollar, remember there's always some risk. Make sure you are aware of the risks and comfortable with them when making a decision to invest. Here are two other popular investment strategies:

529 College Savings

A 529 college savings fund is a good investment vehicle if you know that your children are headed for college. Some of these plans also offer deferred pre-tax options for state taxes that allow you to save even more on your current annual taxable income. Make sure you read all literature and know the limits and possibilities of this investment type before opening an account and contributing.

On a personal note, I know practice owners who elect to contribute to a 529 plan in place of their own retirement savings contributions. While this is a very personal decision, consider the fact that your beneficiary of the college savings account possess their own lifespan of earning potential as you are older and possess less of that potential. One advisor once said to me, "wouldn't you rather be sure you save enough for yourself in retirement so that you don't put your adult child in the position of needing to provide financially for you later on?" Put in that context, it was an easy decision for me. Still, in order to feel like I am helping my children's future, I contribute to their college savings account minimally ($10 a week), until I can afford a larger contribution. Diversifying in this manner works well for me. Consider your values, the facts, and make a good decision that works well for you.

Property Ownership

Another method of diversification of investments consists of purchasing and owning property. Home ownership is perhaps the easiest and most logical form of owning property and often it's less expensive than the rental market. In general, property ownership is a good long-term investment, unless you are in the business of fixing and flipping, which is a side career itself. The general idea for property ownership is to buy low and sell high, and never ever get underneath the property, or behind in mortgage payments. The housing bust in 2007/08 caused many unfortunate property owners to lose their homes not because the market went bad, but mostly because many of these property owners trusted a system that misinformed and improperly educated the buyer/refinancer, putting owners in high risk variable rate home loans they couldn't afford. Again, as with any investment you must make sure you are extremely well informed and know the risks.

I recommend when buying a property to stay away from Adjustable Rate Mortgages (ARM) and instead find a mortgage at a good fixed interest rate. Of course, make certain you are getting the property at a fair market price by looking at recent comparable sales in the area, getting a proper and thorough appraisal of the property and its dwellings, and working with a non-biased real estate professional. Another benefit to home ownership is that interest paid throughout the year on your mortgage is tax deductible—a benefit both to owning your home and to your business' bottom line.

Diversifying Investments

Growing your investment portfolio involves patience, persistence, and a smart diversification process that fits your values and needs. Calculated research and risk is essential. While there are no guarantees, if you are in it for the long haul, you will see your net worth grow over time. Keep in mind that private practice is a marathon and not a sprint. This advice holds quite true when it comes to investing your money. Your step-wise investment strategy of:

1. Securing and reducing your debt
2. Starting a retirement account early and contributing something consistently and often
3. Working toward your 50/50 challenge of saving 20% and maxing out your annual retirement contribution and
4. Building your investment portfolio through smart diverse add-on investments such as property ownership, college savings funds, whole life insurance or others, will allow you to build financial wealth, further securing your financial future.

Securing Your Financial Future

You now understand something about the complexities of your multidimensional step-by-step strategy for managing short-term and long-term financial growth and wealth accumulation. Transfer the exercises you completed throughout this chapter into the general Financial Management and Growth section of your business plan (See Appendix A) for safekeeping. You need not follow these ideas to the letter. Hopefully reading this chapter and engaging in the exercises puts you in the right mindset and creates motivation and serious commitment toward a process of managing, saving, and investing that builds professional and personal sustainability.

Remember, you are not alone. The benefit of help is all around you. As you grow your practice and become more business wise, adding professionals in your support circle like a billing specialist, an accountant, a banker, a bookkeeper, a financial advisor, an insurance agent and others will help you reach your dreams of making a difference and creating a legacy in your profession, while safeguarding your loved ones at the same time.

CHAPTER TEN |
PROFESSIONAL DEVELOPMENT & BURNOUT AVOIDANCE

Have you ever asked yourself, "How am I going to be in it for the long haul?" "What do I need in order to manage through change, not burning out, and creating my own personal work/life balance?" Practice longevity and sustainability are achieved through multiple means. In this chapter, you will learn models for sustainability through avoiding burnout and continuing your professional education throughout your career. You will develop your own professional development and burnout avoidance plan to remind yourself about important practices and choices you can make as you age through your practice.

Over time, you will discover that thriving in practice gets more challenging as you grow older and changes in the industry multiply. New and creative interventions are constantly being fashioned by up-and-coming thinkers from younger generations while the elders of our industry cause shifts in our field through legacies left behind. Keeping up with change in the field while aging, and personally building your life in roles outside of your work is nonetheless challenging. The grind of life can be a great mountain to climb, even for the mentally and physically fittest.

BURNING UP AND NOT BURNING OUT

Many years ago, in the 1980's, when working at my summer camp as a teenager, the challenge of remaining motivated throughout the hot weeks of July and the intense 24/7 work environment and caring for the campers caused myself and many others to experience exhaustion, compassion fatigue, and even burnout. To properly paint the picture, understand that we weren't solving the world's problems by any stretch. Yet nearly all of the staff, myself included took our jobs VERY seriously, sometimes too seriously, and in fact all forms of losing energy described occurred.

That was 30 years ago, and the director of the summer camp had his own version of dealing with burnout. His voice and message gets replayed every time I find myself "burning out." One night, in mid-summer, amid the exhaustion, during our all-camp staff meeting on a Saturday night, the director pulled out a bunch of gimmicky items, including silly eyes, arrow-through-the-head hats, and other novelty toys as each staff member received their own. The experience instantly lifted everyone out of summer exhaustion, fatigue, and burnout. My impression that night included a firm message that when we burn out, we allow ourselves to be controlled by our own listlessness. However, when we "burn-up," we keep our flame alive by taking a different perspective and adding the right amount of wood to our flame as we continue burning, something you do in the form of counsel to your clients.

To this day, the director's message of finding a way to "burn-up" and not "burn-out" resonates in everything I do. I often rely on this message delivered nearly thirty years ago when it comes to giving my clients the same energy on Thursday afternoon as to those who saw me more rested on the Monday after a weekend. I rely on this message when I am down about referrals, or worried about my budget. I rely on it when I question my ethics, or my desire to be in this profession.

Burning up really means balancing and taking proper care. It's about being aware of when you are fatigued by the heaviness of your clients' stories, also known as compassion fatigue. It means recognizing when you are just plain exhausted and need a good night's sleep, even though you can't shut off the mind. Finally, it's knowing and honoring when you are burned out, and haven't allowed joy in your life as a result of long-term responsibilities and work stress.

As you well know, professional helpers are often the worst when it comes to self-care. While we are self-aware, we seem not to do the "self-care" part. Interesting, isn't it?

To survive and thrive in the short term and long haul of private practice, you must create healthy work/life balance. My recipe for burning up and not burning out involves four key elements I call *ZENS*.

DISCOVER YOUR ZENS

You need a fail-proof plan for managing compassion fatigue, avoiding burnout, and experiencing healthy work/life balance in the short term and throughout the course of your career as a helping professional. The following 4 key elements of self-care serve to help make you stronger and more resilient when it comes to the emotional and physical "human factors" of managing and growing your practice.

- **Zzzz's (Sleep)**—Sleep is an extremely important part of healthy functioning. Many people "burn the midnight oil," and sleep very little. Five to six hours a night or less is simply not enough sleep consistently. Those who don't get much sleep tend to be more fatigued and irritable during the day. Also, food cravings increase as quality and quantity of sleep decreases. Finally, poor sleep or not enough sleep can lead to memory and concentration problems, even depression or anxiety.

Sleep Recommendations:

1. 7–8 hours minimum each night before a work day.
2. Go to sleep around the same time each night and wake up around the same time each morning during the work week.
3. Try not to eat within two hours of going to bed (don't give in to nighttime food cravings).
4. Make sure your sleeping environment is calm, quiet, dark enough, and inviting for the relaxing practice of good sleep.
5. Make sure you have a comfortable sleeping surface, including mattress, bedding, and pillows.
6. If a warm shower before bed helps ready you for sleep, do so. Create a calming sleep preparation ritual, such as a warm shower, meditation, or soft music just before lights out.
7. Try to stay off technology, screens etc., during the hour before lights out.

- **Exercise**—What is your workout routine? How often do you exercise and for how long? Most of us in private practice sit in a chair for hours at a time. A sedentary lifestyle during your workweek is definitely not a recipe for a long and healthy life. Studies suggest that a lack of movement and routine exercise in sedentary jobs lead to chronic health problems and lower life expectancy. My suggestion for a longer and healthier life both at work and in life overall is routine exercise and lots of general movement.

Exercise & Movement Recommendations:

1. Try to do at least 30–45 minutes of aerobic/cardio exercise 3–4 times weekly.
2. Stretch your body before and after all workout sessions.
3. Create "movement moments" in-between clients where you stretch and move, such as going for a walk around the building, or if you have a little break in-between a few clients then stretch or run in place for a few moments.

4. If necessary, work with a professional trainer to help you stay in shape and learn how best to work on your physical health.
5. Join a class or sports activity that meets routinely to help with accountability.
6. Use muscles in your body that you wouldn't normally use. Hiking and climbing are good muscle exercises that also have aerobic benefit.
7. There are many mobile applications and devices for tracking progress. Download and use one to help you stay on track.

- **Nutrition**—What is your diet like these days? Are you a "stress eater," someone who eats emotionally and doesn't pay attention to what you are putting into your body? We live in a very health-conscious world when it comes to nutrition these days. You may even preach it in your clinical practice. But how often do you follow your own advice? Whether you pay little attention to what and how much you consume, or you are obsessed with healthy food, it's worth reflecting on unbalanced eating habits. Consider the following recommendations for embracing moderation and re-calibrating your daily nutritional needs.

Nutrition Recommendations:

1. Eat a good balance of healthy foods daily including one serving of fruit, plenty of vegetables, and plenty of protein.
2. Don't overdo it with sweets or heavy carbohydrates like pastas and breads, etc. . . .
3. Don't skip meals or deny yourself eating all day long. Better to eat several small healthy snacks spread throughout the day.
4. Drink plenty of water throughout the day.
5. Stay away from sugared drinks, including all colas.
6. Be mindful of your caffeine intake (caffeine takes 36 hours to fully metabolize in the body).
7. Do not eat late in the evening.
8. Consume alcohol in moderation.
9. If needed, work with a professional nutrition expert to help you stay on track.

- **Spirituality**—How do you replenish, recharge, and nurture your spirit? Has it been a long time since you have taken a vacation? Are you neglecting to take time for yourself because you are so used to helping others, both at work and while at home? If you are not nurturing your spirit enough or properly, you aren't alone. Many practice owners are so busy providing services, running the administrative aspects of the business, and helping with their own families that it's no wonder they can't find time to take a break, go on vacation, or even experience a moment of quiet solitude or partnership with loved ones. While each person is unique, and there are numerous methods of connecting spiritually, here are a few general guidelines to help you get started.

Nurturing the Spirit Recommendations:

1. Engage in a favorite hobby or activity routinely and deliberately.
2. Try a new hobby/activity once a year. If you like it stick with it.
3. If you are religious, take time routinely to connect and practice your religion.
4. Find quiet solitude and just "be" a little bit every day.
5. Get outside a little bit every day, even when it's cold or hot (just be safe about it).
6. Use meditation, yoga, mindfulness, massage or any other calming method that suits you, to connect spiritually.
7. Learn and practice cultural and family customs and rituals, alone, as a family, and within your community.

Finding your *ZENS* actually requires your keen thoughtful lens and a mindful presence of what makes you happy and relaxed. In this next exercise, look into these four areas of your life and jot down what's working well for you and what goals you might have to work on to change how you practice your *ZENS*.

EXERCISE 10.1 | Find Your ZENS!

For each of the following four areas, write what you already do that works, and what you'd like to do in the future to change and/or improve upon your ZENS balance.

ZENS	WHAT I DO NOW	MY NEW GOALS
Z'S(SLEEP)	1. 2. 3. 4. 5.	1. 2. 3. 4. 5.
EXERCISE	1. 2. 3. 4. 5.	1. 2. 3. 4. 5.
NUTRITION	1. 2. 3. 4. 5.	1. 2. 3. 4. 5.
SPIRITUAL	1. 2. 3. 4. 5.	1. 2. 3. 4. 5.

MENTORSHIP

Take a moment and think of how you ended up where you are right now. You didn't get there alone. Whether you are starting your practice, or reading this book to revamp and/or grow in a different direction, others helped you get to where you are today. Mentors are an important component to your success. Past, present and future mentors are necessary, in my opinion.

While previous mentors may not now actively give you advice, your memory and awareness of lessons learned are crucial to success. Personally, for example, countless mentors from my past taught me relevant lessons along the way in my journey. These included former directors, supervisors, professors, therapists, camp counselors, rabbis, authors, coaches, colleagues, friends, parents' friends, family, and others. Their messages resonate today perhaps even louder and more significantly when compared to hearing them in my stubborn younger mind.

EXERCISE 10.2 | My Past Mentors

Take some time think about your past mentors, who they are, what you learned from them, and how their message might help you in your private practice. Write down your top three as a way of getting started with awareness of past mentors.

PAST MENTOR #1:

Mentor Name: _____

What I learned:_____

How it applies to my practice: _____

_____

PAST MENTOR #2:

Mentor Name: _____

What I learned:_____

How it applies to my practice: _____

_____

PAST MENTOR #3:

Mentor Name: _____

What I learned:_____

How it applies to my practice: _____

_____

Current mentors are extremely helpful as well. Consider them as the "go to" people upon whom you can rely in the here and now when it comes to needed advice. Sometimes, these individuals are the very professionals you might pay to help your practice function. Others include those who are in private practice that you trust, even those who may not be practicing in the field. It's good to have different people from variant careers and fresh perspectives in your corner. If you don't already have a diverse network of a few important mentors currently in your life, you might be missing out on needed and relevant advice.

EXERCISE 10.3 | My Current Mentors

Now, list your top three current mentors, what you are learning, and how it applies to your practice.

CURRENT MENTOR #1:

Mentor Name: _____

What I am learning: _____

How it applies to my practice: _____

_____

CURRENT MENTOR #2:

Mentor Name: _____

What I am learning: _____

How it applies to my practice: _____

_____

CURRENT MENTOR #3:

Mentor Name: _____

What I am learning: _____

How it applies to my practice: _____

_____

Future mentors are waiting for you! Though it may be hard to believe, you are actually ripe for meeting new people along the way who will become important in your practice and career development. Pay attention with an open mind and your thirst for learning and you will find the next new mentor, whether it be to help you with some aspect of your business, hone a clinical skill, or provide you with the next needed life lesson that you can implement into your practice.

EXERCISE 10.4 | My Future Mentors

Write three names of individuals or types of people with whom you'd like to learn who don't currently mentor you. Write what you'd like to learn, and make a commitment for when you will contact and/or search for this individual.

FUTURE MENTOR #1:

Mentor Name: _____

What I want to learn: _____

How it might apply to my practice: _____

_____

FUTURE MENTOR #2:

Mentor Name: _____

What I want to learn: _____

How it might apply to my practice: _____

_____

FUTURE MENTOR #3:

Mentor Name: _____

What I want to learn: _____

How it might apply to my practice: _____

_____

PROFESSIONAL DEVELOPMENT

Your ongoing development as a professional includes formal and informal training, education, and even certification beyond your graduate level training. Many states require a minimum number of continuing education clock hours in order to maintain a professional license. In addition to licensure maintenance, your overall clinical competency and business credibility hinges upon continued professional development training and your general experience.

EXERCISE 10.5 | Professional Development Seminars

List three formal clinical training topics you'd like to learn about and attend either as a live seminar or a video training within the next 12 months:

1 _____

2 _____

3 _____

It's important to improve your knowledge about new and innovative therapeutic approaches, how theories change, and know the latest research in your interest area. Equally important are the informal ways we learn. Reading journals, participating in a peer supervision group, and collaborating professionally with colleagues on special projects such as running a group experience are all examples of how to keep the professional growth moving in a forward and upward direction.

EXERCISE 10.6 | Other Professional Development Activities

Write down five activities you'd like to engage in throughout the year that will help you grow professionally. Activities can include reading a book (name the book if you can or the subject/interest area).

1 _____

2 _____

3 _____

4 _____

5 _____

In addition to professional clinical training, it is important to engage in routine business training, whether formal, informal or both. Formal business training in private practice can be found everywhere these days. In addition to this very book, you will find experts like me in just about every state. Business experts in the helping profession each have their own unique lens and a lot of experience to back up their knowledge base. You can learn something of value from just about any of us and maybe something unique from every one of us. Some experts emphasize marketing, while others focus on clinical excellence. There are private practice consultants who have one specialization like online marketing, or making the most of social media presence. Still others offer the full range of practice training tools. Some, like me, offer one-to-one private consulting, while others offer "consulting memberships." Many provide hands-on group trainings. And, you can now find numerous books, audio CDs, and videos on the topic of business improvements.

The important piece is making sure that you find someone to learn from who is a good fit for you. Not every private practice expert will be the right fit. All you need is one really good business expert who is knowledgeable and supportive, has excellent hands-on practice tools (like some in this book), and the other professional supports already discussed.

The main point is in attending to your business training side on an ongoing basis. This book, while comprehensive, should certainly not be your only source of business advice throughout your career in private practice. One practice owner with whom I consult shares that she continues to seek new tools and ways to innovate her practice even though she's already well on her path to success. Though she no longer "needs" private consulting for business development, she still meets with me twice per year for practice updates, business maintenance, growth, and development planning.

EXERCISE 10.7 | Ongoing Private Practice Development Trainings

Write down three specific or general topics you'd like to learn more about when it comes to the business side of growing and managing your practice.

1 _____

2 _____

3 _____

The Three Rs

Managing compassion fatigue, avoiding burnout, developing a solid mentorship program, and building a great professional development plan will help you immensely as you journey through your private practice. While you boldly grow into a confident role as business owner and professional helper, it's important to pay attention to the three R's . . . *Risk, Record and Remember.*

- *Risk*—No good comes from sitting back in your seat and not trying. In baseball, managers don't like to see their batters striking out without swinging. And, a great batting average is .300! This mean that you actually don't get on base due to hitting the ball 7 out of 10 tries at home plate. And, only very rarely are you going to hit that "home run." Most people don't risk enough because they don't like to experience more failure than success, and many are too focused on hitting the homerun. The result is not trying consistently or worse, giving up entirely. So the next time you are faced with an opportunity, take the risk, knowing that you may fail more than once, and learn until one of these risks turns out to be a "base hit." I always say to my students, consultation clients, and trainees the following:

"Failure is the road to success. Risk is the engine. You are the driver!"

- ***Record***—As you are taking these risks, failure or success, write them down. Invest $8 in a journal, or simply type your risks and how each turns out in document on your computer or tablet. Why? Writing down what you plan to do, then doing it, and then recording the outcome of each experience, keeps a living log of your business decisions and outcomes. It's nearly impossible to document every risk or business decision. However, when you keep a log of the relevant choices and risks as well as an "outcome" ledger, you are creating a historical archive of what works and what doesn't which comes in handy as a partial basis for future decisions.

- ***Remember***—Your written record serves a dual purpose. In addition to guiding your future, you must remember your decisions so that you don't make the same mistake twice or more. When you know what works, you will want to repeat that recipe for success as often as you can until it doesn't work well enough anymore. Creating that record helps you remember. Practicing good business decisions also helps you remember. This last step requires a high degree of precision mindfulness, the very kind of awareness you may teach a client to help improve a clinical problem.

CHAPTER ELEVEN |
REAL CLINICIANS, REAL STORIES

I wouldn't want you to simply take my "expert" word for it when it comes to practice building. As I just mentioned near the end of the previous chapter there are many professional business-building experts in our field these days. But, perhaps the most valuable people you can learn from aren't actual experts. They are the common clinicians hanging a shingle on main street, perhaps even near you. You can and should learn from other professionals like you who experienced start-up, growth, management, failure, and success in their own respective practices. This chapter is dedicated to you the reader and those practice owners who work tirelessly to give to their clients while building and growing business in an honorable and ethical manner.

As I was finalizing my outline for this book, my assistant, Veronica, and I were wondering how to properly represent what many go through in their process of practice start-up and development. We came up with a great idea to ask real practitioners who are already in practice to share their stories. So, in an informal online survey, we asked practice owners a series of questions relevant to their practice building philosophy and process. The responses were amazing. They were so honest and helpful that I am now looking into compiling them into a separate book next year. In the meantime, enjoy learning about our survey and what we learned, while getting to know a few of our respondents throughout this chapter.

FINDINGS FROM THE PRIVATE PRACTICE SURVEY

We had over 35 people respond to our survey asking them about their experience building and maintaining private practice and the answers were insightful. You can find the questions we asked listed at the end of the chapter. The clinicians who responded had both diverse and common experiences in their journeys. The range of time in private practice varied from those who recently hung their shingles; 5 respondents were in practice less than a year, to clinicians who made private practice their life-long career; 10 were in private practice over 20 years with 2 of those in practice for 40 years.

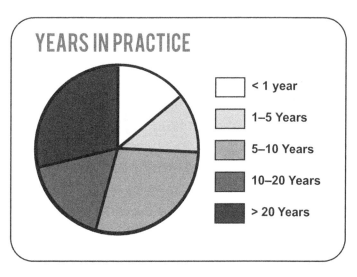

As you know, location is one important factor when choosing where to start. We don't always get to choose where we end up geographically; some of that is happenstance or dependent on other factors such as our family or partner or even where we went to graduate school. The clinicians in our survey live in geographically diverse areas, and many are from Colorado considering it's our home area. We heard from people as far north as Ontario and Toronto Canada and many U.S. practice owners from areas on the East Coast, including New York, New Hampshire, Virginia, North Carolina, the South and Southwest, including Florida, Texas, Arizona, and places in the West including California and Washington.

PHILOSOPHY AND GUIDING PRINCIPLES

One of our first curiosities was the philosophy, mind-set, guiding principles, values and/or beliefs practitioners hold about being successful in their private practice.

While it might be obvious considering we are in the business of helping others that one of the main themes noted by several practitioners was the importance they placed on keeping clients' wellbeing at the forefront of their minds in all aspects of practice, from their own clinical training and preparedness to how business-related transactions are handled and communicated. Maintaining a working balance and understanding both the clinical/healing and business sides of private practice was given much emphasis. Furthermore, finding a niche and an area of passion in the field, and pursuing it in a creative and value-driven way were tantamount to having a successful practice.

In the process of finding and knowing your niche, three key words came up frequently throughout the responses: patience, persistence, and perspective. Clinicians spoke to creating patience with practice building while maintaining trust and understanding that clients, referrals, and connections will come in the right time. Numerous responses throughout identified the idea of persistence and how valuable it is to nurture and engender a willingness to try new things, discovering a process that works for you and your clients while on the other hand keeping flexibility and openness to start over or do something different for the benefit of the your clients, you as a clinician, and your business.

> *"Connection in itself is healing." I explain to my clients I am a partner in their journey. They bring their expertise on them and their world, I bring my listening skills, experience, and training. Therapy is done with someone not to someone.*
>
> *-Philip J. Fauerbach, LMHC*

> *Be yourself and your clients will love you for it. Trying to be all things to all clients or imitating another clinician in your town isn't going to give you the thriving practice that you want. Clients won't believe that you can help them live an authentic life if you're coming across incongruent.*
>
> *-Tammy Whitten, LMFT*

The importance of staying connected became clear in the responses. Many clinicians spoke about connection with regard to traditional ways of networking and marketing in the community via presentations, meet and greets, and more recent trends of staying connected online through websites, social media, and blogs. Others shared about connection on a spiritual level such as how this process is at the core of therapy and guides the development of practice. Lastly on the topic of what brought clinicians practice success, almost every therapist who responded commented that, at the heart of what they do and how they practice, they are true to themselves and their values, and by giving themselves the permission to "just be yourself" they are modeling and creating safety and acceptance for their clients. This advice seems to be the Golden Rule of practice success.

FINANCIAL PRACTICES AND PROFITABILITY

In addition to learning about overall philosophy, we wanted to understand the business and logistical side of practitioner experience. One of the main concerns of many heading into and already in practice centers around finances and how quickly profit comes. Good news! The responses from the clinicians just might assuage some of your fears. Over half of the respondents reported they hit their "break-even" point in one year or less after hanging their shingles. Roughly one quarter of the participants reported hitting their "break-even point" between 2–4 years; however, they explained contributing factors of either other life circumstances or only being in private practice part time. Several clinicians saw a profit early on due to keeping their expenses at a minimum while others credit their immediate return on investment to being well connected within their community, leading to a steady stream of referrals.

FACING CHALLENGES

Eager to learn about the challenges faced along the way and how owners managed or are still managing through them, we asked participants to share their trials and tribulations. Some of the common over-arching challenges faced by practitioners included managing the financial aspects of the business, marketing and networking, person-of-therapist issues, and balancing home and work life. When it comes to finances and other business-related aspects some therapists recognize how their own limited knowledge and training in these areas may create a steep learning curve. Numerous clinicians spoke to being comfortable with money, charging a reasonable fee and that for better or for worse insurance companies played a role in that journey for them. It became clear from the responses that practitioners who work directly with insurance companies seem to experience a love-hate relationship dynamic. Many clinicians chose to engage with insurance companies in order to build their referrals and caseloads, broadening the accessibility of their services. Others shared that they decided to forgo working with insurance in order to have more autonomy and flexibility.

Another frequently-mentioned challenge was the continual and ever-changing face of marketing and networking. For some individuals, this part of their practice has been intimidating while others have come to embrace it, as it has become simply a part of who they are in their

> *I was fortunate in the early phases. There was a need in the community for the services I offered and I was invited to go into practice by a colleague who provided a steady stream of referrals. It has been my experience that 2–3 key relationships of cross referring has provided a strong core to my practice.*
>
> *-Kathy Naman, MA, LPC*

> *Boulder has many many therapists and healers. It was extremely helpful taking courses to define a niche, and to craft my website content so that the people I worked with best could find me. For me, the other challenge is around fees. I have been slow to increase my fees and about a third of my practice is insurance based. I could probably drop the insurance panels. But I don't because they are folks who would not usually seek services. It feels wrong to me to not make space for them. At least so far.*
>
> *-Kathy Naman, MA, LPC*

> *The building part has become less difficult, in that I understand the value and necessity of networking, networking, and networking! Getting out there in front of treatment facilities, other clinicians, and just the general public has become second nature to me. The maintenance is about recognizing there are always going to be ebbs and flows in the practice, and that it's always necessary to engage and attract more clients.*
>
> *-Valerie J. Shinbaum, MS, LPC, MAC, NCC*

community. Additionally, one of the biggest challenges noted was keeping up the motivation to market and network even during times of managing a full case load while also keeping up with how marketing and networking change over the years toward in-person and online. Other clinicians shared how some of their challenges in starting the journey of private practice dealt with understanding their own self-doubts, figuring out how to get out of their own way, and creating a space mentally, physically, spiritually, and relationally in which they could thrive. Lastly, on the topic of early challenges of practice development, many respondents spoke to the ongoing need to exercise intention around how they manage their time in their work and at home so that they can be their best selves for their families and their clients.

After probing about past challenges in the beginning phases, we asked about the current challenges with continuing the building and maintaining of their private practices. These two questions, asked sequentially, invited the respondents to reflect on their own growth, change, and development in a 'then versus now' perspective. The answers received were quite interesting. Responses to the challenges faced in the beginning were similar to many that were illuminated in the struggles faced when expanding the reach and growing their practice in later parts of the journey. A notable theme transpired around learning your ideal client and figuring out how to attract that ideal client by making solid connections with various referral sources to help build a steady flow of ideal clients.

> *The biggest challenge I faced in building my private practice was my own self-doubt. Challenges I have faced in maintaining my private practice is keeping a strong balance between work and fun. The busier I got at work, the more important it was to have fun and rejuvenate myself. That can be a challenge for me as I love what I do and have a difficult time saying "no" to exciting business opportunities.*
>
> *-Barbara Sheehan-Zeidler, MA, LPC*

> *I have identified my preference for "ideal" clients. That doesn't mean I don't have other types of clients in my practice, but for me there are certain types of clients with whom I work best. The challenge therefore is to stay open to all clients in the hope of attracting a majority of those "ideal" clients.*
>
> *- Valerie J. Shinbaum, MS, LPC, MAC, NCC*

> *"Time! There are so many fun things that you can do in private practice. There will never be enough time to do all of the wonderful things that are available to us and our clients."*
>
> *-Tammy Whitten, LMFT*

Several of the respondents shared that building referral relationships with other practitioners and helping professionals in one's community is not only a time-consuming venture but also a process of persistence and patience. Time management came up in many responses as we are reminded of the value and importance of finding a way that works in terms of scheduling your week, determining your priorities and setting aside time to do things that are of value and meaning both at work and home. Several clinicians mentioned how the challenge of not having enough time impacts their goals of diversifying their private practices and giving time and energy to other projects and interests in the field.

The challenge of practicing healthy boundaries, in terms of knowing one's own limits around whom you can help, how you can help, and how many people you can help was another theme. There were clinicians who verbalized challenges around working with insurance companies and trying to make the change to a primarily fee for service practice.

The challenge of licensure and portability when relocating and setting up practice in another state was also voiced. And, as you may imagine, looking to move to another state and continue practicing is a major challenge in terms of figuring out how to proceed. Diane Shelton, a clinician who closed her practice in April of 2015 after being in private practice for 17 years in Colorado, Arizona, California, and Connecticut gives a response to this challenge, highlighting the skill and necessity of learning how to be creative, flexible, and willing to adapt one's business and private practice in order to keep doing what one loves. *"Irregularity in licensing . . . Florida does not recognize the CPQ and has differing PRE doctoral requirements, so getting licensed after moving here was going to require me enrolling in a program, after being licensed in FOUR other states, a nearly 20-year career with a perfectly clean record and volumes of experience. So, I shifted my direction and am using my experience to continue to serve others via coaching. My style as a therapist is well suited for the change, but it requires diligent education to differentiate coaching from therapy, for both potential clients as well as other professionals. I'm currently working beautifully with a client who is in therapy, and I consult with her therapist regularly. The coaching, especially with my clinical experience, is really augmenting her therapy and she's making terrific progress"* —Diane Shelton, PsyD

> *If a psychotherapist has solid strong ethics, and integrity, there will be clients that you have to refer, for one reason or another. That can take a sudden huge bite out of income that you weren't expecting. I think that it takes quite a bit of time to build a private practice that can sustain you financially. I don't have a sliding scale and I don't offer a free first session. Figuring out my business practices around these important issues was hard, but I decided that I had to be comfortable with my business practice in those areas. I find that out of session time takes longer than I would have expected it to, and that is not paid time.*
>
> *-Anonymous, Ontario*

TURNING POINTS IN PRACTICE

Hearing about what clinicians have and continue to find challenging in the building and maintaining of their private practice should shed some light on what you might end up facing in your own process. It can be comforting to realize that you aren't alone in your struggles. Our hope is that some of our participants' truth and wisdom empowers and encourages you to continue on your journey and recognize that, for many out there, success is in private practice is a moving target and often a matter of "trial and error." The responses we heard from clinicians asking about a few of the most critical and/or relevant turning points in their private practice building process revealed just that. When asked about critical turning points, many of the answers we received took on the theme of being open and willing to take risks, performing leaps of faith, and trusting one's intuition when making business and life decisions, ultimately leading them in a meaningful direction. The "turning point" responses focused around three main topics: finding one's niche, building a solid web presence, and building a marketing, networking, and referral process that works. Here are some of the responses we received, categorized by those three topics.

It's All About the Niche

"Deciding on a niche!. When this happened I felt focused, I found peace, and I had direction. I was able to really direct my marketing efforts and my training, and my interactions with my clients improved because I had a model to follow." —Shauna Cavalli, LPC

Online Is Where It's At

"One of the earliest critical turning points was when I invested my marketing budget wisely and hired a web developer. Prior to hiring him, I had designed my own website with zero education and, no surprise to me now, I had no clients contact me. After hiring the web developer and learning as much as I could about creating great content and user friendly web pages, I had six phone calls in one week. Within a month I had 15 regular clients. A later turning point in building my private practice was when I became trained in an evidence-based, trauma focused protocol. This distinguished me from my peers and began my professional identity as a trauma-focused, trauma-informed therapist." —Barbara Sheehan-Zeidler, MA, LPC

"Getting my first website up that was powerful, comprehensive, beautiful and something I could be proud of was the first big step in month two of year one. An important step in year two was focusing on what I love and am best at and owning this boldly." —Laureli Shimayo

It Works, If You Work It . . . the Referral Wheel That Is

"The first (turning point) was learning how to set fees properly, by making a real budget and figuring out what the *numbers* (not other therapists or clients) say is an appropriate fee. The second was learning how to approach possible referral sources with an authentic goal of figuring out how I can help them. It took me a while to realize that the expertise I have is actually *needed* by lots of professional folks. So I wasn't just begging for referrals. I was providing important services and spreading an important message, which naturally led to referrals." —Peg Shippert, MA, LPC

"I attended an ethics training early in my practice as is required in Florida. The speaker talked about one of the greatest frustrations of referral sources, especially from the medical field, is a lack of information. He suggested that I contact each physician, with appropriate authorization, on a monthly basis and give them feedback on the progress the client is making and develop a partnership. My initial reaction was, "yeah, right; a physician is going to take my feedback." Actually the psychiatrists loved it. We now do bi-monthly phone conferences after I emailed them the list of clients I wanted to speak to them about. PCPs, psychiatrists, and pediatricians responded well, we each had our charts in front of us and discussed treatment and progress. That single action of partnering built my practice to a point that I had a waiting list in 18 months." —Philip J. Fauerbach, LMHC

WHAT I LEARNED ON THE JOURNEY

Beyond learning about major turning points clinicians experienced along the way, we wanted to know more about what our respondents learned in their own process of private practice development and asked them to narrow it down to three key points. Here are just some responses of what they learned along the way:

- Make sure the place where you have your office is safe for you and your clients. My first office experience in Colorado was in a toxic environment for me and felt by some of my clients. Be careful in setting up your office environment, and take the time to find that safe space. (Valerie J .Shinbaum, MS, LPC, MAC, NCC)

- Have a good theory of psychopathology and treatment (Susan Heitler, PhD)

- Letting people know what I do and how I do it clearly and simply. (Sandy Jardine, M.S., LPC Certified Emotionally Focused Therapist and Supervisor)

- The best liability insurance, first and foremost, is communicating with your clients. I have always remembered that. Because of the nature and parameters of the relationship, there is no client relationship that is not immersed in countertransference. It's a business and it is my livelihood. (Kathy Naman, MA, LPC)

- Specialize, specialize, specialize. Find your niche, get as much training as possible and sharpen your skills. You cannot be all things to all people and will dilute your therapy by being a generalist. See your client as a person first and a client second. Build on your connection skills as a partner in treatment not a superior. I often joke that I always ask, "What was today like for you?" not because I am insecure but I want to do my best that they walk out of my office better than they walked in. (Philip J. Fauerbach, LMHC)

- Know why you are doing this and don't let others judge you by their standards. (The Rev. Christopher L. Smith, LCAC, LMHC, LMFT)

- Don't be afraid to invest in yourself and your business. From the furniture that is comfy and cozy for sitting . . . to the software to really be able to run your practice easily. Be careful with advertising. Don't use words like "free" and be stingy with your time. Free phone or office consults can result in people wanting free sessions and not understanding that difference. Guard your time and your knowledge and be aware of how you share these things in any advertising that you do. Remember: there's a difference in marketing and advertising. (Tammy Whitten, LMFT)

- Have cards at all times, because you never know who you may run into. (Penny Dahlen, Ed.D., LPC)

- Don't be afraid to be a salesperson. (Emily Marquis)

- Be true to yourself and don't let anyone take advantage of your license, you have worked really hard for it. (Nancy Gunzner, MS, MA, LMFT, CACII)

- Having a trusted psychiatrist and other mental health therapists available for consultation when needed. (Janet G. Nestor, MA, LPC, DCEP)

- Just because you open a private practice and are good at what you do, does not mean that people will flock to you. It's important to get the word out to people and other professionals. (Carol Torgerson)

- Adapt your marketing to your community. (Anne Goshen)

IF I KNEW THEN WHAT I KNOW NOW

We also knew that with time comes wisdom and that with many life journeys—including the process of building a private practice—there are some things that you don't know and *can't* know until you've walked that journey. We asked our respondents to reflect on what they now know that they wished they would have known much earlier along the journey in private practice. The responses we received were pretty incredible as they highlight how making the choice to be in private practice and build a career as a mental health professional is all at once demanding and inspiring, life giving, and humbling. If they had only known then what they know now:

- Growth doesn't happen every year and there are years when you take a step back. (Richard Huttner)

- I wish I had listened to the advice about choosing a specialty, and not worried so much about choosing the "right" specialty. (Anonymous)

- That building a good website was imperative! Going the cheap route cost me time and money! (Leah Leynor, MA, LMFTA, LMBT)

- Be prepared to say no to a prospective client when you smell trouble—there are nice ways to say no. (Anonymous)

- Business skills are essential—As essential as being a skillful therapist. (Sandy Jardine)

- Block off time every week for organizing, planning, and marketing activities. Stick to these, just as if they were a session. (Tammy Whitten, LMFT)

- How to be very direct about financial matters and to set clear practice boundaries with clients immediately. (Anonymous)

- Don't always trust that people will do the right thing regarding paying you for services, (Donna Schwartz, MA, CAC III)

- It'll be okay; actually, better than okay! You are supported with each step you dare to take so it's okay to dare yourself a little bit a little more often. (Barbara Sheehan-Zeidler, MA, LPC)

- Take your time; be cautious when people ask you to see difficult clients. (Nancy Gunzner, MS, MA, LMFT, CACII)

- The importance of networking. (Anonymous)

- That it is ok not to have a sliding scale but instead set a fee that you can live on and create an ideal client so all of your marketing and networking is reaching out to them. (Robbin Rockett, Psy.D)

BALANCE AND BURNOUT PREVENTION

In case you haven't noticed from what you've heard from the clinicians who responded to our survey, it is clear that building a private practice and serving the community is demanding on many different levels and in various ways. We found ourselves curious about how these helping professionals choose to manage those demands and what they do to nurture and sustain themselves both in and out of the office. There were many commonalities in the responses in both categories.

In terms of what is most significant and meaningful in tending to one's professional side of self-care as it relates to private practice, the following points were emphasized: Clinicians realize that finding other outlets and making time to do other things besides seeing clients all day is energizing, allows them to access other parts of their professional interests, prevents burnout, and keeps them connected to colleagues and the field in meaningful ways. Some of the outlets that were mentioned included: teaching, mentoring or providing supervision, speaking and/or presenting at conferences, and being active in networking and supervision groups.

> *I have a private practice and I teach and supervise. Creating a niche and reducing my private practice hours has allowed me to continue to be available for my children and not burn out.*
>
> *-Robbin Rockett, Psy.D*

Numerous mental health professionals underscored the importance of keeping firm boundaries around the hours and days they spend seeing clients and being strict about not going outside those boundaries. "It is very hard. I could work 100 hours a week if I wanted to. I have set personal boundaries and block off specific time while repeating affirmations."—Emily Marquis

Repeatedly, the concept of having clarity and a strong awareness of one's own limits; knowing who they want to help, how they want to help and why; and having an understanding of their own expectations and needs as a clinician came up in the responses. Knowing how and being comfortable with these areas allows them to run their practice in alignment with their own values and ethics.

When it came to reflecting on what sustains clinicians in their personal lives, it was clear from the responses that practicing what we preach and modeling for our clients in own lives what we are helping them do for themselves is paramount. The three primary ways these clinicians keep themselves grounded in their personal lives are through hobbies, making self-care and "me-time" a priority, and having a strong support system in their family and friend group. Below are some quotes from the respondents about their personal self-care approach.

> *I have a very specific niche, which helps with so many things: self confidence, picking appropriate training, effective marketing and networking, ending up with clients who I can really help, etc.*
>
> *-Peg Shippert,* MA, LPC

> *I have learned to say "no" to some referrals*
>
> *-Zena Havelock,* MSW

- I love what I do. This is what sustains me the most. I feel energized doing my work. I do other things as I want to. I trust this balance. —Laureli Shimayo

- I am a yoga teacher and my own practice is really important and helpful. I also need to connect with other people who understand me and support me, so I have to build that in. I have definitely found that private practice feels lonely and I have to be strategic in getting in time with friends and supports.—Jamie Justus, LCSW, RYT

- I pay attention to my body and certain traits that show up letting me know I am working too hard and need to back it down. —Philip J. Fauerbach, LMHC

- Know your limits and respect what you need. Consider all dimensions of your life and regularly evaluate how balanced you are. If you need to, use others for accountability.—The Rev. Christopher L. Smith, LCAC, LMHC, LMFT

PRIVATE PRACTICE REFLECTIONS AND ADVICE

The final question we asked in our survey invited clinicians to reflect on their experience and journey in private practice as a whole. While it is often not the case that clinicians give advice to their clients, we were eager to know what advice they could offer practitioners getting started with their practice building process. The responses we received were inspiring and reveal the passion and drive behind people who choose to go into private practice. The advice was not only encouraging and empowering to others struggling to get their feet steady in their business, it was also practical and constructive. The overarching themes mentioned were to surround yourself with the support you need on the business and clinical side of things by getting good clinical supervision, hiring a billing specialist and accountant, finding a mentor, and connecting with other mental health professionals to build strong networking, marketing, and referral relationships. In addition, the responses encouraged clinicians to get the training needed to have a practice that you feel confident in, using both your business and clinical skills. In other words the learning is never done. Lastly, we heard from numerous practitioners urging patience and trust in the process of practice building. There were other pieces of advice given from our respondents that could not simply be summarized and doing so would detract from their power, so we decided to include more direct quotes from the clinicians who so generously shared their experiences with us.

- Get clear about what you want. It's hard to ignore the voices that tell you you shouldn't want it, can't achieve it, etc. Then make a plan. Persist. When things don't work out, regroup, change the plan and keep moving. Get comfortable with money. You can get there.—Stephen Adair Vernon, MFT

- Seek your own therapy as a client. It will be the greatest gift you give yourself. Form a peer consultation/support group. You cannot do this alone. Examine and heal your relationship with money. Learn basic business skills. Do what you love. Understand your limits = respect your energy. Find some way to undo the damage of sitting. Keep learning. Ask for help. Take time to rest, relax and renew.—Anonymous

- Give yourself time to build a practice. Don't expect it to happen overnight. Be realistic with your income goals. Continue to hone your skills and to pick your specialty. You don't do yourself or your clients any favors by trying to be all things to all people. Focus on those issues and groups that you are passionate about and expect that to vary some over the course of your practice. Have some friends that you can share with. It's hard building a business. It's scary, and you face your own fears and weaknesses about yourself. Even if these friends are in other fields, use them to help encourage each other on the hard days. Learn about building a business. Look at things on mental health private practices and from the business world. In graduate school, you learned the basics on how to help people. But you didn't learn anything on how to build a private practice. And even if you did take a course on it (if you were lucky enough to have one available in your grad school program), consider the source. Is the person teaching it as a successful private practice owner, one who can solely rely on their practice for their income? Or are they someone who's been in academia for the majority of their career? Things change in the business world a lot.—The Rev. Christopher L. Smith, LCAC, LMHC, LMFT

- Stay true to yourself. Follow your heart's intuition. Use an online management program for notes, scheduling, etc. Be flexible, and be gentle with yourself. Not everything that works for someone else will work for you. Allow yourself room to try things, make mistakes, and try again. Allow yourself to grow as a practitioner and as a business person. Don't expect perfection. Find a tribe. It can be online or in person, but align your self with a group with similar values and similar situations/circumstances. Try a few to see what works, and don't feel bad if some of them don't work out.—Tammy Whitten, LMFT

- If it's a calling and you are spiritually open and seeking, it's amazing what and who shows up when you least expect it. Get to know marketers of treatment centers who are networkers extraordinaire!—Anonymous

- Realize that this is your livelihood, and treat it like the business that it is. Charge a fair fee for your skill, give some time away to those in need, and set money aside for the future as well. Too many therapists don't know how to think about money, and so they don't succeed. It is possible to be an excellent therapist, and a financially successful therapist.—Shauna Cavalli, LPC

Note to the reader: These practice owners took time and made themselves quite vulnerable in sharing their experiences of their journey into and through private practice. We are extremely grateful to all who participated in the survey.

CHAPTER TWELVE |
THE ULTIMATE ENTREPRENEUR

By now, you've learned so many different lessons about what it takes to successfully start, manage, and even improve your practice. Congratulations on your work thus far. Now, we're going to bring it all together, which is why there is one thing I don't want you to EVER forget—that you started this whole journey because you want to make a difference in the lives of those you help and those who benefit from those you help. In doing so, whether you are willing to take credit or not, you are indeed creating a legacy.

Your legacy hinges on becoming "entrepreneurial" in a way not generally associated with the word. Entrepreneurs are commonly thought of as creating a business at great financial risk. You should redefine the word to mean something much more than taking a financial risk to grow your business. While the entrepreneur is simply a businessperson wired to build and measure success financially, the *ultimate entrepreneur* is much more.

This is why I want you to seriously think about your legacy. What impression would you like to leave when you are all done working in your field as a private practitioner? As you read this last chapter, think about your own motto for success and the legacy that is yours. One day you will leave your beloved practice and when you do, you want to leave the field better than when you arrived, hopefully with the pride and humility that you added something from your corner in the world.

To become your own ultimate entrepreneur means thinking multi-dimensionally, practicing proper diversified decision-making strategies in many areas, risking, failing, and constantly refining and redefining. Let's look at the key steps for making this happen.

DIVERSIFICATION OVER TIME

I promised to emphasize diversification as a meaningful and important part of business building. People are different when it comes to their own process of diversification. You may be ready to build a website sooner than your colleague down the hall. Your colleague may diversify in their services by offering groups before you figure out that you are ready to start a therapy group. Remember, you are the decision-maker of your own diversification process, and it's okay to hold off if you want, or to move forward when you may not be entirely ready. Either way, you will learn and your practice will adjust over time. Just make sure your risks and diversifications are not so far out of your comfort zone that you cannot recover. That's why I refer to these decisions as "calculated" risks.

The next charts show many of the areas in which you learned where and how to diversify. The work you do preparing for diversified business movement is essential to being an ultimate entrepreneur and creating your legacy as a professional in practice.

FIGURE 12.1 | Eleven Areas of Diversification

The 11 areas are core to the foundation of your practice.

SERVICES **CLINICAL** **MARKETING** **NETWORKING**

PROFESSIONAL SUPPORT **SYSTEMS OF ORGANIZATION** **ASSET PROTECTION** **ASSET GROWTH**

PROFESSIONAL TRAINING **WORK/LIFE BALANCE** **PERSONAL INTERESTS**

FIGURE 12.2 | Diversification Examples

Below are three samples in each core area.

SERVICES
1. Relationship Counseling
2. Men's Individual Counseling
3. Family Counseling

CLINICAL
1. Depression & Anxiety
2. Emotional Trauma
3. Child/Adolescent Development

MARKETING
1. Website
2. Blog
3. Business Cards

NETWORKING
1. Visit Physician Offices and provide Lunch and Learns
2. Create a consultation group
3. Network at professional conferences

PROFESSIONAL SUPPORT
1. Attorney
2. Medical Biller
3. Accountant

SYSTEMS OF ORGANIZATION
1. Monthly Tracking Form
2. Electronic Calendar
3. Medical Record Keeping

ASSET PROTECTION
1. Limited Liability Company (LLC)
2. Malpractice Insurance
3. Other Insurances

ASSET GROWTH
1. Retirement Savings
2. College Savings
3. Property Ownership

PROFESSIONAL TRAINING
1. Mindfulness Training
2. Relationship Intervention Training
3. Trauma Intervention Training

PERSONAL INTERESTS
1. Exercise/Outdoors
2. Travel
3. Writing/Speaking

WORK/LIFE BALANCE
1. Family and Friends
2. Develop weekly schedule
3. Carve out time for hobbies

The example above is really a starting point for going into greater depth. The more you define and refine your core areas, the better your overall business plan. You can use this exercise as a separate business plan or integrate it into the body of your overall plan. You can take any of these objectives and expand further, delineating steps you must take to reach a particular goal in each area.

EXERCISE 12.1 | Diversification Examples

In each of the 11 areas, make a diversification outline of at least three goals in each area.
You can use information from previous exercises.

SERVICES

1. _____
2. _____
3. _____

CLINICAL

1. _____
2. _____
3. _____

MARKETING

1. _____
2. _____
3. _____

NETWORKING

1. _____
2. _____
3. _____

PROFESSIONAL SUPPORT

1. _____
2. _____
3. _____

SYSTEMS OF ORGANIZATION

1. _____
2. _____
3. _____

ASSET PROTECTION

1. _____
2. _____
3. _____

ASSET GROWTH

1. _____
2. _____
3. _____

PROFESSIONAL TRAINING

1. _____
2. _____
3. _____

PERSONAL INTERESTS

1. _____
2. _____
3. _____

WORK/LIFE BALANCE

1. _____
2. _____
3. _____

> ## EXERCISE 12.2 | Diversification Timeline
>
> Now, create a timeline in each of these 11 core areas. You can make one timeline or 11 separate lines. The idea is to create a tentative schedule for rolling out different phases of your practice in each of these areas.

BUSINESS PLAN REVIEW

The ultimate entrepreneur creates . . .

- An amazing **Mission Statement**
- A cool **Tagline and Logo**
- Awareness of **Capabilities, Challenges, Chances, and Concerns** (4C's)
- Awesome **Services**
- Crisp **Marketing/Networking**
- Thorough and trusting **Administration** practices and relationships
- Solid **Financial Management and Growth** practices
- Interesting **Professional Growth and Development** learning opportunities
- Fail-proof and well-balanced **Personal Growth and Burnout Avoidance** activities
- Comprehensive community **References and Resources** lists for practitioner and clients
- A brief and thorough **Executive Summary** to assist others in understanding the general nature of your overall plan

> ## EXERCISE 12.3 | Business Plan Review and Executive Summary
>
> Now it's time to review your business plan. Take time to go through your entire plan, add more definition or specific information, and then implement your core areas and the timeline that follows. Finally, write an Executive Summary that describes the plan in a general way.

Once your plan is complete, keep a "working" digital copy of your plan that you can revisit, modify, and update as needed. You may want to print and bind your main completed template and keep as a hardcopy of your humble beginnings, something to reference when needed. You'd be surprised at how often you will look at your ideas and think about them even years after you created success in your practice.

AND SO I LEAVE YOU WITH A FEW FINAL THOUGHTS...

Dr. Dan Siegel (2012) discussed the whole person as an integrated being who is properly differentiated and well linked. As a well-integrated practitioner, one who shows uniqueness by being individuated professionally and differentiated by the specialized set of services and business practices offered, and one who is linked to others in a healthy fashion, including clients, colleagues, teachers, and students in the field, can claim to be an ultimate entrepreneur.

In all of this, one must make sense of practice growth and development not from the lens of fearing scarce resources, nor from the misnomer that there are abundances of clients for the taking. Rather, the best recipe for success comes from being and doing *enough!* Brown (2012) defined doing enough as "wholehearted," which brings us back to our passions, and genuine nature. Your genuine wholehearted nature is enough and at the core of what connects you to your business and your business to you.

Go forward with fervency and always remember . . .

"The ultimate entrepreneur does not live by the gains received from others. Rather, such a person is concerned with the art and passion of creating and giving, and any gains received are primarily put back into further creations, fueling a perpetually positive and powerful engine of change and growth."

In service . . . *Howard Baumgarten*

AFTERWORD

Upon reflection, this book is the culmination of my many years of work in the area of professional practice business development. It is the integration of the past 17 plus years of lived private practice experience, a graduate curriculum on private practice building I developed and taught for nearly fifteen years, building and growing one of the largest group therapy practices in Denver between 2002 and 2010, national trainings on practice growth and development created and delivered between 2012 and 2014, and individual professional business consultation provided since 2010. All of this work along with my humble beginnings shared in the first chapter created what seemed to be the next step in this great passionate area of interest.

Despite my years of diverse experience and preparations that are at the roots of this book, creating this project was indeed a laborious process. Sandwiched between a full-time private practice and growing family responsibilities, among other commitments, I managed to write a manuscript that I am proud of. I hope it helps my readers grow a meaningful practice and allows me to experience satisfaction and appreciation that I helped in some way. The accomplishment of completion is somewhat bittersweet. There is so much anticipation during the process that it became difficult to imagine a finishing point. While writing, I often felt in a groove, a rhythm of passion for my message as I typed away at my keyboard. Occasionally, the moments dragged on, staring at a paragraph that I deemed sloppy, and out of place, stuck in the mud of wondering whether this project would even work or ever become complete.

As the doubts crept in, so too did my propensity for procrastination. Busy with work, especially doing speaking events and trainings in my own community and around the country, time got away from me, and I couldn't get a consistent writing rhythm going. I wrote less than 50 pages in the first 18 months, with two deadline extensions. There I was writing a book about proper practice development, including healthy work/life balance, and I, its author, was living my own story of what NOT to do, overwhelmed by over committing, under doing, spread way too thin, not enjoying the process of writing, while other areas suffered!

I had to dig deep, and take a page or two out of my own book, literally! The time to re-prioritize, make a plan, be more selective of opportunities, and say "no" when most needed was NOW. Instead of intermittent writing sessions, I applied myself during large blocks of time and rattled out two thirds of the book during the last eight months before the editing phase. Of course, it's immensely helpful when you have an understanding publisher supporting the writing process!

Emotionally, the roller coaster of highs and lows leveled out over time. I think about this project much like an intimate relationship that leads to marriage and eventually making a child. In the very beginning, you have no children, no worries, and are filled with the excitement, and the highs and lows of something new. Then the glitz wears off, and you must deal with the realities of being in this relationship—a marriage in this case to an idea and the process of literally giving birth to that idea. As you settle in the emotional extremes slowly wane, and realism kicks in. A baby is coming. In this case, the baby is the completion of the book. So again there's more excitement and challenge preparing for that fateful 9th month (in this case more like 24 months). And then it's done.

Being on the back half (I hope) of raising my two boys and well settled in my marriage, I cannot help but wonder and be excited about how this new "baby" will make a difference in the world and fit in the ever-changing and quickly growing fields of professional helping. I can only marvel momentarily at the accomplishment, my own process of diversification, knowing that it's not accomplished for the money, but for the love and passion of teaching others what I know. And, then that moment passes and like you, . . . I move on to the next endeavor!

APPENDIX A:

Private Practice Business Plan & Program Goals/ Timeline Template

The Business Plan Template is a categorical summary of all sections of the business plan discussed in Chapter 2. The Program Goals/Timeline Template is your blueprint to creating specific clinical programs within your business that promote your strengths, help your target population, and improve the overall value of your practice.

MY PRIVATE PRACTICE BUSINESS PLAN

Executive Summary: _____

_____

_____

_____

_____

_____

Mission Statement: _____

_____

_____

Tagline: _____

_____

_____

The Four Cs:

• Capabilities (Strengths): _____

_____

_____

• Challenges (Weaknesses): _____

_____

_____

• Chances (Opportunities): _____

_____

_____

• Concerns (Threats): _____

_____

_____

Services (Describe—Who, What, When, Where, Why, How):_____

_____

_____

_____

_____

_____

Marketing/Networking:_____

_____

_____

_____

_____

Administration

- What professionals involved? _____

    _____

    _____

- What procedures?_____

    _____

    _____

Financial Management and Growth: _____

_____

_____

_____

Professional Growth: _____

_____

_____

Personal Growth & Burnout Avoidance: _____

_____

_____

_____

Diversity Inclusion Statement/Plan:_____

_____

_____

_____

Advocacy: _____

_____

_____

_____

References and Resources: _____

_____

_____

_____

_____

_____

_____

_____

_____

_____

_____

_____

PROGRAM GOALS/TIMELINE TEMPLATE

Program Name/Title: _____

Overall Goal: _____

_____

_____

General Objective and Method(s) #1: _____

_____

General Objective and Method(s) #2: _____

_____

General Objective and Method(s) #3: _____

_____

Specific Clinical Goal #1:_____

_____

_____

Objective/Method #1: _____

_____

Objective/Method #2: _____

_____

Specific Clinical Goal #2:_____

_____

_____

Objective/Method #1: _____

_____

Objective/Method #2: _____

_____

Financial Goal #1: _____

_____

_____

    Objective/Method #1: _____

        _____

    Objective/Method #2: _____

        _____

Financial Goal #2: _____

_____

_____

    Objective/Method #1: _____

        _____

    Objective/Method #2: _____

        _____

Marketing Goal #1: _____

_____

_____

    Objective/Method #1: _____

        _____

    Objective/Method #2: _____

        _____

Marketing Goal #2: _____

_____

_____

    Objective/Method #1: _____

        _____

    Objective/Method #2: _____

        _____

Timeline for achieving objectives/goals:

Overall Goal: _____

Specific Clinical Goal #1: _____

Specific Clinical Goal #2: _____

Financial Goal #1: _____

Financial Goal #2: _____

Marketing Goal #1:_____

Marketing Goal #2:_____

Written Evaluation _____

_____

_____

_____

_____

_____

_____

_____

_____

_____

_____

_____

_____

_____

Resources

APPENDIX B:

Sample Clinical Paperwork: Fee for Service Forms

The following forms are merely samples of various forms clinicians might use in a private practice. Please note that the state you practice in may dictate the content that must be included in your statement of disclosure as well as requirements regarding record keeping. See Appendix F (Professional Counselor Licensing by State) for information about where to find these requirements in your state.

CLIENT ADMISSION FORM

Client Name:_____ Gender:_____

Date of Evaluation:_____ Date of Birth: _____

Reason for seeking counseling including background information:

_____

_____

_____

Check current clinical symptoms:

- ○ Addictive Behavior
- ○ Aggression/Violence
- ○ Alcohol/Substance Abuse
- ○ Alcohol/Substance Dependence
- ○ Anger/Irritability
- ○ Anxiety/Panic
- ○ Appetite Problems/Restricting Intake
- ○ Binge Eating w/o Compensatory Behaviors
- ○ Binging/Purging
- ○ Bizarre Behavior

- ○ Chronic Medical Problems
- ○ Depression
- ○ Destructive Behavior
- ○ Gender Identity Concerns
- ○ Grief/Loss
- ○ Homicidal Ideation
- ○ Isolation/Withdrawal
- ○ Suicidal Ideation
- ○ Self-Harming Behaviors
- ○ Mood Swings
- ○ Obsessions/Compulsions
- ○ Phobia/Fear

- ○ Poor Impulse Control
- ○ Post Traumatic Stress
- ○ Problems Thinking/ Concentrating
- ○ Sexual Activity Concerns
- ○ Sexual/Intimacy Issues
- ○ Sexual Identity Issues
- ○ Sleep Disturbance
- ○ Stress/Feeling Overwhelmed
- ○ Tearful/Crying Spells

Check current psychosocial and environmental concerns:

- ○ Academic/Educational Problems
- ○ Acculturation Difficulty
- ○ Bereavement
- ○ Career/Job Dissatisfaction
- ○ Communication/Trust Problems
- ○ Disruption of Family by Separation/Divorce
- ○ Domestic Violence
- ○ Exposure to Disaster, War, or other Hostilities

- ○ Family Relationship Conflict
- ○ Financial Stressors/Hardship
- ○ History of Military Deployment
- ○ Homelessness
- ○ Housing Problems
- ○ Intense Family Distancing
- ○ Legal Problems or Problems related to the Legal System
- ○ Parenting Issues
- ○ Phase of Life Problems

- ○ Physical Impairment
- ○ Perpetrator of Abuse
- ○ Problem related to Current Military Deployment Status
- ○ Religious/Spiritual Issues
- ○ Target of Adverse Discrimination/ Persecution
- ○ Victim of Abuse
- ○ Victim of Crime

If client is under 18, check current symptoms below in addition to those above:

- ○ Aggression
- ○ Autism Spectrum Disorder
- ○ Bed Wetting
- ○ Blended Family Issues
- ○ Destruction of Property
- ○ Divorce/Separation
- ○ Fire-setting
- ○ Tantrums
- ○ Hyperactivity

- ○ Inattention
- ○ Impulse Control Issues
- ○ Learning Disorder
- ○ Lying/Manipulative Behavior
- ○ Night Terrors
- ○ Oppositional Behavior
- ○ School Problems
- ○ Stealing
- ○ Risk-Taking Behavior

- ○ Running Away
- ○ Separation Anxiety
- ○ Perpetrator of Bullying
- ○ Unusual birth/pregnancy events
- ○ Victim of Bullying
- ○ Victim of Abuse/Neglect

Previous Treatment: ○ **Yes** ○ **No**

If yes, please indicate dates, whether inpatient/outpatient, problem for which you were treated, and name of treating professional:

_____

_____

_____

_____

Please list any allergies/drug sensitivities: _____

Indicate Current Medications and Dosage: _____

Name and Phone Number of Prescribing Professional: _____

If not on medication, is a referral for a medication evaluation needed? ○ **Yes** ○ **No**

Name and Phone # of Primary Care Physician: _____

Permission to contact Primary Care Physician regarding treatment: ○ **Yes** ○ **No**

Please list past & present tobacco, alcohol, and drug use:_____

_____

_____

_____

List Strengths/Accomplishments: _____

_____

_____

_____

Client Signature_____ Date _____

[Your Practice Name, Revised Month/Year]

[YOUR PRACTICE NAME]
CLIENT CONTACT INFORMATION FORM

Client Name:_____Date of Birth:_____

Parent/Guardian (if client is under 16): _____

Mailing Address: _____

City/State/Zip: _____

Email Address:_____
Okay to email for scheduling appointments? ○ **Yes** ○ **No**

Home Phone:_____ Okay to leave detailed message? ○ **Yes** ○ **No**

Work Phone: _____ Okay to leave detailed message? ○ **Yes** ○ **No**

Other Phone: _____ Okay to leave detailed message? ○ **Yes** ○ **No**

Emergency Contact Name: _____

Phone: _____

Mailing Address: _____

City/State/Zip: _____

By signing below, I agree to the following: (1) I understand that the client is ultimately responsible for the cost of all services rendered. (2) I will pay the appropriate fee at the time service is rendered. (3) I understand that I will be billed for missed appointments that are not cancelled at least 24 hours in advance and that I am responsible for paying those charges. (4) I agree to pay for all costs of collection of the client's delinquent accounts including reasonable attorney fees. (5) I agree that if my mailing address is written incorrectly, has changed since the date of this form, or is missing from this form, I may receive a bill at a current and verifiable address for any outstanding charges.

Client Signature_____ Date _____

[Your Practice Name, Revised Month/Year]

CLINICAL EVALUATION & TREATMENT PLAN

Client Name:_____ ID#:_____

DOB:_____Date of Evaluation: _____

Initial Payment Due:_____ Amount Paid:_____ Insurance: _____

Brief Mental Status Exam:

Affect:

○ reactive and mood congruent   ○ labile   ○ blunted
○ normal range   ○ tearful   ○ expansive
○ constricted   ○ flat

Mood:

○ anxious   ○ depressed   ○ elevated
○ irritable   ○ euthymic

Thought Processes:

○ goal-directed and logical   ○ disorganized

Thought Content:

○ hallucinations   ○ phobias
○ delusions   ○ obsessions/compulsions

DSM-5 DIAGNOSIS:

Risk factors:_____

Problem 1: _____

   Goal 1: _____

      Objective: _____

      Intervention: _____

      Objective: _____

      Intervention: _____

      Objective: _____

      Intervention: _____

Problem 2: _____

    Goal 2: _____

        Objective: _____

        Intervention: _____

        Objective: _____

        Intervention: _____

        Objective: _____

        Intervention: _____

Approximate number of sessions to reach treatment goals: _____

Recommended frequency of visits: _____

Counseling Modality: ○ Individual ○ Family ○ Couple ○ Group

Types of therapeutic intervention: _____

_____

_____

Adjunct referrals needed: _____

Client involved in treatment planning: _____

Clinical Summary/Notations: _____

_____

_____

_____

[Provider/Counselor] Signature_____ Date_____

[Your Practice Name, Revised Month/Year]

CONSENT FOR TREATMENT OF MINOR

Child's Name: _____

ID#: _____

Child's Date of Birth: _____

I/We _____am/are the legal custodial parent(s) of
_____ and give my/our permission to [Service Provider Name] to provide psychological services to my/our child (children). I understand that the counseling sessions will be confidential and that no information or records concerning those sessions will be divulged to any person, including parents or legal guardians, without the prior consent of the individual receiving counseling services and this counselor or pursuant to the laws of the state of Colorado.

Authorization Option 1:

Parent 1: _____Date: _____/_____/ _

and (both signatures required by law)

Parent 2: _____Date: _____/_____/ _

Authorization Option 2:

Parent 1: _____Date: _____/_____/ _

and (signature and documentation required by law)

○ Attached copy of court order declaring sole decision-making powers.

[Your Practice Name, Revised Month/Year]

Please note that the state you practice in may dictate requirements for the authorization to treat a minor.

DISCLOSURE, TREATMENT, AND FEE AGREEMENT

Name
Business Address
Business Telephone Number

Degrees, Credentials, and Certifications
Degree and Emphasis (Year)
Example: M.A. in Counseling Psychology (1997)
Licenses and/or Certifications (Year)
Example: Licensed Professional Counselor (1999)

CLIENT RIGHTS AND IMPORTANT INFORMATION

Method of Treatment: You may receive information about the methods of treatment, techniques used, duration of therapy if known, and the fee structure. At any time you may seek a second opinion or terminate treatment. Please be advised that in a professional relationship, sexual intimacy is never appropriate and should be reported to the board that licenses, registers, or certifies the licensee, registrant or certificate holder.

Sessions and Fees: Sessions are billed by the 45-minute hour at a rate of $$$ per session (60-minute follow-up sessions are $$$, and 90-minute follow-up sessions are $$$). The initial evaluation session is $180 (60 min), $250 (90 Min). Payment for each session is due at the time of each therapy session. If you carry mental health insurance, arrangements will be made for payment of services from the insurance company and you will be held responsible for deductibles, co-payments, non-covered services, or unpaid balances. You will be billed $100 for missed sessions ($175 if a 90-minute session) unless you cancel at least 24 hours prior to your scheduled session. There is a $30 processing fee for checks returned "non-sufficient funds."

Confidentiality: Sessions are confidential. Information regarding treatment may be shared with a third party only with written consent from the client. Exceptions to confidentiality include when the client is in imminent danger of harming self or others, or when child or elder abuse is suspected. In the case of working with minors, legal guardians will know about the treatment, though privacy will be respected as much as possible. When treating couples and/or families, confidentiality among family members is not a guarantee. *****Please note there may be additional limits of confidentiality and these vary depending on your state. For example in Colorado the other exceptions to confidentiality include if there is a court order and if threats are being made to a public entity***.

Emergencies: In a mental health emergency dial 911or go to your nearest urgent care or emergency center. Paging the therapist regarding an urgent matter is available provided your call back number is not blocked. Urgent calls are returned within the hour.

Crisis Coverage: In my absence or in the event of medical or family emergency an on-call clinician will be provided. By signing this agreement you permit information to be shared with the on-call clinician regarding your treatment.

REGULATORY REQUIREMENTS APPLICABLE TO MENTAL HEALTH PROFESSIONALS

The practice of licensed or registered persons in the field of psychotherapy is regulated by the Mental Health Licensing Section of the Division of Registrations. The board of Licensed Professional Counselors Examiners can be reached at 1560 Broadway, Suite 1350, Denver, Colorado 80202, (303) 894.7800.

The practice of licensed or registered persons in the field of psychotherapy is regulated by the Mental Health Licensing Section of the Division of Registrations. The board of Licensed Marriage and Family Therapy Examiners can be reached at 1560 Broadway, Suite 1350, Denver, Colorado 80302, (303) 894.7800.

The practice of licensed or registered persons in the field of psychotherapy is regulated by the Mental Health Licensing Section of the Division of Registrations. The Board of Certified Addictions Counselor III (CAC III) can be reached at 1560 Broadway, Suite 1350, Denver, Colorado 80302, (303) 894.7800.

Registered psychotherapist is a psychotherapist listed in the State's database and is authorized by law to practice psychotherapy in Colorado but is not licensed by the state and is not required to satisfy any standardized educational or testing requirements to obtain a registration from the state.

Certified Addiction Counselor I (CAC I) must be a high school graduate, complete required training hours and 1,000 hours of supervised experience.

Certified Addiction Counselor II (CAC II) must complete additional required training hours and 2,000 hours of supervised experience.

Certified Addiction Counselor III (CAC III) must have a bachelor's degree in behavioral health, complete additional required training hours and 2,000 hours of supervised experience.

Licensed Addiction Counselor must have a clinical master's degree and meet the CAC III requirements.

Licensed Social Worker must hold a masters degree in social work.

Psychologist Candidate, a Marriage and Family Therapist Candidate, and a Licensed Professional Counselor Candidate must hold the necessary licensing degree and be in the process of completing the required supervision for licensure.

Licensed Clinical Social Worker, a Licensed Marriage and Family Therapist, and a Licensed Professional Counselor must hold a masters degree in their profession and have two years of post-masters supervision.

A Licensed Psychologist must hold a doctorate degree in psychology and have one year of post-doctoral supervision.

I have read the preceding information, it has also been explained to me orally by the therapist, and I understand my rights as a client or as the client's responsible party. I agree to the conditions stated above, including policies regarding fees, insurance, cancellations, confidentiality, crisis coverage, and client rights.

Print Client's Name: _____

Client's or Responsible Party's Signature _____

Date_____

If signed by Responsible Party, please state relationship to client and authority to consent:

Witness:_____ Date _____

*Please note that the state you practice in may dictate the content that must be included in your statement of disclosure. See listing of Professional Counselor Licensing by State in Appendix F.

[Your Practice Name, Revised Month/Year]

MISSED APPOINTMENT/LATE CANCELLATION CHARGES FORM

Name
Business Address
Business Phone Number

By signing below, I acknowledge that I am responsible for payment of charges by [Business Name] for not showing up to an appointment without at least 24-hour notice of cancellation. I acknowledge that effective [Date], the amount for which I am responsible in the event of a late canceled or missed appointment is $_____ per 45/60-minute session, and $_____ per 90-minute session. I agree to pay this amount within 30 days of my late canceled or missed appointment.

Signature of Client (Parent if under age 18) _____

Date_____

Your Business Name, Revised Month/Year]

NOTICE OF PRIVACY PRACTICES

Name
Business Address

In compliance with the Health Insurance Portability and Accountability Act of 1996 (HIPAA), this notice describes how health information about you is protected, and also how it may be used and disclosed. During the process of providing services, [Your Name Here], will obtain, record and use mental health and medical information about you that is protected health information. Ordinarily, that information is confidential and will not be used or disclosed, except as described below. Colorado law provides strict protections for patient confidentiality, which together with ethical restrictions and standards often will be more private than HIPAA guidelines. This notice takes effect on April 15, 2003 and will remain in effect until it is replaced.

USES, DISCLOSURES, AND COMMUNICATION OF PROTECTED INFORMATION

A. General Uses and Disclosures Not Requiring the Patient's Consent.

1. **Treatment**: Treatment refers to the provision, coordination, or management of healthcare (including mental healthcare) and related services. During treatment, the provider may consult with other providers, without identifying you by name, and also not disclosing any other identifying information about you, in order to ensure the best care possible for your concerns.

2. **Payment**: Payment refers to the activities undertaken by the provider to obtain or provide reimbursement for the provision of healthcare. For example, the provider will use your information to develop accounts receivable information, to bill you, and with your consent, to bill third parties. If you elect to have a third party pay for your treatment, the information provided to the third party may include information that identifies you as well as your diagnosis, type of service, date of service, and other information about your condition and treatment.

3. **Contacting the Patient**: The provider may contact you to remind you of appointments, or to change or cancel appointments. The provider may leave messages on voicemail or with other parties, identifying the name and phone number of the provider. The provider will use best judgment in the details left on a voicemail. If you do not want the provider leaving messages, or if you wish to restrict the messages in any way, please notify the provider in writing.

4. **Required by Law**: The provider will disclose protected health information when required by law or when necessary for healthcare oversight. This includes, but may not be limited to: (a) reporting child abuse or neglect; (b) when court ordered to release information; (c) when there is a legal duty to warn or take action regarding imminent danger to others; (d) when the patient is a danger to self or others or gravely disabled; (e) when a coroner is investigating the patient's death.

5. **Family Members**: Except for certain minors, protected health information cannot be provided to family members without the patient's consent. In situations where family members are present during a discussion with the patient, and it can be reasonably inferred from the circumstances that the patient does not object, information may be disclosed in the course of that discussion. However, if the patient objects, protected health information will not be disclosed.

6. **Emergencies**: In life-threatening emergencies, the provider will disclose information necessary to avoid serious harm or death.

B. Patient Authorization or Release of Information:

The provider may not use or disclose protected information in any other way without a signed authorization or release of information. When you sign an authorization, or a release of information, it may later be revoked, provided that the revocation is in writing. The revocation will apply, except to the extent the provider has already taken action in reliance thereon.

C. Alternative Means of Receiving Confidential Information:

You have the right to request that you receive communications of protected health information from the provider by alternative means or at alternative locations. For example, if you do not want the provider to mail statements or other materials to your home, you can request that this information be sent to another address. There are limitations to the granting of such requests. You will also have to pay any additional costs that may be associated with such a request.

Protection of Confidential Information: The provider has taken steps to protect the confidentiality of your information, including the use of name-codes, password protection of computer files, locked file cabinets, paper shredding, and other security measures. Your files will be destroyed (shredded or incinerated) when past the time required for the maintenance of such records. If you have further questions, please contact the Privacy Officer, [Name] at [phone number].

I hereby acknowledge that I have received a copy of the provider's Notice of Privacy Rights.

Client or Parent/Guardian Signature _____

Date_____

[Your Practice Name, Revised Month/Year]

AUTHORIZATION FOR RELEASE OF INFORMATION

Name
Business Address
Business Phone Number
Business Fax Number

I, _____, hereby authorize [Your Business Name] and _____

(Name of Person/Hospital/Agency/Company), at Street Address/City/State/Zip _____

Telephone:_____Fax: _____ to exchange information, regarding the treatment

of_____ , whose date of birth is_____.

The type of information to be disclosed:

○ Evaluations   ○ Test Results   ○ Summary
○ Medical/Hospital   ○ Diagnosis   ○ Course of Treatment
○ Records   ○ Treatment Plan   ○ Psychotherapy Notes
○ Psychological/Medical   ○ Mental Health Record   ○ Other:_____

The purpose of such disclosure:

○ Ongoing Treatment   ○ Transfer of Care   ○ Utilization
○ Medical Care   ○ Legal Issues   ○ Other:_____
○ Consultation   ○ Coordination of Care
○ Evaluation   ○ Health Benefit

The designated information about me ○ **may** ○ **may not** be transmitted by fax, electronic mail or other electronic file transfer mechanisms. [Your Name] and the above designated person ○ **may** ○ **may not** discuss by telephone the content of the information released.

This consent is in effect until_____. I understand that I may revoke this authorization, in writing, at any time unless action based on it has already taken place.

I hereby release all parties stated herewith from any liability resulting from the release of this information. I agree that a photocopy of this release shall be as valid as the original. I understand that my communications in therapy are protected under federal and state confidentiality regulations and cannot be disclosed without my written authorization. The information provided by a client during therapy sessions is legally confidential in the case of licensed professional counselors, except as provided in section 12.43.218 CRS and except for certain legal exceptions. In general, these exceptions pertain to matters of danger to self or others, and to assault or neglect of a child or elder.

I further understand that the potential exists for re-disclosure of my private mental health information, and that it may no longer be protected under the HIPAA privacy regulations.

This is to certify that I have given consent freely and voluntarily, and that the benefits and disadvantages of releasing the information, if known, have been explained to me.

Signature of Client or Personal Representative _____

Date _____

FEDERAL REGULATIONS PROHIBIT THE RECIPIENT OF THIS INFORMATION FROM MAKING ANY FURTHER DISCLOSURES OF THIS INFORMATION.

[Your Business Name, Revised Month/Year]

Resources

APPENDIX C:

Sample Clinical Paperwork: Insurance/Managed Care Forms

The following forms have been created for clients utilizing their insurance benefits and have been found useful to organize, manage, and document the necessary information required when working with insurance/managed care organizations. These forms are similar to those found in Appendix B and may be modified to fit your needs as clinician. As a reminder, the state you practice in may dictate the content that must be included in your statement of disclosure as well as requirements regarding records required to be kept.

CLIENT ADMISSION FORM

Client Name:_____ Gender:_____

Date of Evaluation:_____ Date of Birth: _____

Reason for seeking counseling including background information:

_____

_____

_____

Check current clinical symptoms:

- Addictive Behavior
- Aggression/Violence
- Alcohol/Substance Abuse
- Alcohol/Substance Dependence
- Anger/Irritability
- Anxiety/Panic
- Appetite Problems/Restricting Intake
- Binge Eating w/o Compensatory Behaviors
- Binging/Purging
- Bizarre Behavior

- Chronic Medical Problems
- Depression
- Destructive Behavior
- Gender Identity Concerns
- Grief/Loss
- Homicidal Ideation
- Isolation/Withdrawal Suicidal Ideation
- Self-Harming Behaviors
- Mood Swings
- Obsessions/Compulsions
- Phobia/Fear

- Poor Impulse Control
- Post Traumatic Stress
- Problems Thinking/ Concentrating
- Sexual Activity Concerns
- Sexual/Intimacy Issues
- Sexual Identity Issues
- Sleep Disturbance
- Stress/Feeling Overwhelmed
- Tearful/Crying Spells

Check current psychosocial and environmental concerns:

- Academic/Educational Problems
- Acculturation Difficulty
- Bereavement
- Career/Job Dissatisfaction
- Communication/Trust Problems
- Disruption of Family by Separation/Divorce
- Domestic Violence
- Exposure to Disaster, War, or other Hostilities

- Family Relationship Conflict
- Financial Stressors/Hardship
- History of Military Deployment
- Homelessness
- Housing Problems
- Intense Family Distancing
- Legal Problems or Problems related to the Legal System
- Parenting Issues
- Phase of Life Problems

- Physical Impairment
- Perpetrator of Abuse
- Problem related to Current Military Deployment Status
- Religious/Spiritual Issues
- Target of Adverse Discrimination/ Persecution
- Victim of Abuse
- Victim of Crime

If client is under 18, check current symptoms below in addition to those above:

- Aggression
- Autism Spectrum Disorder
- Bed Wetting
- Blended Family Issues
- Destruction of Property
- Divorce/Separation
- Fire-setting
- Tantrums

- Hyperactivity
- Inattention
- Impulse Control Issues
- Learning Disorder
- Lying/Manipulative Behavior
- Night Terrors
- Oppositional Behavior
- School Problems

- Stealing
- Risk-Taking Behavior
- Running Away
- Separation Anxiety
- Perpetrator of Bullying
- Unusual birth/pregnancy events
- Victim of Bullying
- Victim of Abuse/Neglect

Previous Treatment: ○ **Yes** ○ **No**

If yes, please indicate dates, whether inpatient/outpatient, problem for which you were treated, and name of treating professional:

_____

_____

_____

_____

Please list any allergies/drug sensitivities: _____

Indicate Current Medications and Dosage: _____

Name and Phone Number of Prescribing Professional: _____

If not on medication, is a referral for a medication evaluation needed? ○ **Yes** ○ **No**

Name and Phone # of Primary Care Physician: _____

Permission to contact Primary Care Physician regarding treatment: ○ **Yes** ○ **No**

Please list past & present tobacco, alcohol, and drug use:_____

_____

_____

_____

List Strengths/Accomplishments: _____

_____

_____

_____

Client Signature_____ Date _____

[Your Practice Name, Revised Month/Year]

[BUSINESS NAME]
CLIENT INFORMATION FORM

Client Name:_____ Date of Birth:_____

Parent/Guardian (if client is under 16): _____

Mailing Address: _____

City/State/Zip: _____

Email Address:_____
Okay to email for scheduling appointments? ○ **Yes** ○ **No**

Home Phone:_____ Okay to leave detailed message? ○ **Yes** ○ **No**

Work Phone: _____ Okay to leave detailed message? ○ **Yes** ○ **No**

Other Phone: _____ Okay to leave detailed message? ○ **Yes** ○ **No**

Emergency Contact Name: _____ Phone:_____

Mailing Address: _____ City/State/Zip:_____

Primary Insured: _____ Relation to Client:_____

Employer: _____ Date of Birth:_____

Street Address: _____ City/State/Zip:_____

Primary Insurance: _____Phone#:_____

Visits Authorized:_____ Co-pay/Co-insurance:_____

Member ID#: _____ Deductible:_____

Authorization #: _____ Group Number:_____

By signing below, I agree to the following: (1) I understand that the client is ultimately responsible for the cost of all services rendered. (2) I will pay the appropriate fee at the time service is rendered. (3) I understand that I will be billed for missed appointments that are not cancelled at least 24 hours in advance and that I am responsible for paying those charges. (4) I agree to pay for all costs of collection of the client's delinquent accounts including reasonable attorney fees. (5) I agree that if my mailing address is written incorrectly, has changed since the date of this form, or is missing from this form, I may receive a bill at a current and verifiable address for any outstanding charges.

Signature of Client/Guardian_____ Date _____

[Your Business Name, Revised Month/Year]

CLINICAL EVALUATION & TREATMENT PLAN

Client Name:_____ ID#:_____

DOB:_____ Date of Evaluation: _____

Initial Payment Due:_____ Amount Paid:_____ Insurance: _____

Brief Mental Status Exam:

Affect:

○ reactive and mood congruent   ○ labile   ○ blunted
○ normal range   ○ tearful   ○ expansive
○ constricted   ○ flat

Mood:

○ anxious   ○ depressed   ○ elevated
○ irritable   ○ euthymic

Thought Processes:

○ goal-directed and logical   ○ disorganized

Thought Content:

○ hallucinations   ○ phobias
○ delusions   ○ obsessions/compulsions

DSM-5 DIAGNOSIS:

Risk factors:_____

Problem 1: _____

     Goal 1: _____

         Objective: _____

         Intervention: _____

         Objective: _____

         Intervention: _____

         Objective: _____

         Intervention: _____

Problem 2: _____

Goal 2: _____

Objective: _____

Intervention: _____

Objective: _____

Intervention: _____

Objective: _____

Intervention: _____

Approximate number of sessions to reach treatment goals: _____

Recommended frequency of visits: _____

Counseling Modality: ○ Individual   ○ Family   ○ Couple   ○ Group

Types of therapeutic intervention: _____

_____

_____

Adjunct referrals needed: _____

Client involved in treatment planning: _____

Clinical Summary/Notations: _____

_____

_____

_____

[Provider/Counselor] Signature_____ Date_____

[Your Practice Name, Revised Month/Year]

CONSENT FOR TREATMENT OF MINOR

Child's Name: _____

ID#: _____

Child's Date of Birth: _____

I/We _____ am/are the legal custodial parent(s) of _____ and give my/our permission to [Service Provider Name] to provide psychological services to my/our child (children). I understand that the counseling sessions will be confidential and that no information or records concerning those sessions will be divulged to any person, including parents or legal guardians, without the prior consent of the individual receiving counseling services and this counselor or pursuant to the laws of the state of Colorado.

Authorization Option 1:

Parent 1: _____ Date: _____ /_____ /_

and (both signatures required by law)

Parent 2: _____ Date: _____ /_____ /_

Authorization Option 2:

Parent 1: _____ Date: _____ /_____ /_

and (signature and documentation required by law)

○ **Attached copy of court order declaring sole decision-making powers.**

Please note that the state you practice in may dictate requirements for the authorization to treat a minor.

[Your Practice Name, Revised Month/Year]

DISCLOSURE, TREATMENT, AND FEE AGREEMENT

Name
Business Address
Business Telephone Number

Degrees, Credentials, and Certifications
Degree and Emphasis (Year)
Example: M.A. in Counseling Psychology (1997)
Licenses and/or Certifications (Year)
Example: Licensed Professional Counselor (1999)

Client Rights and Important Information

Method of Treatment: You may receive information about the methods of treatment, techniques used, duration of therapy if known, and the fee structure. At any time you may seek a second opinion or terminate treatment. Please be advised that in a professional relationship, sexual intimacy is never appropriate and should be reported to the board that licenses, registers, or certifies the licensee, registrant or certificate holder.

Sessions and Fees: Sessions are billed by the 45-minute hour at a rate of $$$ per session (60-minute follow-up sessions are $$$, and 90-minute follow-up sessions are $$$). The initial evaluation session is $180 (60 min), $250 (90 Min). Payment for each session is due at the time of each therapy session. If you carry mental health insurance, arrangements will be made for payment of services from the insurance company and you will be held responsible for deductibles, co-payments, non-covered services, or unpaid balances. You will be billed $100 for missed sessions ($175 if a 90-minute session) unless you cancel at least 24 hours prior to your scheduled session. There is a $30 processing fee for checks returned "non-sufficient funds."

Confidentiality: Sessions are confidential. Information regarding treatment may be shared with a third party only with written consent from the client. Exceptions to confidentiality include when the client is in imminent danger of harming self or others, or when child or elder abuse is suspected. In the case of working with minors, legal guardians will know about the treatment, though privacy will be respected as much as possible. When treating couples and/or families, confidentiality among family members is not a guarantee. ***Please note there may be additional limits of confidentiality and these vary depending on your state. For example in Colorado the other exceptions to confidentiality include if there is a court order and if threats are being made to a public entity.***

Emergencies: In a mental health emergency dial 911or go to your nearest urgent care or emergency center. Paging the therapist regarding an urgent matter is available provided your call back number is not blocked. Urgent calls are returned within the hour.

Crisis Coverage: In my absence or in the event of medical or family emergency an on-call clinician will be provided. By signing this agreement you permit information to be shared with the on-call clinician regarding your treatment.

Regulatory Requirements Applicable to Mental Health Professionals

The practice of licensed or registered persons in the field of psychotherapy is regulated by the Mental Health Licensing Section of the Division of Registrations. The board of Licensed Professional Counselors Examiners can be reached at 1560 Broadway, Suite 1350, Denver, Colorado 80202, (303) 894.7800.

The practice of licensed or registered persons in the field of psychotherapy is regulated by the Mental Health Licensing Section of the Division of Registrations. The board of Licensed Marriage and Family Therapy Examiners can be reached at 1560 Broadway, Suite 1350, Denver, Colorado 80302, (303) 894.7800.

The practice of licensed or registered persons in the field of psychotherapy is regulated by the Mental Health Licensing Section of the Division of Registrations. The Board of Certified Addictions Counselor III (CAC III) can be reached at 1560 Broadway, Suite 1350, Denver, Colorado 80302, (303) 894.7800.

Registered psychotherapist is a psychotherapist listed in the State's database and is authorized by law to practice psychotherapy in Colorado but is not licensed by the state and is not required to satisfy any standardized educational or testing requirements to obtain a registration from the state.

Certified Addiction Counselor I (CAC I) must be a high school graduate, complete required training hours and 1,000 hours of supervised experience.

Certified Addiction Counselor II (CAC II) must complete additional required training hours and 2,000 hours of supervised experience.

Certified Addiction Counselor III (CAC III) must have a bachelor's degree in behavioral health, complete additional required training hours and 2,000 hours of supervised experience.

Licensed Addiction Counselor must have a clinical master's degree and meet the CAC III requirements.

Licensed Social Worker must hold a masters degree in social work.

Psychologist Candidate, a Marriage and Family Therapist Candidate, and a Licensed Professional Counselor Candidate must hold the necessary licensing degree and be in the process of completing the required supervision for licensure.

Licensed Clinical Social Worker, a Licensed Marriage and Family Therapist, and a Licensed Professional Counselor must hold a masters degree in their profession and have two years of post-masters supervision.

A Licensed Psychologist must hold a doctorate degree in psychology and have one year of post-doctoral supervision.

I have read the preceding information, it has also been explained to me orally by the therapist, and I understand my rights as a client or as the client's responsible party. I agree to the conditions stated above, including policies regarding fees, insurance, cancellations, confidentiality, crisis coverage, and client rights.

Print Client's Name: _____

Client's or Responsible Party's Signature _____

Date _____

If signed by Responsible Party, please state relationship to client and authority to consent:

Witness:_____ Date _____

*Please note that the state you practice in may dictate the content that must be included in your statement of disclosure. See listing of Professional Counselor Licensing by State in Appendix F.

[Your Practice Name, Revised Month/Year]

NOTICE OF PRIVACY PRACTICES

Name
Business Address

In compliance with the Health Insurance Portability and Accountability Act of 1996 (HIPAA), this notice describes how health information about you is protected, and also how it may be used and disclosed. During the process of providing services, [Your Name Here], will obtain, record and use mental health and medical information about you that is protected health information. Ordinarily, that information is confidential and will not be used or disclosed, except as described below. Colorado law provides strict protections for patient confidentiality, which together with ethical restrictions and standards often will be more private than HIPAA guidelines. This notice takes effect on April 15, 2003 and will remain in effect until it is replaced.

USES, DISCLOSURES, AND COMMUNICATION OF PROTECTED INFORMATION

A. **General Uses and Disclosures Not Requiring the Patient's Consent.**

1. **Treatment**: Treatment refers to the provision, coordination, or management of healthcare (including mental healthcare) and related services. During treatment, the provider may consult with other providers, without identifying you by name, and also not disclosing any other identifying information about you, in order to ensure the best care possible for your concerns.

2. **Payment**: Payment refers to the activities undertaken by the provider to obtain or provide reimbursement for the provision of healthcare. For example, the provider will use your information to develop accounts receivable information, to bill you, and with your consent, to bill third parties. If you elect to have a third party pay for your treatment, the information provided to the third party may include information that identifies you as well as your diagnosis, type of service, date of service, and other information about your condition and treatment.

3. **Contacting the Patient**: The provider may contact you to remind you of appointments, or to change or cancel appointments. The provider may leave messages on voicemail or with other parties, identifying the name and phone number of the provider. The provider will use best judgment in the details left on a voicemail. If you do not want the provider leaving messages, or if you wish to restrict the messages in any way, please notify the provider in writing.

4. **Required by Law**: The provider will disclose protected health information when required by law or when necessary for healthcare oversight. This includes, but may not be limited to: (a) reporting child abuse or neglect; (b) when court ordered to release information; (c) when there is a legal duty to warn or take action regarding imminent danger to others; (d) when the patient is a danger to self or others or gravely disabled; (e) when a coroner is investigating the patient's death.

5. **Family Members**: Except for certain minors, protected health information cannot be provided to family members without the patient's consent. In situations where family members are present during a discussion with the patient, and it can be reasonably inferred from the circumstances that the patient does not object, information may be disclosed in the course of that discussion. However, if the patient objects, protected health information will not be disclosed.

6. **Emergencies**: In life-threatening emergencies, the provider will disclose information necessary to avoid serious harm or death.

B. Patient Authorization or Release of Information:

The provider may not use or disclose protected information in any other way without a signed authorization or release of information. When you sign an authorization, or a release of information, it may later be revoked, provided that the revocation is in writing. The revocation will apply, except to the extent the provider has already taken action in reliance thereon.

C. Alternative Means of Receiving Confidential Information:

You have the right to request that you receive communications of protected health information from the provider by alternative means or at alternative locations. For example, if you do not want the provider to mail statements or other materials to your home, you can request that this information be sent to another address. There are limitations to the granting of such requests. You will also have to pay any additional costs that may be associated with such a request.

Protection of Confidential Information: The provider has taken steps to protect the confidentiality of your information, including the use of name-codes, password protection of computer files, locked file cabinets, paper shredding, and other security measures. Your files will be destroyed (shredded or incinerated) when past the time required for the maintenance of such records. If you have further questions, please contact the Privacy Officer, [Name] at [phone number].

I hereby acknowledge that I have received a copy of the provider's Notice of Privacy Rights.

Client or Parent/Guardian Signature _____

Date _____

[Your Practice Name, Revised Month/Year]

MISSED APPOINTMENT/LATE CANCELLATION CHARGES FORM

Name
Business Address
Business Phone Number

By signing below, I acknowledge that I am responsible for payment of charges by [Business Name] for not showing up to an appointment without at least 24-hour notice of cancellation. I acknowledge that effective [Date], the amount for which I am responsible in the event of a late canceled or missed appointment is $_____ per 45/60-minute session, and $_____ per 90-minute session. I agree to pay this amount within 30 days of my late canceled or missed appointment.

Signature of Client (Parent if under age 18) _____

Date _____

[Your Business Name, Revised Month/Year]

AUTHORIZATION FOR RELEASE OF INFORMATION

Name
Business Address
Business Phone Number
Business Fax Number

I, _____, hereby authorize [Your Business Name] and _____

(Name of Person/Hospital/Agency/Company), at Street Address/City/State/Zip _____

Telephone:_____Fax: _____ to exchange information, regarding the treatment

of_____ , whose date of birth is_____.

The type of information to be disclosed:
- ○ Evaluations
- ○ Medical/Hospital
- ○ Records
- ○ Psychological/Medical

- ○ Test Results
- ○ Diagnosis
- ○ Treatment Plan
- ○ Mental Health Record

- ○ Summary
- ○ Course of Treatment
- ○ Psychotherapy Notes
- ○ Other: _____

The purpose of such disclosure:
- ○ Ongoing Treatment
- ○ Medical Care
- ○ Consultation
- ○ Evaluation

- ○ Transfer of Care
- ○ Legal Issues
- ○ Coordination of Care
- ○ Health Benefit

- ○ Utilization
- ○ Other: _____

The designated information about me ○ **may** ○ **may not** be transmitted by fax, electronic mail or other electronic file transfer mechanisms. [Your Name] and the above designated person ○ **may** ○ **may not** discuss by telephone the content of the information released.

This consent is in effect until_____. I understand that I may revoke this authorization, in writing, at any time unless action based on it has already taken place.

I hereby release all parties stated herewith from any liability resulting from the release of this information. I agree that a photocopy of this release shall be as valid as the original. I understand that my communications in therapy are protected under federal and state confidentiality regulations and cannot be disclosed without my written authorization. The information provided by a client during therapy sessions is legally confidential in the case of licensed professional counselors, except as provided in section 12.43.218 CRS and except for certain legal exceptions. In general, these exceptions pertain to matters of danger to self or others, and to assault or neglect of a child or elder.

I further understand that the potential exists for re-disclosure of my private mental health information, and that it may no longer be protected under the HIPAA privacy regulations.

This is to certify that I have given consent freely and voluntarily, and that the benefits and disadvantages of releasing the information, if known, have been explained to me.

Signature of Client or Personal Representative _____

Date_____

FEDERAL REGULATIONS PROHIBIT THE RECIPIENT OF THIS INFORMATION FROM MAKING ANY FURTHER DISCLOSURES OF THIS INFORMATION.

[Your Business Name, Revised Month/Year]

APPENDIX D:

Sample Clinical Paperwork: Supplemental Forms

The following forms are common forms used by mental health clinicians in private practice. Please note that these forms are meant to serve as templates and may need to be modified to fit the needs of your practice.

CANCELLATION OF COUNSELING DAY NOTICE

Date:

Clients of [Your name here]:

Due to a family emergency all counseling sessions are canceled for the day. You will be called at my earliest convenience for rescheduling your appointment. Thank you for your patience and understanding. I apologize for any inconvenience.

Thank you,

[Your name/signature here]

Please note that if you schedule clients via email, this form could be emailed to clients, with a signed electronic communication disclosure form on file.

[Business Name, Created month, year]

CLIENT CONTACT SUMMARY SHEET

CLIENT NAME:_____ ID: _____

DATE	NATURE OF CONTACT

[Business Name, Created month, year]

[BUSINESS NAME]
DAP PROGRESS NOTE

Client Name:_____ Case #: _____

Session #:_____ Date: _____

Counseling Modality: ○ Individual ○ Family ○ Couple ○ Group

Description: (Subjective information such as problems, needs and strengths reported by client through contextual lens, themes, counselor interventions and objective data. Review of any extra-therapeutic work.)

_____

_____

_____

_____

Assessment: (Evaluation by counselor of current status and/or progress toward meeting treatment goals, therapeutic alliance, perceived client insights. Counselor's current hypothesis.)

_____

_____

_____

_____

Plan: (Next session date and time, preliminary plan for next session and/or extra-therapeutic work. Document any referrals.)

_____

_____

_____

Counselor Name(s):

Counselor Signature(s): _____Date: _____

[Business Name, Revised month/year]

GROUP CONFIDENTIALITY CONTRACT

I, _____, acknowledge that I am engaging in a group therapy experience under the facilitation of [Counselor's Name]. The members and facilitator of this group are responsible for maintaining confidences discussed within group sessions. As a member of this group, I agree to keep confidential all material discussed within group sessions.

Group Participant_____ Date _____

[Business Name, created month/year]

[PRIVATE PRACTICE/BUSINESS NAME HERE] SAFETY PLAN

Case #_____

I, _____ agree to use the following plan and resources to help myself through a difficult time.

Below are some coping skills I can use if I need to while waiting for a support person to be reached:

1. _____

2. _____

3. _____

Reasons to live:

• _____

• _____

• _____

I will speak with the following people (please use family members or friends):

Name:_____Phone:_____
OR

Name:_____Phone:_____
OR

If I need to, I will speak with a crisis line staff member at one of the numbers below, or I will admit myself to a hospital where I will be safely cared for: (* Use your community crisis information below)

• Colorado Crisis Services: 1-844-493-8255 *
• Suicide Crisis: 1-800-273-TALK *
• Suicide.org: 1-800-784-2423
• Denver Health Psychiatric ER: 303-602-7221 *
• Denver Health Mobile Crisis Services: 303-602-7220 *

I have willingly participated in the process of creating the safety plan and received a copy. I intend to follow the plan and follow up with a mental health provider.

Client's Signature_____ Date _____

Counselor Signature _____ Date _____

[Business Name, Created month/year]

CONTRACT FOR SAFETY

I,_____, promise to refrain from injuring or attempting to kill myself, inflicting harm on, or attempting to kill others. If I feel my dangerousness to perform any of these acts is so high that it is imminent that I will follow through, I will immediately call 911 or go to my nearest hospital emergency room to ask for help. This contract is in full force as of this day_____, and shall remain in effect indefinitely.

Signature of Client_____ Date _____

[Clinician Name]_____ Date _____

[Business Name, Created month/year]

SESSION NOTE

Client Name: _____ Insurance and ID#: _____

Date: _____ Session #_____ of authorized _____ (Total to date:_____)

Type of Service:_____ Copay/Fee: _____ Paid Today: _____

Session Start Time:_____ End Time: _____

Assessment: _____

_____

_____

Follow-ups from previous session: _____

_____

_____

Progress towards Treatment Goals/Objectives:

    1. _____

    2. _____

    3. _____

Risk factors:_____ Mental Status: _____

Medications: _____ Diagnosis:_____

Other relevant data:

Plan/Follow-up/Referrals: _____ Next Appointment: _____

Homework: _____

_____

Issues to address next session: _____

_____

Therapist Signature_____ Date_____

[Business Name, Revised month/year]

[PRIVATE PRACTICE BUSINESS NAME] TERMINATION SUMMARY NOTE

Client Name:_____ Case #: _____

DOB:_____ Date: _____

Counseling Modality: ○ Individual   ○ Family   ○ Couple   ○ Group

_____

Client System's Presenting Problem: _____

_____

Treatment Goals:

    1. _____

    2. _____

    3. _____

Treatment Objectives:

    1. _____

    2. _____

    3. _____

Case Progress Summary (number of session attended, prominent themes addressed, other notable factors about treatment):

_____

_____

_____

Treatment Outcome (progress towards treatment goals):

_____

_____

_____

Follow Up:

_____

_____

_____

Was it known prior to or during the last session with the client that the session would indeed be the "final session" in treatment?   ○ Yes   ○ No

Primary Reason for Termination of Services:

- ○ Client deceased
- ○ The client attended the Intake Session only (no additional session)
- ○ The client chose to discontinue treatment
- ○ The client stopped participating (e.g., no shows)
- ○ The client was referred to continue counseling services at another facility
- ○ The client was referred to increase their level of care (e.g., inpatient, specialized treatment)
- ○ The client was referred to receive services not available at [your business name] (e.g., medication)
- ○ The Planned Treatment was completed
- ○ There was little or no progress in treatment
- ○ This was a planned, extended pause in treatment (e.g., client vacation)

If "The client was referred," the client was referred to:

_____

_____

Optional: Additional notes regarding the reason for termination:

_____

_____

Source of termination decision:

- ○ Client-initiated or determined
- ○ Therapist-initiated or determined
- ○ Mutual decision

Were additional, optional, referral options presented at any time over the course of treatment to supplement the client's counseling services?   ○ Yes   ○ No

If Yes, please list all of the supplemental referral options that were offered:

_____

_____

Counselor Signature: _____Date: _____

[Business Name, Created month/year]

CLINICAL TREATMENT SUMMARY

Counselor/Private Practice Name
Business Address
Business Phone Number
Business Fax Number

Client Name: _____

Date of Birth:_____ ID#: _____

_____

History & Initial Evaluation:

_____

_____

_____

_____

Current Diagnosis & Treatment Plan

DSM-5 Diagnosis: _____

_____

Treatment Plan Goals:

    1. _____

    2. _____

    3. _____

Treatment Progress: _____

_____

_____

Clinical Recommendations: _____

_____

_____

Counselor's Name:_____ Date: _____

[Business Name, Revised month, year]

APPENDIX E:

Sample Administrative Paperwork: Business-Related Forms

These forms are for purposes of organizing and conducting administrative procedures related to billing, payment tracking, monthly revenue assessment, and general communications.

FAX TEMPLATE

[Street Address]
[City, ST Zip Code]
[phone]
[fax]
[Web address]

[COMPANY NAME]

FAX

To: _____   From: _____

Fax: _____   Pages: _____

Phone: _____   Date: _____

Re: _____   cc: _____

○ Urgent   ○ For Review   ○ Please Comment   ○ Please Reply   ○ Please Recycle

Comments:

This message is confidential and may be privileged. If you believe that this FAX has been sent to you in error, please reply to the sender that you received the message in error; then please destroy this FAX. Thank you

[Business Name, Revised month, year]

PATIENT ACTIVITY REPORT
IN-NETWORK INSURANCE

Service Provider Name:_____ **Date Range:** _____

PATIENT NAME	DIAGNOSIS (1ST TIME)	DOS	CPT CODE	CO-PAY COLLECTED	INSURANCE (1ST TIME)	NOTES

90791—Initial Evaluation; **90834**—45 Min. follow-up; **90837**—60-Min. follow-up; **90847**–Family/Couple appointment; **90839**—60-Min. crisis appointment; **99241**—15-Min. Consult; **99242**—30-Min. Consult; **99243**—40-Min. Consult; **99244**—60-Min. Consult; **99245**—80-Min. Consult

INVOICE

Business Name
Business Address
Business Phone Number
Business Email Address
Tax ID: Number

Date:

BILL TO:
Name:
Mailing Address:

DATE OF SERVICE	CLIENT NAME	DESCRIPTION	FEE FOR SERVICE

Total Amount Due	

Please remit the total amount due within 30 days.
Please make your check payable to: **Business Name.**

Thank You

[Business Name, Revised month, year]

MONTHLY TRACKING FORM

Month _____ Year_____

	INS A	INS B	INS C	INS D	INS E	INS F	INS G	INS H	INS I	TOTAL
# Sessions PPO										
#Sessions HMO										
% of Sessions										
# of Clients PPO										
# of Clients HMO										
% of Clients										
Revenue										
Total Revenue										
% of Revenue										
Avg session per day										
Avg session per week										
Avg $$ per hr										
Total served										
Total Closed										

PATIENT ACTIVITY REPORT
OUT-OF-NETWORK PATIENTS

Service Provider Name:_____Date Range: _____

PATIENT NAME	DIAGNOSIS (1ST TIME)	DOS	CPT CODE	AMOUNT CHARGED	AMOUNT COLLECTED	DATE COLLECTED	CHECK/ CC#

SB = Superbill Receipt
FS or HS = Flexplan or Health Savings Receipt
BC = Billing Charge

90791—Initial Evaluation; **90834**—45-Min. follow-up; **90837**—60-Min. follow-up; **90847**–Family/ Couple appointment; **90839**—60-Min. crisis appointment; **99241**—15-Min. Consult; **99242**—30-Min. Consult; **99243**—40-Min. Consult; **99244**—60-Min. Consult; **99245**—80-Min. Consult_____

APPENDIX F:

Professional Counselor Licensing Boards by State

The following listing was compiled by the American Counseling Association and is available online at http://wwwcounseling.org/knowledge-center/licensure-requirements/state-professional-counselor-licensure-boards. Another useful resource in searching for regulations and requirements in your state regarding licensing requirements is Counselor-License.com (http://www.counselor-license.com/).

PROFESSIONAL COUNSELOR LICENSING BOARDS BY STATE

ALABAMA

Board of Examiners in Counseling
950 22nd Street North, Suite 765
Birmingham, AL 35203
800/822-3307
205/458-8716
205/458-8718 (fax)
www.abec.alabama.gov
Licensed Professional Counselor (LPC)
Associate Licensed Counselor (ALC)

ALASKA

Board of Professional Counselors
P.O. Box 110806
Juneau, AK 99811-0806
907/465-2551
907/465-2974 (fax)
www.commerce.state.ak.us/occ/ppco.htm
Licensed Professional Counselor (LPC)

ARIZONA

Board of Behavioral Health Examiners
3443 N. Central Avenue, Suite 1700
Phoenix, AZ 85012
602/542-1882
602/364-0890 (fax)
information@azbbhe.us
http://azbbhe.us
Licensed Professional Counselor (LPC)
Licensed Associate Counselor (LAC)

ARKANSAS

Board of Examiners in Counseling
P.O. Box 70
Magnolia, AR 71754
870/901-7055
870/234-1842 (fax)
arboec@sbglobal.net
www.arkansas.gov/abec
Licensed Professional Counselor (LPC)
Licensed Associate Counselor (LAC)

CALIFORNIA

On October 11, 2009 the California counselor licensure bill was signed into law, establishing licensure of professional clinical counselors (LPCCs).
California Licensure Implementation Dates:

- **January 1, 2010:** The bill becomes law and the CA Board of Behavioral Sciences then has the responsibility for developing the rules and regulations to implement the bill and it will gear up to accept LPCC applications.
- **January 1, 2011:** Applications for grandparenting and reciprocity will be available through the Board of Behavioral Sciences. These requirements are posted on CALPCC's website.
- **January 1, 2012:** Applications for regular licensure will be available for those not eligible for grandparenting or reciprocity. These requirements are posted on CALPCC's website.

COLORADO

Board of Licensed Professional
Counselor Examiners
1560 Broadway, Suite 1350
Denver, CO 80202
303/894-7766
303/894-7764 (fax)
MentalHealth@dora.state.co.us
www.dora.state.co.us/mental-health
Licensed Professional Counselor (LPC)

CONNECTICUT

Department of Public Health
Professional Counselor Licensure
410 Capitol Avenue, MS #12APP
P.O. Box 340308
Hartford, CT 06134-0308
860/509-7603
860/509-8457 (fax)
oplc.dph@ct.gov
http://www.ct.gov/dph/
Licensed Professional Counselor (LPC)

DELAWARE

Board of Mental Health and Chemical
Dependency Professionals
Cannon Building
861 Silver Lake Boulevard, Suite 203
Dover, DE 19904-2467
302/744-4500
302/739-2711 (fax)
http://dpr.delaware.gov/
Licensed Professional Counselor of Mental Health (LPCMH)
Licensed Associate Counselor of Mental Health (LACMH)

DISTRICT OF COLUMBIA

Board of Professional Counseling
717 14th Street, NW, Suite 600
Washington, DC 20005
877/672-2174
202/727-8471 (fax)
http://hpla.doh.dc.gov/hpla/site/default.asp
Licensed Professional Counselor (LPC)

FLORIDA

Board of Clinical Social Work,
Marriage & Family Therapy, and
Mental Health Counseling
4052 Bald Cypress Way, BIN C-08
Tallahassee, FL 32399
850/245-4474
850/921-5389 (fax)
mqa_491@doh.state.fl.us
www.doh.state.fl.us/mqa/491
Licensed Mental Health Counselor (LMHC)
Provisional Mental Health Counselor
Registered Mental Health Counselor Intern

GEORGIA

Composite Board of Professional
Counselors, Social Workers, and
Marriage & Family Therapists
237 Coliseum Drive
Macon, GA 31217
478/207-2440
866/888-7127 (fax)
http://sos.georgia.gov/plb/counselors/
Licensed Professional Counselor (LPC)
Associate Licensed Professional
Counselor (LAPC)

HAWAII

Department of Commerce and Consumer
Affairs–PVL
Mental Health Counselor Program
P.O. Box 3469
Honolulu, HI 96801
(808) 586-2693
counselor@dcca.hawaii.gov
www.hawaii.gov/dcca/areas/pvl/
programs/mental/
Licensed Mental Health Counselor
(LMHC)

IDAHO

State Licensing Board of Professional
Counselors and Marriage & Family
Therapists
700 W. State Street, First Floor
PO Box 83720
Boise, ID 83720
208/334-3233
208/334-3945 (fax)
cou@ibol.idaho.gov
http://www.ibol.idaho.gov/
Licensed Clinical Professional
Counselor (LCPC)
Licensed Professional Counselor (LPC)
Registered Counselor Intern

ILLINOIS

Professional Counselor Licensing and
Disciplinary Board
320 W. Washington Street, 3rd Floor
Springfield, IL 62786
217/785-0800
217/524-6735 (TDD)
217/782-7645 (fax)
www.idfpr.com/dpr/who/prfcns.asp
Licensed Clinical Professional
Counselor (LCPC)
Licensed Professional Counselor (LPC)

INDIANA

Behavioral Health & Human Services
Licensing Board
402 W. Washington Street, Room
W072
Indianapolis, IN 46204
317/234-2064
317/233-4236 (fax)
pla5@pla.in.gov
www.in.gov/pla/social.htm
Licensed Mental Health Counselor
(LMHC)

IOWA

Board of Behavioral Science
Lucas State Office Building, 5th Floor
321 E. 12th Street
Des Moines, IA 50319
515/281-4422
515/281-3121 (fax)
www.idph.state.ia.us/licensure/
Licensed Mental Health Counselor
(LMHC)

KANSAS

Behavioral Sciences Regulatory Board
712 S. Kansas Avenue
Topeka, KS 66603
785/296-3240
785/296-3112 (fax)
http://www.ksbsrb.org/
Licensed Clinical Professional
Counselor (LCPC)
Licensed Professional Counselor (LPC)

KENTUCKY

Board of Licensed Professional
Counselors
P.O. Box 1360
Frankfort, KY 40602
502/564-3296, x239
502/564-4818 (fax)
http://lpc.ky.gov
Licensed Professional Clinical
Counselor (LPCC)
Licensed Professional Counselor
Associate (LPCA)

LOUISIANA

Licensed Professional Counselors Board
of Examiners
8631 Summa Avenue
Baton Rouge, LA 70809
225/765-2515
225/765-2514 (fax)
lpcboard@eatel.net
www.lpcboard.org
Licensed Professional Counselor (LPC)
Counselor Intern

MAINE

Board of Counseling Professionals
Licensure
35 State House Station
Augusta, ME 04333
207/624-8674
888/577-6690 TTY
207/624-8637 (fax)
http://www.maine.gov/pfr/
professionallicensing
Licensed Clinical Professional
Counselor (LCPC)
Licensed Professional Counselor (LPC)
Conditional LCPC
Conditional LPC
*Registered Counselor *As of August 1,*
2008, the Board is no longer issuing
initial licenses in this category; however,
current Registered Counselors may
continue to renew.

MARYLAND

Board of Examiners of Professional
Counselors and Therapists
4201 Patterson Avenue, 3rd Floor
Baltimore, MD 21215
410/764-4732
410/358-1610 (fax)
http://dhmh.maryland.gov/bopc
Licensed Clinical Professional
Counselor (LCPC)
Certified Professional Counselor (CPC)
As of 10-01-08 this credential is no
longer available to new applicants,
however current CPCs may continue
to renew.
Licensed Graduate Professional
Counselor

MASSACHUSETTS

Board of Registration of Allied
Mental Health & Human Services
Professionals
Division of Professional Licensure
1000 Washington Street, Suite 710
Boston, MA 02118
617/727-3080
617/727-2197 (fax)
www.mass.gov/dpl/boards/mh
*Licensed Mental Health Counselor
(LMHC)*

MICHIGAN

Board of Counseling
P.O. Box 30670
Lansing, MI 48909
517/335-0918
517/373-2179 (fax)
bhphelp@michigan.gov
www.michigan.gov/healthlicense
Licensed Professional Counselor (LPC)
*Limited Licensed Professional
Counselor (LLPC)*

MINNESOTA

Board of Behavioral Health &
Therapy
2829 University Avenue SE, Suite 210
Minneapolis, MN 55414
612/617-2178
800/627-3529 TTY
612/617-2187 (fax)
bbht.board@state.mn.us
www.bbht.state.mn.us
*Licensed Professional Clinical
Counselor (LPCC)*
Licensed Professional Counselor (LPC)

MISSISSIPPI

State Board of Examiners for Licensed
Professional Counselors
P.O. Box 1497
129 E. Jefferson Street
Yazoo City, MS 39194
662/716-3932
888/860-7001
662/716-3021 (fax)
www.lpc.state.ms.us
Licensed Professional Counselor (LPC)

MISSOURI

Committee for Professional
Counselors
3605 Missouri Boulevard
P.O. Box 1335
Jefferson City, MO 65102
573/751-0018
800/735-2966 TTY
573/751-0735 (fax)
profcounselor@pr.mo.gov
http://pr.mo.gov/counselors.asp
Licensed Professional Counselor (LPC)
*Provisional Licensed Professional
Counselor (PLPC)*

MONTANA

Board of Social Work Examiners and
Professional Counselors
301 S. Park, 4th Floor
P.O. Box 200513
Helena, MT 59620
406/841-2391 or 2392
406/841-2305 (fax)
dlibsdswp@mt.gov
http://bsd.dli.mt.gov/license/bsd_
boards/swp_board/board_page.asp
*Licensed Clinical Professional
Counselor (LCPC)*

NEBRASKA

Board of Mental Health Practice
P.O. Box 94986
Lincoln, NE 68509
402/471-2117
402/471-3577 (fax)
www.dhhs.ne.gov/crl/mhcs/mental/
mentalindex.htm
*Licensed Independent Mental Health
Practitioner-Certified Professional
Counselor or Licensed Professional
Counselor (LIMHP-CPC/LPC)*
*Licensed Mental Health Practitioner-
Certified Professional Counselor or
Licensed Professional Counselor
(LMHP-CPC/LPC)*
*Licensed Mental Health Practitioner
(LMHP)*
*Provisional Licensed Mental Health
Practitioner (PLMHP)*

NEVADA

Board of Examiners for Marriage
& Family Therapists & Clinical
Professional Counselors
P.O. Box 370130
Las Vegas, NV 89137-0130
702-486-7388
702-486-7258 (fax)
nvmftbd@mftbd.nv.gov
http://marriage.state.nv.us/
*Licensed Clinical Professional
Counselor (LCPC)*
Licensed Clinical Counselor Intern

NEW HAMPSHIRE

Board of Mental Health Practice
117 Pleasant Street
Concord, NH 03301
603/271-6762
800/735-2954 TDD
603/271-3950 (fax)
www.nh.gov/mhpb
*Licensed Clinical Mental Health
Counselor (LCMHC)*

NEW JERSEY

Board of Marriage and Family
Therapy Examiners
Professional Counselor Examiners
Committee
P.O. Box 45007
Newark, NJ 07101
973/504-6582
973/648-3536 (fax)
www.njconsumeraffairs.gov/proc
Licensed Professional Counselor (LPC)
Licensed Associate Counselor (LAC)

NEW MEXICO

Counseling and Therapy Practice
Board
2550 Cerrillos Road
Santa Fe, NM 87505
505/476-4610
505/476-4633 (fax)
counselingboard@state.nm.us
www.rld.state.nm.us/counseling
*Licensed Professional Clinical
Mental Health Counselor (LPCC)*
*Licensed Professional Mental Health
Counselor (LPC) *The Board is no
longer issuing initial licenses in this
cateogry, however current LPCs may
continue to renew.*
*Licensed Mental Health Counselor
(LMHC)*

NEW YORK

State Board for Mental Health
Practitioners
89 Washington Avenue
Albany, NY 12234-1000
518/474-3817, x450
518/486-2981 (fax)
mhpbd@mail.nysed.gov
http://www.op.nysed.gov/prof/mhp/
mhclic.htm
*Licensed Mental Health Counselor
(LMHC)*

NORTH CAROLINA

Board of Licensed Professional
Counselors
P.O. Box 77819
Greensboro, NC 27417
844/622-3572 or 336/217-6007
336/217-9450 (fax)
LPCInfo@ncblpc.org
http://www.ncblpc.org
Licensed Professional Counselor (LPC)
*Licensed Professional Counselor
Associate (LPCA)*
*Licensed Professional Counselor
Supervisor (LPCS)*

NORTH DAKOTA

Board of Counselor Examiners
2112 10th Ave SE
Mandan, ND 58554
701/667-5969
*same number for both phone and fax
ndbce@btinet.net
www.ndbce.org
*Licensed Professional Clinical
Counselor (LPCC)*
Licensed Professional Counselor (LPC)
*Licensed Associate Professional
Counselor (LAPC)*

OHIO

Counselor, Social Worker, and
Marriage & Family Therapist Board
50 West Broad Street, Suite 1075
Columbus, OH 43215
614/466-0912
614/728-7790 (fax)
cswmft.info@cswb.state.oh.us
http://cswmft.ohio.gov
*Licensed Professional Clinical
Counselor (LPCC)*
Licensed Professional Counselor (LPC)
*Professional Counselor/Clinical
Resident*

OKLAHOMA

State Board of Licensed Professional
Counselors
1000 N.E. 10th Street
Oklahoma City, OK 73117
405/271-6030
405/271-1918 (fax)
nenaw@health.ok.gov
http://pcl.health.ok.gov
Licensed Professional Counselor (LPC)

OREGON

Board of Licensed Professional
Counselors and Therapists
3218 Pringle Road, SE, Suite 250
Salem, OR 97302-6312
503/378-5499
503/373-1427 (fax)
lpct.board@state.or.us
www.oregon.gov/oblpct
Licensed Professional Counselor (LPC)
Registered Intern

PENNSYLVANIA

State Board of Social Workers,
Marriage & Family Therapists, and
Professional Counselors
P.O. Box 2649
Harrisburg, PA 17105-2649
717/783-1389
717/787-7769 (fax)
st-socialwork@state.pa.us
www.dos.state.pa.us/social
Licensed Professional Counselor (LPC)

PUERTO RICO

Board of Examiners of Professional
Counselors
P.O. Box 10200
San Juan, PR 00908
787/765-2929
www.salud.gov.pr
Licensed Professional Counselor (LPC)
*Professional Counselor with
Provisional License (PCPL)*

RHODE ISLAND

Board of Mental Health Counselors and
Marriage & Family Therapists
3 Capitol Hill, Room 104
Providence, RI 02908
401/222-2828
401/222-1272 (fax)
www.health.ri.gov/hsr/professions/
mf_counsel.php
*Licensed Clinical Mental Health
Counselor (LCMHC)*

SOUTH CAROLINA

Board of Examiners for Licensure of
Professional Counselors, Marriage
& Family Therapists, and Psycho-
Educational Specialists
P.O. Box 11329
Columbia, SC 29211-1329
803/896-4665
803/896-4719 (fax)
www.llr.state.sc.us/pol/counselors
To obtain an application for licensure
please contact the Center for
Credentialing and Education (CCE),
an affiliate of NBCC, at:
(888) 817-8283
cce@cce-global.org
www.cce-global.org
Licensed Professional Counselor (LPC)
Professional Counselor Intern (LPC/I)

SOUTH DAKOTA

Board of Examiners for Counselors and
Marriage & Family Therapists
P.O. Box 2164
Sioux Falls, SD 57101
605/331-2927
605/331-2043 (fax)
sdbce.msp@midconetwork.com
http://dhs.sd.gov/brd/counselor
*Licensed Professional Counselor–
Mental Health (LPC-MH)*
Licensed Professional Counselor (LPC)

TENNESSEE

Board for Professional Counselors,
Marital & Family Therapists, and
Clinical Pastoral Therapists
227 French Landing, Suite 300
Nashville, TN 37243
615/532-3202, x 25138
800/778-4123, x 25138
615/532-5369 (fax)
http://health.state.tn.us/boards/
PC_MFT&CPT/
*Licensed Professional Counselor–
Mental Health Service Provider
(LPC/MHSP)*
Licensed Professional Counselor (LPC)

TEXAS

State Board of Examiners of
Professional Counselors
P.O. Box 149347, MC 1982
Austin, TX 78714
512/834-6658
512/834-6677 (fax)
lpc@dshs.state.tx.us
www.dshs.state.tx.us/counselor
Licensed Professional Counselor (LPC)
Licensed Professional Counselor
Intern (LPC-I)

UTAH

Professional Counselor Licensing Board
P.O. Box 146741
Salt Lake City, UT 84114-6741
801/530-6628
866/275-3675 (Utah toll-free number)
801/530-6511 (fax)
http://dopl.utah.gov/licensing/
professional_counseling.html
Licensed Professional Counselor (LPC)
Associate Professional Counselor
Associate Professional Counselor
Extern

VERMONT

Board of Allied Mental Health
Practitioners
National Life Building, North Floor 2
Montpelier, VT 05620-3402
1-800-439-8683 (in-state)
802/828-2390
802/828-2465 (fax)
http://vtprofessionals.org
Licensed Clinical Mental Health
Counselor (LCMHC)

VIRGINIA

Board of Counseling
Perimeter Center
9960 Mayland Drive, Suite 300
Richmond, VA 23233
804/367-4610
804/527-4435 (fax)
coun@dhp.virginia.gov
www.dhp.virginia.gov/counseling
Licensed Professional Counselor (LPC)

WASHINGTON

Licensed Mental Health Counselors,
Marriage and Family Therapists and
Social Workers
Advisory Committee
P.O. Box 47877
Olympia, WA 98504-7877
360/236-4700
360/236-4818 (fax)
hpqa.csc@doh.wa.gov
http://www.doh.wa.gov/licensing/
Licensed Mental Health Counselor
(LMHC)
Licensed Mental Health Counselor
Associate (LMHCA)
Certified Counselor (CC)
Certified Adviser (CA)
Agency Affiliated Counselor (AAC)

WEST VIRGINIA

Board of Examiners in Counseling
815 Quarrier Street, Suite 212
Charleston, WV 25301
304/558-5494
800/520-3852
304/558-5496 (fax)
counselingboard@msn.com
www.wvbec.org
Licensed Professional Counselor (LPC)

WISCONSIN

Examining Board of Marriage &
Family Therapists, Professional
Counselors and Social Workers
P.O. Box 8935
Madison, WI 53708
608/266-2112
608/261-7083 (fax)
http://drl.wi.gov/board_detail.
asp?boardid=32&locid=0
Licensed Professional Counselor (LPC)
Professional Counselor Trainee

WYOMING

Mental Health Professions Licensing
Board
1800 Carey Avenue, 4th Floor
Cheyenne, WY 82002
307/777-3628
307/777-3508 (fax)
WyoMHPLB@wyo.gov
http://plboards.state.wy.us/
mentalhealth/index.asp
Licensed Professional Counselor (LPC)
Provisional Professional Counselor
(PPC)

APPENDIX G:

Online Therapist Directory

The following list is comprised of various online directories for counselors and other mental health professionals/providers. The most frequently used online directories are listed below in alphabetical order. This list is in no way comprehensive; a Google search will provide access to other options not listed below. Individuals may be eligible to join certain directories based on memberships with national associations. Location-specific directories are also available, such as the Denver Therapists Network or Counseling California.

ONLINE THERAPIST DIRECTORY

BREAK THROUGH
WWW.BREAKTHROUGH.COM

About: An online resource that connects individuals to mental health providers for online counseling and psychiatric care. Breakthrough.com is not a referral service. Breakthrough currently operates in the following US states: Alabama, Alaska, Arizona, Arkansas, California, Colorado, Connecticut, Delaware, District of Columbia, Florida, Georgia, Hawaii, Idaho, Illinois, Indiana, Iowa, Kansas, Kentucky, Louisiana, Maine, Maryland, Massachusetts, Michigan, Minnesota, Mississippi, Missouri, Montana, Nebraska, Nevada, New Hampshire, New Jersey, New Mexico, New York, North Carolina, North Dakota, Ohio, Oklahoma, Oregon, Pennsylvania, Rhode Island, South Carolina, South Dakota, Tennessee, Texas, Utah, Vermont, Virginia, Washington, West Virginia, Wisconsin, and Wyoming.

Fees: There is no set-up cost or on-going fees for service providers. In exchange for the services provided by Breakthrough, providers are charged $6 per session. Providers are expected to conduct a minimum of 5–15 sessions per month.

Who is eligible to join? To be eligible to join Breakthrough's provider network you must carry a current behavioral health license in a state where Breakthrough is operating as well as have a current NPI (National Provider Identifier) and professional liability insurance.

OPEN PATH PSYCHOTHERAPY COLLECTIVE
OPENPATHCOLLECTIVE.ORG

About: An online directory of therapists who have agreed to provide in-office treatment at low client fees ranging between $30 and $50. Membership includes a customizable profile page where you can include a photo, link to your website, basic information about your practice as well as list qualifications, client focus and treatment approach. Open Path requires members to see a minimum of one client at any given time at this reduced rate. Open Path has partnered with numerous organizations/businesses to offer members discounts on products as a benefit for member therapists.

Fees: There is no fee to be a member and set up a profile.

Who is eligible to join? Open Path Psychotherapy Collective welcomes licensed or provisionally licensed (Pre-Licensed/License Eligible) mental health clinicians with graduate degrees in psychotherapy, counseling, or a related field from an accredited institution. They also accept "unlicensed professionals practicing in jurisdictions where it is legal to practice counseling and psychotherapy without a license." All applicants must pass the peer-reviewed online application process and provide proof of liability insurance.

THE FAMILY & MARRIAGE COUNSELING DIRECTORY
FAMILY-MARRIAGE-COUNSELING.COM

About: An online, multidisciplinary directory of helping professionals categorized by state and city. The website states that is one of the "most popular" directories on the internet and encourages helping professionals to join and become "advertisers" to begin getting referrals. "Advertisers" are listed by city and state. Listings are basic and include name, website, address, phone number, and special interests. The website claims that the "simple nature" of the listings lowers the chance of consumers "talk(ing) themselves out of therapy by reading lengthy "profiles" trying to decide if you are the right therapist for them."

Fees: $9.95 per month for an individual listing or $11.95 for a group, organization or agency listing. There is no contract or obligation and listings can be cancelled at any time.

Who is eligible to join? To list with the directory, one must have a master's degree in a counseling-related field from an accredited university and be licensed, or undergoing the licensing process, in their respective state. "Advertisers" must also be free from any disciplinary action by their profession's respective licensing body. The website states that degree qualifications are checked periodically.

FIND-A-THERAPIST.COM
WWW.FIND-A-THERAPIST.COM

About: An online directory of "verified therapists, psychologists, marriage and family counselors, social workers, licensed professional counselors and psychiatrists." Membership includes benefits such as receiving statistics about your profile, freedom to edit your own listing, ability to accept payments or sell products via PayPal through your listing, and ability to "connect with patients through an integrated micro-blog." The site offers members a guarantee of high visibility for their listing and states "we guarantee that your listing will be viewed at least 365 times per year or your listing will be kept active without charge until it reaches 365 views!"

Fees: There are three plans available. The standard listing is $99 a year; the enhanced listing is $199 a year; and the premium listing is $299 a year.

Who is eligible to join? Find-a-Therapist.com asserts that it verifies the following for each listing: name and contact details of the professional; that the professional holds a valid license (if applicable) in the practicing state; and that there are no restrictions on the professional's license.

GOODTHERAPY.ORG
WWW.GOODTHERAPY.ORG

About: GoodTherapy.org touts itself as one of the highest-ranked therapist directories on the internet. The directory claims to be "an association of mental health professionals in over 30 countries who support efforts to reduce harm in therapy and provide ethical, collaborative therapy services." Membership is open to mental health counselors, psychotherapists, social workers, marriage and family therapists, psychologists, psychoanalysts, psychiatrists, physicians, and nurse practitioners. GoodTherapy.org guarantees referrals and states that if ,within the first three months, you have not received a client, they will waive their fee until you receive a client as well as "work with you to correct whatever is causing your profile listing to underperform."

Fees: There are two options for membership: a monthly fee of $24.95 or $269 for the year.

Who is eligible to join? Members are required to have received graduate-level academic training and a degree in psychotherapy, counseling, or a related field from an accredited institution. One must also be licensed or pre-licensed practicing legally under the supervision of a licensed professional. You may also be "an unlicensed professional in a jurisdiction in which it is legal to practice counseling and/or psychotherapy without a license." All applicants must pass a peer-reviewed online application process, which they guarantee is done within one business day.

Additional Benefits of Membership: GoodTherapy.org offers its members access to online continuing education events with CE credits at no additional cost. Other benefits promoted by GoodTherapy.org include: publication opportunities, media relations, and eligibility to receive special offers and/or reduced rates from other service providers and manufacturers.

GOOGLE MY BUSINESS

About: Google My Business complements your existing website by giving your business a public identity and presence on Google. The information you provide about your business can appear on Google Search, Maps and Google+.

Fees: There is no cost.

Who is eligible to join? This service is open to the general public and not regulated by any governing body. Information that is published here is not necessarily verified.

MY THERAPIST MATCH
WWW.MYTHERAPISTMATCH.COM

About: An online directory in which users complete a questionnaire and receive a list of therapists who are deemed "compatible" based on the users' "personality, community style, and personal preferences." To start the process, one must complete the matching survey, choose a subscription plan, complete a profile and lastly have credentials verified by the "MyTherapistMatch.com Team."

Fees: There are three pricing options available: $297 for a one-year subscription, $400 for a two-year subscription, and $400 for an 18-month subscription. Each plan includes the following services and benefits: "personality-based client matching, listing in our therapist directory, premium content to grow your practice, include a video on your profile, free listing on MyCoachMatch.com, and exclusive discounts on Industry-leading service providers."

Who is eligible to join? MyTherapistMatch.com welcomes the following professions: counselors, psychotherapists, social workers, marriage & family therapists, psychologists, psychoanalysts or psychiatrists. Members must have graduate-level academic training and a degree in psychotherapy, counseling, or a related field from an accredited institution. Additionally, members are required to be licensed. Unlicensed interns under the supervision of a licensed professional are permitted. They also extend membership to unlicensed professionals who are practicing counseling and psychotherapy in a jurisdiction where it is legal.

Additional Benefits of Membership: Members are eligible for special discounts on service providers.

NETWORK THERAPY.COM
WWW.NETWORKTHERAPY.COM

About: A provider directory for psychologists, counselors, marriage and family therapists, and other mental health providers. A profile/listing includes: "full contact information; additional in-depth practice information; up to 4 searchable practice locations; a powerful and unique search technology; an optional photo; an optional video or audio introduction; a custom website address; 12 extra pages for posting articles, therapy groups, office photos; opportunity to publish articles linked to and from your profile; a link to your website; email contact form with spam protection; profile counters; friendly support via phone or email; and a 90-day satisfaction guarantee."

Fees: Membership costs $179 a year.

Who is eligible to join? To list in the directory, one must be a state licensed or registered mental health professional (psychologists, psychiatrists, social workers, marriage and family therapists, counselors, psychoanalysts, creative arts therapists, and psychiatric nurse practitioners). Pre-licensed mental health professionals, under the supervision of a licensed professional, are also welcome to join. All professionals must have at least a master's degree in a counseling-related field (psychology, social work, counseling, etc.) from an accredited institution. License information is verified at the time of joining the directory and annually thereafter. A professional's license must be active and in good standing.

PSYCHOLOGY.COM
WWW.PSYCHOLOGY.COM

About: Claims to be the first online counseling and therapy directory. The directory lists licensed clinical psychologists, social workers, counselors and other professionals with a variety of specialties.

Fees: There are two options. The basic listing is $99.95/year and includes basic demographic information and ability for individual to contact you through the site. The expanded listing for $14.95/month or $149.95/year includes basic demographic information, ability for individuals to contact you through the site; expanded profile page with information about your practice, ability to add a photo, ability to link to an external website; an automatic map to your location; preferred placement in search results and the ability to offer professional advice online.

Who is eligible to join? Only licensed therapists can join the network. When you register, a current license number will need to be provided and this will be validated.

PSYCHOLOGY TODAY.COM
THERAPISTS.PSYCHOLOGYTODAY.COM

About: Online professional listings for psychologists, psychiatrists, therapists, counselors, group therapy and treatment centers in the United States and Canada. Psychology Today's Therapy Directory lists clinical professionals, psychiatrists and treatment centers who provide mental health services in the US and internationally.

Fees: 29.95/month

Who is eligible to join? Name and contact details as well as professional license, if applicable, are all verified upon initial registration. Registration is not limited to licensed professionals. If practicing under the clinical supervision and license of another professional, that professional's credentials need to be provided to register.

PSYCH CENTRAL
PSYCHCENTRAL.COM

About: Pscyh Central uses the online directory Theravive (more information below). They also offer professionals an opportunity to connect with one another online through Psych Central Clinical Connection, which is a closed professional social network only available for professionals in clinical psychotherapy practice with a license. For more information about Psych Central's Clinical Connection visit them online at threapists.pyschcentral.com.

THERAPISTLOCATOR.NET
WWW.THERAPISTLOCATOR.NET

About: TherapistLocator.net is an online directory of marriage and family therapists. All therapists listed in this directory are Clinical Fellows and Members of the American Association for Marriage and Family Therapy (AAMFT), and as such must meet stringent training and education requirements established by AAMFT. In order to list in the directory, the professional must be a member of AAMFT.

Fee: Free with membership; Membership dues vary based on level of membership.

Who is eligible to join? Membership in AAMFT is open to a broad range of individuals in six different categories based on education and professional experience/status. For more information about membership visit www.aamft.org.

THERAPY TRIBE.COM
WWW.THERAPYTRIBE.COM

About: The unique feature of this directory is the geo-targeting technology, which matches the location of a visitor on any of their support websites to a therapist listed in the directory. List your individual or group practice on the TherapyTribe online therapist directory and help prospective clients and referral sources learn more about you and the services you offer. Communicate in detail your unique credentials and expertise. Connect to over 150,000 relevant visitors a month.

Fee: Choose a Monthly or Annual Membership: Monthly Listing: ($20 Month) Sign up today and get your 1st Month FREE, Cancel Anytime. Annual Listing: ($199 Year) All annual sign-ups get a 30-day Money Back Guarantee.; special offers for members of the following associations: American Psychological Association (APA), American Counseling Association (ACA), National Association of Social Workers (NASW), and American Association for Marriage and Family Therapy (AAMFT).

Who is eligible to join? Anyone professional can list their counseling practice.

Additional Benefits of Membership: Searchable office locations, Personalized URL: www.therapytribe.com/listing/YourName, Link to your website—with click-thru stats, links to your personal TherapyTribe blogs, E-mail contact form to protect you from unwanted emails, and Smart search shows your profile in nearby zip code searches.

THERAVIVE
WWW.THERAVIVE.COM

About: Theravive is an online listing of licensed and professional clinical counselors, therapists, and psychologists.

Fee: The yearly cost for standard listing is $247–397. The enhanced and VIP listing prices are not advertised and you must call to inquire. Theravive offers numerous features that you may choose to include or opt out of; thus pricing varies.

Who is eligible to join? Theravive claims registrants hold advanced degrees and are fully licensed to practice counseling. The registration process asks professionals to check a box stating "I certify I am a credentialed therapist with at least a Masters level education bound by, and in good standing with, regulatory bodies that govern my professional practice."

THRIVEWORKS
THRIVEWORKS.COM/FIND-COUNSELOR

About: Developed by Anthony Centore, a counselor and private practice consultant for the American Counseling Association. He had a vision to develop a free counselor directory, similar to that of "Psychology Today" to help counselors promote their practices online. He has also developed an online platform called Thriveworks (www.thriveworks.com) that connects individuals to licensed counselors and coaches at a Thriveworks Counseling office near them. Thriveworks also offers online and telephone counseling.

Fee: Free

Who is eligible to join? Anyone professional can list their counseling practice.

THERAPIST SITES
WWW.THERAPISTSITES.COM

About: A free web page is available for all mental health professionals, including Marriage and Family Therapists, Social Workers, Nurse Practitioners, Pastoral Counselors, Licensed Professional Counselors, Psychologists, and Psychiatrists.

Fee: Free basic courtesy web page or $100/year for a custom designed web page which includes search engine optimization using unique keywords, choice of templates, up to 7 Links, customized text/bio, enhanced directory display and toll-free tech support.

Who is eligible to join? Anyone professional can list their counseling practice.

Resources

APPENDIX H:

Government Mental Health Agency Directory

The following listings are for government or government-related agencies where mental health resources such as listings of providers, provider panel application and information, and other helpful resources may be found.

GOVERNMENT MENTAL HEALTH AGENCY DIRECTORY

AGENCY FOR HEALTHCARE RESEARCH AND QUALITY
WWW.AHRQ.GOV

This site, housed within the U.S. Department of Health & Human Services, is all about creating advances in healthcare through improving healthcare quality. Housed within this site you will find information on healthcare for professionals as well as policy makers. There's information about grants and funding as well. So, if you are building a non-profit program or agency, you can look into funding through this site. Additionally, this site has information that will help you in your advocacy role in private practice.

CENTERS FOR MEDICARE AND MEDICAID SERVICES
WWW.CMS.GOV

This site is the home for all things Medicare, Medicaid, Children's Health Insurance Plan (CHIP), and the Health Insurance Marketplace.

MEDICARE
WWW.MEDICARE.GOV

This site is the official U.S. government website for the Medicare plan. It's a helpful site to understand and send your Medicare clients to for information about their plan. Also, it's helpful as a practice owner to utilize this site to access more specific information about Medicare. You can find providers who accept Medicare through this site. And, you can file complaints of fraud/abuse through this site.

MEDICAID
WWW.MEDICAID.GOV

This site houses further information about Medicaid and the Children's Health Insurance Plan (CHIP).

SUBSTANCE ABUSE AND MENTAL HEALTH SERVICES ADMINISTRATION (SAMHSA)
WWW.SAMHSA.GOV

A federal government website with specific information on substance abuse and mental health services, including a comprehensive state-specific behavioral treatment program locator, as well as information on suicide prevention, behavioral health equity, mental health and substance abuse data, and other helpful information.

TRICARE
WWW.TRICARE.MIL

A part of the U.S. Department of Defense, Tricare is the insurance plan for military personnel. A provider search is available on this site for helping to develop a referral network of other providers. And, you can obtain information on how to become a provider by scrolling to the bottom of the home page and clicking on "For Providers."

U.S. DEPARTMENT OF HEALTH AND HUMAN SERVICES
WWW.HHS.GOV

An overall healthcare-related site that has information on healthcare laws and regulations, grants and contracts, programs and services.

Resources

APPENDIX I:

Other Business Tools for Helping Professionals

These tools will help you build and continue to grow your practice. I want you to have choices, so I included different options in each category to help you. Please note that these listings are not an endorsement nor a guarantee of the company listed, nor their products or services. They are simply well researched and viable options to use as helping tools.

OTHER BUSINESS TOOLS FOR HELPING PROFESSIONALS

LIABILITY INSURANCE PROTECTION

HPSO—(http://www.hpso.com/)

CPH & Associates—(http://www.cphins.com/)

Lockton Affinity—(http://locktonmedicalliabilityinsurance.com)

LEGAL ENTITY RESOURCES AND FEES BY STATE

Limited Liability Company (LLC) Filing Fees by State—(https://thecorpsec.files.wordpress.com/2012/03/llc-annual-costs-by-state2.pdf)

Incorporate Fast Inc.—(https://www.incorporatefast.com/state-filing-fees/)

BUSINESS TRAININGS/ CONSULTATION FOR PRIVATE PRACTICE

Be a Wealthy Therapist (www.beawealthytherapist.net)

Coaching with Annie (www.coachingwithannie.com)

Higher Practice (www.higherpractice.com)

Private Practice From the Inside Out (www.tamarasuttle.com)

Practice of the Practice (www.practiceofthepractice.com)

Private Practice Success (www.privatepracticesuccess.com)

Smart Practice Central (www.smartpracticecentral.com)

Zynnyme (www.zynnyme.com)

MENTAL HEALTH PRACTICE MANAGEMENT SOFTWARE

Simple Practice (www.simplepractice.com)

TherapyNotes.com (www.therapynotes.com)

Therapy Partner (www.therapypartner.com)

Therapist Helper (www.helper.com)

Therapy Mate (www.therapymate.com)

Therabill (www.therabill.com)

WEBSITE DESIGN AND ONLINE PRESENCE FOR THERAPISTS

Counseling Wise (www.counselingwise.com)

Design For Therapists (http://www.designfortherapists.com/)

Weston Graphics (www.westongraphicsinternet.com/web-design/sites-for-therapists/)

Therapysites (www.therapysites.com)

In Session (insession.io)

Ignite Therapy Sites (http://www.ignitecustomwebsites.com/websites-for-counselors-therapists.php)

Brighter Vision Web Solutions (http://www.brightervision.com/)

SCHEDULING SOFTWARE FOR THERAPISTS

Appointments Plus (https://www.appointment-plus.com/industries/counseling-appointment-scheduling-software)

Yellow Schedule (https://www.yellowschedule.com/about/for-business/therapists/)

VIRTUAL ASSISTANT RESOURCES

My Solution Services—(Virtual Assistant for Therapists!)—(http://mysolutionservices.com/)

Virtual Assistant Networking—Global Virtual Assistant Networking Organization (http://www.vanetworking.com/)

Psych Assistant (http://www.psychassistant.com.au/index.html)

CONTINUING EDUCATION RESOURCES FOR MENTAL HEALTH PROFESSIONALS

PESI (www.pesi.com)

i-counseling (https://www.i-counseling.net/home)

Hazelden (https://www.hazelden.org/web/public/professional_education.page)

The Gottman Institute (https://www.gottman.com.)

The Mindsight Insititute (https://www.mindsightinstitute.com/)

Aspira Continuing Education (https://aspirace.com/)

Psychotherapy.net (https://www.psychotherapy.net/continuing-education/counseling)

COUNSELING RESOURCE MATERIALS

Child Play Therapy Toys (http://www.childtherapytoys.com/store/index.html)

Self Help Warehouse (www.selfhelpwarehouse.com)

Therapist Aid—Worksheets and Tools for Mental Health Professionals (http://www.therapistaid.com/)

APPENDIX J:

National Professional Associations for Mental Health Professionals

This list of national professional associations will assist you in providing additional support for your clinical practice. Some are specific to your clinical specialty area and others include your general professional association(s). Not listed are state level professional associations. You are encouraged to contact and join your state level professional association as well.

NATIONAL PROFESSIONAL ASSOCIATIONS FOR MENTAL HEALTH PROFESSIONALS

Academy for Eating Disorders (AED): www.aedweb.org

American Art Therapy Association (AATA): www.arttherapy.org

American Association of Christian Counselors: www.aacc.net/

American College Counseling Association (ACCA): http://www.collegecounseling.org/

American Association of Sexuality Educators, Counselors, and Therapists (ASSECT): www.aasect.org/

American Association for Marriage and Family Therapists (AAMFT): www.aamft.org

American Counseling Association (ACA): www.counseling.org

American Group Psychotherapy Association (AGPA): www.agpa.org

American Medical Association (AMA): www.ama-assn.org/ama

American Mental Health Counselors Association (AMHCA): www.amhca.org/home.html

American Music Therapy Association (AMTA): www.musictherapy.org

American Psychiatric Association: www.psych.org

American Psychological Association (APA): www.apa.org

American Rehabilitation Counseling Association (ARCA): www.arcaweb.org

American School Counselors Association (ASCA): www.schoolcounselor.org

Association for Adult Development and Aging (AADA): www.aadaweb.org

American Society of Group Psychotherapy and Psychodrama: http://www.asgpp.org/

Association for Counselor Education and Supervision (ACES): www.acesonline.net

Association for Counselors and Educators in Government (ACEG): acegonline.org

Association for Creativity in Counseling (ACC): www.creativecounselor.org/

Association for Lesbian, Gay, Bisexual, and Transgender Issues in Counseling (ALGBTIC): www.algbtic.org/

Association for Humanistic Counseling (AHC) : afhc.camp9.org/

Association for Multicultural Counseling and Development: www.multiculturalcounseling.org/

Association for Specialists in Group Work: www.asgw.org/

Association for Spiritual, Ethical, and Religious Values in Counseling (ASERVIC): www.aservic.org/

Association for Play Therapy (APT): http://www.a4pt.org/

Association for Women in Psychology: www.awpsych.org

British Association for Counselling and Psychotherapy: http://www.bacp.co.uk/

Chi Sigma Iota: https://www.csi-net.org/

Counseling Association for Humanistic Education and Development (C-AHEAD): http://afhc.camp9.org/

Counselors for Social Justice: https://counseling-csj.org/

Dialectical Behavioral Therapy National Certification and Accreditation Association (DBTNCAA): www.dbtncaa.com

European Branch of the American Counseling Association: http://eb-aca.jimdo.com/

International Society for Mental Health Online: http://ismho.org/

International Association of Addiction and Offender Counselors (IAAOC): http://www.iaaoc.org/

International Association of Marriage and Family Counselors (IAMFC): http://www.iamfconline.org/

National (USA) Association of Social Workers: www.naswdc.org

National (USA) Association for Drama Therapy: www.nadt.org

National Association for Addiction Professionals: www.naadac.org

National Association of School Psychologists: https://www.nasponline.org/

National Board for Certified Counselors (NBCC): www.nbcc.org

National Career Development Association (NCDA): http://www.ncda.org/

National Employment Counseling Association (NECA): http://www.employmentcounseling.org/

Society for Industrial and Organizational Psychology (SIOP): www.siop.org

REFERENCES

Baumgarten, H. (2014, May 21). *The Affordable Care Act: What Every Mental Health Professional Needs to Know About Obamacare's Impact on Your Practice.* Lecture presented at Wyndham Philadelphia–Mt. Laurel, Mount Laurel, NJ. Retrieved May 17, 2016, from http://www.pesi.com/ECommerce/ItemDetails.aspx?ResourceCode=RNV046745

Baumgarten, H. (2014). Need a Website. Retrieved April 10, 2016, from http://smartpracticecentral.com/wp/need-a-website/

Baumgarten, H. (2014, September 17). *Smart Business Strategies & Solutions for the Clinician: Improve Client Care, Increase Revenue, and Secure Your Financial Future.* Lecture presented at Courtyard Cromwell Marriott in Cromwell, CT. Retrieved May 15, 2016, from https://catalog.pesi.com/item/smart-business-strategies-solutions-clinician-improve-client-care-increase-revenue-secure-financial-future-6524.

Behavioral Health Services. (2016). Retrieved April 03, 2016, from https://www.medicaid.gov/medicaid-chip-program-information/by-topics/benefits/mental-health-services.html

Breakthrough: Confidential video counseling and online therapy. (n.d.). Retrieved September 18, 2015, from https://www.breakthrough.com/for-providers/general-faq

Brown, B. (2012). *Daring greatly: How the courage to be vulnerable transforms the way we live, love, parent, and lead.* New York, NY: Gotham Books.

Burns, D. D. (2009). Feeling good: the new mood therapy. New York: Harper.

CAQH—ProView—Final. (2015, April 07). Retrieved March 06, 2016, from http://www.caqh.org/

Centore, A. (2016, March). A warning for your counseling practice: Be different or die. *Counseling Today, 58*(9), 12–13.

Civic Impulse. (2016). H.R. 2759—114th Congress: Mental Health Access Improvement Act of 2015. Retrieved from https://www.govtrack.us/congress/bills/114/hr2759

Civic Impulse. (2016). H.R. 3662—113th Congress: Mental Health Access Improvement Act of 2013. Retrieved from https://www.govtrack.us/congress/bills/113/hr3662

Civic Impulse. (2016). S. 562—113th Congress: Seniors Mental Health Access Improvement Act of 2013. Retrieved from https://www.govtrack.us/congress/bills/113/s562

Client Guarantee! We guarantee you at least one paying client. (n.d.). Retrieved September 18, 2015, from http://www.theravive.com/forcounsellors/sign-up/welcome-page.aspx

Copeland, M. (2014). *Retirement on the brain: a prescription for healthy retirement* [PowerPoint slides]. Retrieved June 29, 2016, from StanCorp Equities, Inc. via e-mail September, 19, 2014.

Counselor Licensing. (n.d.). Retrieved September 15, 2015, from http://www.counselor-license.com/

DeGrossa, B. (2016, March 25). How to build your ultimate website! [Telephone interview].

Engel, M. (2015, March 25). Doctors' office wait times get shorter: Study. Retrieved September 05, 2016, from http://www.nydailynews.com/life-style/health/doctors-office-wait-times-shorter-study-article-1.2161945

Eveleigh, R. (2016, April 05). Mention 2nd Wind in Book [E-mail to the author].

FIND A MENTAL HEALTH PROFESSIONAL. (n.d.). Retrieved September 18, 2015, from http://www.therapistsites.com/

Find-a-Therapist.com :: List your practice on Find-a-Therapist.com, statistics, ecommerce support, personal blog. (n.d.). Retrieved September 18, 2015, from http://www.find-a-therapist.com/pages/listpract

Find a therapist. (n.d.). Retrieved September 18, 2015, from http://www.mytherapistmatch.com/

For Our Providers. (n.d.). Retrieved March 19, 2016, from https://www.colorado.gov/hcpf/our-providers

Frankl, V. (1984). *Man's search for meaning.* New York, NY. Washington Square Books.

Franz, D.A. (2011). *The private practice field guide: How to build your authentic and successful counseling practice.* Plymouth, IN. Author.

FY 2014 Unduplicated Number of Children Ever Enrolled in . . . (n.d.). Retrieved April 3, 2016, from https://www.medicaid.gov/chip/downloads/fy-2014-childrens-enrollment-report.pdf

Gladwell, M. (2011). *Outliers: the story of success.* New York, NY. Little, Brown and Company.

Griswold, B. (2015). *Navigating the insurance maze: The therapist's complete guide to working with insurance—and whether you should, 6th Edition.* San Jose, CA: Paper Street Press.

Grodzki, L. (2015). *Building Your Ideal Private Practice, 2nd Edition A Guide for Therapists and Other Healing Professionals.* New York, NY: W.W. Norton.

Grodzki, L. (2000). *Building your ideal private practice: how to love what you do and be highly profitable too.* New York, NY. W.W. Norton.

Grodzki, L. (2009). *Crisis-proof your practice: How to survive and thrive in an uncertain economy.* New York, NY. W.W. Norton.

Hansen, M.V. & Allen, R. G. (2009). *The one minute millionaire: The enlightened way to wealth.* New York, NY. Crown Publishing.

HIPAA Administrative Simplification: Regulation Text (2013). (n.d.). Retrieved April 17, 2016, from http://www.hhs.gov/sites/default/files/ocr/privacy/hipaa/administrative/combined/hipaa-simplification-201303.pdf

H.R.2759—114th Congress (2015-2016): Mental Health Access Improvement Act of 2015. (n.d.). Retrieved June 19, 2016, from https://www.congress.gov/bill/114th-congress/house-bill/2759

Information for Providers. (2016, February 4). Retrieved April 03, 2016, from http://tricare.mil/Providers/ProviderTypes.aspx

John F. Kennedy: "Special Message to the Congress on Mental Illness and Mental Retardation.," February 5, 1963. Online by Gerhard Peters and John T. Woolley, *The American Presidency Project.* http://www.presidency.ucsb.edu/ws/?pid=9546.

Johnson, L. (2016, January 6). Internet Marketing and SEO Strategies [Telephone interview].

Join GoodTherapy.org. (n.d.). Retrieved September 18, 2015, from http://www.goodtherapy.org/welcome-therapists-counselors.html

Klontz, B., Klontz, T., & Kahler, R. (2009). *Wired for wealth: Change the money mindsets that keep you trapped and unleash your wealth potential.* Deerfield Beach, FL: Health Communications.

Licensure & Certification—State Professional Counselor Licensure Boards. (n.d.). Retrieved September 15, 2015 from http://www.counseling.org/knowledge-center/licensure-requirements/state-professional-counselor-licensure-boards

List Your Practice. (n.d.). Retrieved September 18, 2015, from http://www.networktherapy.com/providers/list_practice.asp

List Your Practice—TherapyTribe Member Registration. (n.d.). Retrieved September 18, 2015, from https://www.therapytribe.com/list-your-practice/

LLC Annual Costs by State—Updated. (2012). Retrieved August 30, 2016, from https://thecorpsecblog.com/2012/03/27/llc-annual-costs-by-state-updated/

Lovett, R. A. (2013, July 15). Desk jobs can be killers, literally. *The Washington Post.* Retrieved July 17, 2016, from https://www.washingtonpost.com/national/health-science/desk-jobs-can-be-killers-literally/2013/07/15/ce61f9e8-e59b-11e2-aef3-339619eab080_story.html

Mapp, C. (2011). *Ethical marketing for therapists, counselors, and the helping professions.* Kennydale, TX. Author.

My Business. (n.d.). Retrieved September 18, 2015, from https://www.google.com/business/

Open Path Psychotherapy Collective—Open Path Psychotherapy Collective is a network of mental health therapists dedicated to helping individuals, families, children, and couples attain affordable psychotherapy. (n.d.). Retrieved September 18, 2015, from http://openpathcollective.org/

Paterson, R. J. (2011). *Private practice made simple: Everything you need to know to set up and manage a successful mental health practice.* Oakland, CA. New Harbinger Publications.

Patient Protection and Affordable Care Act, 42 U.S.C. § 18001 et seq. (2010).

Pear, R. (2017, January 1). Job No. 1 When New Congress Meets? Dismantling Obama's Health Law. The New York Times, pp. 13-16.

Professional Marriage and Family Therapists. (n.d.). Retrieved September 18, 2015, from http://www.therapistlocator.net/iMIS15/therapistlocator/Professionals/Shared_Content/Therapistlocator/Professional.aspx?hkey=55b4dbcb-d018-49bf-b02a-9519949d2a5d

Psych Central Clinician Connection. (n.d.). Retrieved September 18, 2015, from http://therapists.psychcentral.com/

Psychology Today Therapists. (n.d.). Retrieved September 18, 2015, from https://therapists.psychologytoday.com/rms/content/about.html

Ratey, J. J. (2008). *Spark: the revolutionary new science of exercise and the brain.* New York, NY. Little, Brown and Company.

Real, T. (1997). *I don't want to talk about it: Overcoming the secret legacy of male depression.* New York: Scribner.

Reynolds, G. P. (2010). *Private practice: Business considerations.* Retrieved from http://counselingoutfitters.com/vistas/vistas10/Article_36.pdf

Rovner, J. & Cornish, A. (2013, November 8). White House releases long-awaited rules on mental health. In M. Block (Host) All Things Considered. Washington DC: National Public Radio. Retrieved from http://www.npr.org.

Sanok, J. R. (2012). *Practice of the practice: A start-up guide to launching a counseling private practice.* (3rd ed.). Traverse City, MI. Sanok Counseling PLLC.

Siegel, D. (2012) *The developing mind: How relationships and the brain interact to shape who we are.* (2nd ed.). New York, NY. Guilford Press.

Steele, D. (2012). *The million dollar private practice: Using your expertise to build a business that makes a difference.* Hoboken, New Jersey: John Wiley & Sons.

Stout, C. E. & Cope Grand, L. (2005). *Getting started in private practice: the complete guide to building your mental health practice.* Hoboken, New Jersey. John Wiley & Sons.

Stout, C. E. (Ed.). (2012). *Getting better at private practice.* Hoboken, New Jersey. John Wiley & Sons.

Streisand Quote — http://www.brainyquote.com/quotes/quotes/b/barbrastre578549.html?src=t_diversified—accessed 11/30/2015 Streisand information—http://www.barbrastreisand.com/us/home & https://en.wikipedia.org/wiki/Barbra_Streisand—Accessed 11/30/2015

Sultz, H. & Young, K. (2013). *Healthcare USA: Understanding its organization and delivery, 8ᵗʰ Ed.* Burlington, Massachusetts. Jones & Bartlett Learning.

Tate, N. (2013). *ObamaCare survival guide: The affordable care act and what it means for you and your healthcare.* West Palm Beach, Florida. Humanix Books.

The Family & Marriage Counseling Directory: Mental Health, Counselor, and Therapist Advertising. (n.d.). Retrieved September 18, 2015, from http://family-marriage-counseling.com/advertise.htm

Therapist Directory Registration. (n.d.). Retrieved September 18, 2015, from http://www.psychology.com/therapy/

Therapist FAQs—Open Path Psychotherapy Collective. (n.d.). Retrieved September 18, 2015, from http://openpathcollective.org/therapists/faq/

Todd, T. (2009). *Practice building 2.0 for mental health professionals: strategies for success in the digital age.* New York, NY. W.W. Norton.

Truffer, C. J., Wolfe, C. J., & Rennie, K. E. (2014). Department of Health & Human Services 2014 ACTUARIAL REPORT ON THE FINANCIAL OUTLOOK FOR MEDICAID. Retrieved April 3, 2016, from https://www.medicaid.gov/medicaid-chip-program-information/by-topics/financing-and-reimbursement/downloads/medicaid-actuarial-report-2014.pdf

Tunis, V. (Comp.). (2016, June 01). Clinic Forms [Intake and Miscellaneous Forms for Practicum Students]. University of Colorado, Denver. Adapted from University of Colorado, Denver Counseling Clinic Forms

Varney, S. (2013, October 24). Therapists explore dropping solo practices to join groups. In S. Inskeep (Host), Morning Edition. Washington DC: National Public Radio. Retrieved from http://www.npr.org.

What's Medicare? (n.d.). Retrieved March 19, 2016, from https://www.medicare.gov/sign-up-change-plans/decide-how-to-get-medicare/whats-medicare/what-is-medicare.html

Why We're Here. (n.d.). Retrieved April 06, 2016, from http://www.thesecondwindfund.org/why-were-here

Zur, O. (2015). *Modern Day Digital Revenge: Responding to the Emerging Problem of Online Negative Reviews by Disgruntled or Discontent Psychotherapy Clients,* Online Publication by Zur Institute. Retrieved September/12/2016 from http://www.zurinstitute.com/online_reviews_negative.html

95935479R10151